STRAIGHT THROUGH THE HEART

STRAIGHT THROUGH THE heart

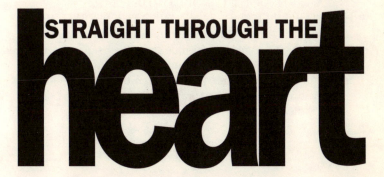

How the Liberals Abandoned the Just Society

MAUDE BARLOW & BRUCE CAMPBELL

A Phyllis Bruce Book
HarperCollins*Publishers*Ltd

First Edition

Canadian Cataloguing in Publication Data

Barlow, Maude
Straight through the heart :
how the Liberals abandoned the just society

"A Phyllis Bruce book".
Includes index.
ISBN 0-00-255306-6

1. Liberal Party of Canada.
2. Canada — Politics and government — 1993–   .*
3. Canada — Social policy.
I. Campbell, Bruce, 1948–   .
II. Title.

FC635.B37 1995   971.064'8   C95-931372-9
F1034.2.B37 1995

95 96 97 98 99 ❖ HC 10 9 8 7 6 5 4 3 2 1

Printed and bound in the United States

To our colleagues in Canada and around the world who work tirelessly for social and environmental justice—from whom we draw our inspiration.

"The only Canada I want to preserve is a Canada that can do something: for its own people, for the hungry two-thirds of the world, for the survival of the planet; not a phantom that can only watch helplessly as we all tumble down a steep place to destruction."

Eugene Forsey

CONTENTS

ACKNOWLEDGMENTS

As always, many people gave generously of their time and expertise for this book. I am most grateful to them and have acknowledged them individually or by group in the chapter notes at the end of the book. However, I would like to particularly thank Tony Clarke for his constant advice, guidance, and inspiration, and David Robinson for his excellent background research.

Once again, I am indebted to the wonderful staff at the Council of Canadians whose patience and unswerving support made this book possible: Peter Bleyer, Joanne Polsky (and her computer genius partner David), Alex Boston, David Robinson, Anne Boys, Jill Anderson, Patricia Armstrong, and Neil Parekh. You are the best.

Bruce joins me in thanking Phyllis Bruce of HarperCollins for her inspiration and Charis Wahl, our fearless editor, for her professionalism and brilliance.

I also wish to thank my family: my husband, Andrew, who has been enormously supportive; my father and mother, Bill and Flora; my sisters, Pat, Christine, and Carole Anne; and my sons and their partners, Charles and Lynn, and Bill and Pam.

Maude Barlow

This book draws on the work and ideas of many people. Some of these are acknowledged in the chapter notes. Here I would like to thank my colleagues at the Canadian Centre for Policy Alternatives for their intellectual sustenance, and for covering for me during the months of writing: Ed Finn who read various drafts, Duncan Cameron who read the entire manuscript, Paul Browne, Larry Brown, Diane Touchette, and Agathe Gauthier. This book would not have been possible without them. I am grateful to Lisa Shaw for her statistical assistance, and to Laura Sky for her comments on a draft of the medicare chapter. Thanks as well to Nelson Riis for his support during the researching of the book.

Maude and I are also indebted to the following colleagues whose work has helped shape our understanding of economic and social policy issues: John Dillon, Sam Gindin, Andrew Jackson, John Loxley, Heather-jane Robertson, Ian Robinson, Matt Sanger, Jim Stanford, Scott Sinclair, Michelle Swenarchuk, Ken Traynor, and Armine Yalnizyan.

Finally, I would like to thank my family for their patience and understanding during a time when my preoccupation with this project made me not always easy to live with: my partner Nathalie, my son Ryan, and my daughter Marie-Claire. I would also like to acknowledge Peter and Sarah of my extended family, and my late parents, Hazel and Ken.

Bruce Campbell

INTRODUCTION

*S*traight Through the Heart tells the story of the building of the just society, the sustained attack on it by big business, and the capitulation to corporate might by the current Liberal Party. It is a book we thought we would never have to write. We did not imagine we would ever have to document how the Liberals—the party of Mackenzie King, Lester Pearson, and Pierre Trudeau—have set out to dismantle the just society they were instrumental in creating. Yet the Liberal Party of Jean Chrétien is bringing about the biggest changes to social policy since the creation of the social programs of the 1960s.

When the Liberals are finished, social security in Canada will be unrecognizable. Federally enforced national standards and universality will be gone. So too will the notion that all Canadians have, by right of citizenship, access to basic social security. The party that built our social safety net is now shredding it; the party that gave us the just society is turning its back on its history and its people.

As we use the term, the "just society" is a covenant between a people and its government. It establishes a social environment in which citizens are responsible for one another and government sets up institutions to provide for the well-being of the community. Although Canadians have yet to achieve fully the just society, we have learned to use democracy to demand economic rights from government, which we believe can and should operate as a positive force for social justice. Social security and full employment are key instruments of the just society—a goal that can be achieved only when the populace is neither fearful nor in need, and when the state has the independent means of achieving the desires of its citizens.

Post-war advances in social security were established largely under Liberal governments, yet Liberals themselves were not historically the driving force behind reform. Rather, Liberals have tended to react to the power centre of their day and to follow prevailing political fashion. The political leanings of Liberal leaders have been remarkably similar: the times influenced the men, more than the other way around. Given their common fiscal conservatism, they are interchangeable. Thus, if Mackenzie King were prime minister now, he would probably be dismantling social security; had Jean Chrétien been prime minister in the 1940s, he would be creating social programs, not destroying them.

The 1930s put capitalism on trial. The economic system had clearly failed all but a small élite, and calls for radical reform were rampant. Militant grassroots social and labour movements were threatening the old order with calls for minimum social rights. The Second World War was a galvanizing force for the next step in nation-building; the state's success in managing the economy for the war effort enhanced its power and legitimacy to act as an instrument of positive change for its citizens. Buffeted by populist demands for reform on one side and, on the other, by a business sector more than prepared to compromise with the citizenry to save capitalism, the Liberal government of Mackenzie King prepared the way for the great social reforms of the 1960s under Lester Pearson.

Finance Minister Paul Martin explains how his father, a key architect of social security under three Liberal prime ministers, described the motivation behind the changes: "He said Canada in 1946 was on the precipice of a tremendous decline. So what did they do? They redefined the role of the national government. What they did was lay down the foundation for the social programs that in fact enabled us to go from one era to another."

By the 1990s, the picture had changed dramatically. Now the concept of the nation-state is on trial. National borders everywhere are being overridden and the power of national governments is being usurped by global financial institutions and transnational corporations. Corporate power has been consolidated by its ability to escape national law; the deal between the corporate sector and citizens, which gave rise to the welfare state, is no longer in business's interest. Corporations set out to exchange the social agenda of our country with their own, subverting democracy in the process. We document how they did this and identify their hallmark policies, including free trade and high-unemployment monetary policy.

Instead of acting as a buffer against a hostile global economy or a voice for global economic reform, the Liberal government under Jean Chrétien, like the Tories under Brian Mulroney, has become the political agent of big business interests and the neoliberal ideology that sustains them. They are stripping government of its powers to enforce social, cultural, and environmental standards, but greatly empowering it to enforce a doctrine of economic survival-of-the-fittest on its citizens.

Paul Martin couches his changes—including huge cuts to social programs and massive decentralization—in the language of reform used by his father: "My father said: 'What we did, the Canadians of my generation, is we built one of the great countries in the world.' Then he said: 'The time surely has come for the Canadians of your generation to do the same thing.'"

But the reinvention of Canada taking place under Paul Martin and Jean Chrétien is not one of nation-building. They are sweeping power from the public to the private sector; slashing, downloading, or privatizing social services; trashing the public sector; leaving families to cope on their own.

The reinvention of Canada under the Liberals and those provincial governments who share their view is a return to the bad old days: good services for the wealthy, what's left over for the rest—means-testing, impoverished public schools and public hospitals, relief camps, food banks. Governments are off-loading their "problems"—the federal to the provinces, the provinces to one another and to overworked charities, all levels to families.

Not even health care is safe. We show how, no matter how

much they deny it, that the Liberals are complicit in the systematic, step-by-step dismantling of medicare—perhaps the most central social bond of the nation.

This is not, as the Liberals claim, the only choice for Canadians. We have a choice between two very different futures: as a corporate nation-state, with limited government, an entrenched underclass, a struggling middle class, and privatized social security; or as a social nation-state within a remodelled global system that recognizes our common need to share our resources for survival.

The federal Liberals have made their choice. They have abandoned the promises made in a decade of opposition and during their 1993 election campaign. This is not surprising, given their historical acquiescence to power. But if they succeed in carrying out their current policies, our nation will be greatly diminished. Jean Chrétien has turned his back on the policy positions he articulated so passionately in his autobiography, *Straight from the Heart.* In so doing, he has left the millions of Canadians committed to the bonds of common purpose symbolized by our national social programs without a political voice.

Straight Through the Heart tells the story of how the Liberals are abandoning the just society, what this will mean to Canadians, and what we can and must do to stop it.

PART ONE

THE RISE AND FALL OF THE JUST SOCIETY

1
BUILDING THE
JUST SOCIETY

"In my thinking, the value with the highest priority in the pursuit of a Just Society had become equality."

Pierre Trudeau

In 1968, flush from a year-long bash celebrating the nation's hundredth birthday, Canadians felt young, in love with our country, and ready for a future filled with hope and tempered by justice. "For many years I have been fighting against the tyranny of the group, and for a just distribution of our national wealth," Pierre Elliott Trudeau told an adoring audience the night he won the Liberal leadership. He called on "young and old, the famous and the unknown" to join him in shouldering the burdens of global injustice. Years later, he would remember his tenure with pride. "We fought for a fairer, more humane Canada, in which the power of government was a necessary instrument in the quest for a more Just Society."

In 1993, Canadians again gave a majority government to a Liberal who promised compassion, hope, and justice. Although we were a much chastened people, without the unbounded faith in the future that characterized the late 1960s, we believed Jean Chrétien when he promised his would not be the party "of the big corporations...[but] the party of the little people in Canada."

When his government set out, less than eighteen months later, to dismantle the central structures of the just society, Canadians were caught off guard. After all, this was no Brian Mulroney, boasting that he would restructure and downgrade every Canadian institution in a decade. Finance Minister Paul Martin—who cited the role his beloved father played in establishing Canada's social programs as the inspiration for his "reforms"—was no Michael Wilson, who, as Tory finance minister, displayed appalling lack of sympathy for the unemployed. So synonymous is the Liberal Party with social progress that even now we cannot recognize the wolf in sheep's clothing. We appear ready to allow the Liberals to finish what we demolished the Mulroney Conservatives for starting.

The explanation for this curious behaviour lies in our mistaken notion that Liberals invented the just society and proactively created universal social structures to benefit all Canadians. The truth is that Liberals almost always created—or destroyed—social programs in reaction to external pressures; for social policy has always been hotly debated within the party. While every Liberal government and opposition has had its social justice champions—among them some of the most committed and articulate social advocates in the country—big business has always had a powerful voice in the party. Free-market, continentalist, pro-American forces have found their historic home most often in the Liberal Party.

The Liberal Party is, and always has been, a compromise between conflicting visions of government. "Business" Liberals and "social" or "welfare" Liberals have worked, ruled, and fought together for most of the party's history, reaching out to a diverse cross-section of Canadians to maintain power. Since the party has held power at the federal level for more than two-thirds of this century, internal Liberal debate about the appropriate role of government has been the backdrop against which most great social change in Canada has taken place.

Liberals of all stripes support free enterprise, individual rights, and market competition. It is a fundamental tenet within the party that economic growth is crucial to the nation's success, and that government's role should be limited to establishing positive conditions in which private markets can create wealth. But within these parameters, there are some very real divisions. Big business Liberals are concerned with profit; they want to hand corporations the tools—low taxes, minimal social responsibilities, and friendly competition policy—with which they can prosper. They believe that a free market is a necessary condition of a free society, and that less government is better government. They favour free trade and limited regulations on the conduct of capital. For them, a healthy private sector equals a healthy nation.

While most social Liberals support the fundamental principles of a market economy, they want to compensate the inevitable losers. (Some business Liberals deny there are losers.) They argue that government has a moral responsibility to provide the poor, the unemployed, the young, and the old with a social safety net to mitigate against the harsh and inequitable consequences of a competitive system. Similarly, individual liberty, which is central to all Liberal ideology, must be tempered by collective rights. Thus, while generally rejecting a class analysis of society, social Liberals accept that extraparliamentary citizen advocacy groups promote democracy and social progress. It is under Liberal governments that feminists, environmentalists, farmers, aboriginal peoples, peace activists, and a variety of other social advocates have been funded.

Business Liberals tend to be continentalist, preferring to let market forces determine resource and industry ownership. They balk at protectionist policies and align themselves with powerful corporate interests, irrespective of their country of origin. Social Liberals have a more nationalist approach, calling on government to protect Canadian industry, resources, and culture. They know that distinct Canadian social programs require Canadian control over the economy. Social Liberals see a direct equation between social security and Canadian sovereignty. The more strongly they believe in the principles of national standards and universality, the more likely they are to oppose continental economic integration.

Time and again these two sides have clashed, sometimes bitterly. Usually, they keep their disputes internal, and the public sees only the resulting compromise. Liberals prefer incremental change. Now and then, however, the Liberal Party has done a complete turnabout on a policy of major consequence, like free trade, demonstrating a total victory of one side over the other. Such is the case with the current about-face on the issue of social security. Social Liberals have been routed, and the national social programs put in place under former Liberal governments are being abandoned. But in an attempt to convince Canadians that these changes represent the old compromise and not a victory of one side over the other, the party assures us that it is merely doing "better with less," and denies the radical shift we can see with our own eyes.

Of course, the great compromises, such as funding both big business and social-advocacy groups at the same time, were easier in times of economic prosperity. When money is tight, choices have to be made, and the rifts show. At all times, the political leanings of the leader are crucial to the policy direction of the government.

Most Liberal leaders, even those popularly thought to be "progressives," have been small "c" conservatives. Their place on the political spectrum has generally been accepted as occupying the "centre" of Canadian political life. But this centre can shift, sometimes dramatically, even under the same leader, indicating that external political conditions, rather than ideology, have informed Liberal policy direction and social legislation. With rare exceptions, Liberals have followed, not led.

Before the turn of the century, there was no such thing as social security in Canada, and no recognition of social rights. Child labour was common. Churches, private charities, and minimal municipal assistance provided the only relief for the poor. The destitute, the ill, the insane, the homeless, criminals—all were sheltered together in poorhouses. Some communities contracted out the care of their poor to the lowest bidder; some held an annual public auction of "paupers." This custom, which resulted in much mistreatment and many deaths, persisted in New Brunswick until the end of the nineteenth century.

Our current social system has its origins in two different ideologies. Almost everyone subscribed to the notion of a distinction between the "deserving poor"—the very young, very old, sick, or disabled—and the "undeserving poor," the able-bodied unemployed. However, nuances were forming. Upper Canada based welfare on the idea that the primary social and economic unit was the family, and responsibility for poverty was largely individual, not collective.

A collective framework for action was being formed in what is now Quebec, Atlantic Canada, and parts of the West, where a fusing of Loyalist sentiment, agrarian collective values, traditions of feudal hierarchy, and concern for the group—and later, social gospel teachings—produced a counterforce to free-enterprise individualism. The resulting mix would form the basis for the just society and anticipate future lines of contention. Interrelationships developed everywhere between private charities, churches, municipalities, and governments, as public monies were increasingly sought by those providing relief; this in turn required government monitoring and regulation. (The notion of the "deserving poor" is fundamentally at odds with that of universality, and is at the heart of the social program debate of the 1990s.)

By Confederation, prairie farmers were transcending racial, religious, and language differences, and gathering into agrarian collectives. Taking on the powers of the CPR and Hudson's Bay Company, grain growers formed co-operatives, the first step toward the formation of later political movements and parties. At the same time, the population was shifting to urban centres, where fierce battles to establish decent working conditions in the burgeoning industrial sector would lead to the eventual growth of a powerful labour movement. (Trade union membership grew from 20,000 in 1890 to more than 120,000 by 1910, and to almost 400,000 by 1920.)

Unfettered, unregulated capitalism was not working for the majority of Canadians. Anger at the old class structure—a privileged few dominating government and the economic and social lives of millions—exploded at the end of the First World War. The propertied classes had become richer from a war that had cost so many working families their sons. The élites used their power to suppress political dissension, fully expecting to return to the pre-war status quo and resisting the working class's demands.

But Canadians had changed. Women had fought for and won the right to vote. Men who had been prepared to die for their country had rethought their place in society. Western farm radicalism was growing; rejecting the two mainstream political parties, farmers' parties were forming provincial governments in Ontario and Alberta; they captured sixty-five seats in the federal election of 1921. Labour-union members were demanding more radical political stands from their leadership, recognizing that conditions in the factories and the mines were only a part of larger social reforms.

The Winnipeg General Strike of 1919 confirmed for many just who the government served. Thirty-five thousand workers walked off their jobs to demand the right to collective bargaining and a living wage. The federal Tory government sided with the Winnipeg business community in opposing the strikers: the RCMP charged at the demonstrators, killing one and injuring several others. Leaders were arrested in midnight raids on their homes. J.S. Woodsworth, then a Methodist minister in Winnipeg, was charged with seditious libel for quoting a passage on poverty from Isaiah.

The pre–First World War Liberal Party embodied laissez-faire business thinking. It opposed economic nationalism and collective bargaining rights for working people; it was isolationist in foreign policy, and strengthened provincial rights to safeguard against encroachment by central government. Liberalism was guided by two dominant themes: freedom from restrictions on liberty, and the rights of all individuals to seek opportunity and enterprise.

An important Liberal mentor, Goldwin Smith, articulated principles that still echo in business Liberal circles today. An avid annexationist, he saw Canada as an irrational concept based on sentiment. Canada was an American community, and any political interference in north–south trade patterns was a "desperate war against nature." He believed that political decisions were artificial and, by definition, interfered with the "natural" forces of economics. Influenced by such thinking, the Liberal government led by Prime Minister Wilfrid Laurier pursued free trade with the United States. Laurier boasted that he was "of the old school...of Provincial Rights" and rejected any move to restrict natural market forces "in favour of the great interests of the mechanic, the labourer, the farmer, the lumberman." But the political dynamics of the country were too complicated to tolerate such simplistic maxims for long.

At the leadership convention of 1919, Mackenzie King committed himself to the construction of a welfare state that would include medicare, unemployment insurance, and pensions—programs he had advocated in his early written works—but, in action, he remained dedicated to a free-market economy, and it would be decades before such reforms would be realized. His old-age-pension legislation of 1927 was passed only under pressure from J.S. Woodsworth and two other independent labour members, contingent on the creation of provincial programs. Similarly, while he recognized the legitimacy of trade unions, he steadfastly denied the existence of any class conflict so vexed that it required them; nor did he see the need for the state to regulate the economy to benefit workers.

On the eve of the great financial crash of 1929, the two competing ideologies would meet head to head in their struggle to influence the development of Canadian social policy: on one side, individual initiative, free enterprise, private charities and families providing for those in need; on the other, the belief that Canadians were becoming deeply divided by class, and only collective action, backed by proactive government intervention to ensure equality of opportunity and social rights, could eradicate chronic poverty, disease, and want. This ideology was fermenting in slums, in universities, on the factory floor, in mines and lumber camps, at rural revival meetings, in churches and kitchens. It would become the major influence on social policy development in the terrible years ahead, anticipating the concept of universal social rights, and forever changing the way Canadians live and work together.

If the Great War represented the maturation and international recognition of the young nation, the Depression was its crucible. Canadians were hit as hard as any group in the world. Atlantic Canada was devastated; fish exports plummeted and unemployment soared. In Ontario, unemployment rose from 2 percent in 1929 to 36 percent in 1936.

Buffeted by drought and shrinking world wheat markets, the Prairies suffered total economic collapse. They became one vast drifting desert where 40,000 families fought to survive—travelling miles for a little drinking water, reduced to starvation diets, forced to pull children out of school when no more patching could salvage worn-out clothing. By 1936, one-third of Saskatchewan farmers were on relief; a year later, the number rose to two-thirds. In some districts, every single family was on relief.

At the height of the Depression, half the wage earners in Canada were on some form of relief—a greater number than all who had enlisted in the First World War. Intense competition for scarce jobs gave employers almost unlimited power to exploit their workforce: wages as low as two cents an hour, work weeks as long as one hundred hours. Employers terrorized their employees, docking pay for failure to meet impossible production quotas, strictly limiting washroom visits, telling part-time workers when or if they would be called in only at the last moment, firing without notice. There was no sick leave, paid holidays, or insurance for unemployment or hospitals. Yet these workers were still the lucky ones. By 1932, almost 100,000 homeless men were wandering the country, sleeping in alleys, riding the rails, growing restless in relief camps.

Federal transfers to the provinces did grow dramatically in these years. Spending on social welfare as a percentage of government expenditures grew from 2.5 percent in 1910 to 25.7 percent in the mid-1930s. This is crucial to the debate over universality. In the absence of any coherent national plan or notion of social rights, this money was often wasted. Relief was administered by the provinces and municipalities, who were generally punitive in their approach to welfare. Standards varied widely. Several provinces were unable to meet their relief obligations, and assistance was minimal even by the standards of the day. In 1936, Quebec dropped relief payments altogether, forcing all recipients onto workfare.

There was a terrible stigma attached to the "dole." To be eligible for relief, a family had to demonstrate that it was nearly destitute. Inspectors would come to the home, and if they found any signs of food, new clothes, liquor, or, in some cases, even a radio, relief was denied. Most municipalities had a one-year residency requirement even for emergency health care, and immigrants were not only turned down for help but deported for requesting it. Medical aid was scarce and far too expensive for many Canadians. And, of course, there was no universal health care.

William Lyon Mackenzie King was completely incapable of rising to the crisis of the Depression. King governed Canada (with a brief interruption in the summer of 1926) from 1921 to 1930, and again from 1935 to 1948, through the nation's transition to a welfare state. By the end of his life, the views of the majority of Canadian people regarding the role of government had fundamentally changed, but not because King led the way; rather, the transformation of the Liberal Party was brought about by the Canadian people, with King a reluctant convert.

King was a self-made millionaire and fiscal conservative whose instinct was to let the market play itself out. As a politician, he was always reluctant to enact specific measures until he was convinced either that the majority of Canadians favoured them or that his political survival was at stake. Insisting that there was "no evidence" of an unemployment emergency, King called federal relief an "orgy of public expenditures."

Granted, it had been a bit much to hear Conservative prime minister R.B. Bennett suddenly declare on the eve of the 1935 election that the capitalist system lay in ruins and that it was time to replace laissez-faire economics, free competition, and "corporate evils" with government regulation and economic controls. King charged that Bennett's New Deal would require jurisdictional powers that would not likely be granted by the courts, and correctly relied on the scepticism and ill will Canadians harboured for the divided Tories. Posing as a moderate in a sea of left-wing radicalism, King openly espoused pro-business economic policies and recruited C.D. Howe, future keeper of the business Liberal flame. Business showered the Liberals with donations.

Once in office again, King came to be obsessed with balanced budgets, reducing aid to the provinces by 25 percent in 1936 and by 34 percent in 1937. He convinced himself that the worst was over and, with one eye to the growing business support for his party, made it clear that relief was a provincial matter. Federal social reform would have to await constitutional clarification. It was under his orders that violent crackdowns on strikers and demonstrators intensified in the years before the war. In this, King was supported by most of the mainstream press, which spoke almost exclusively for business interests. The newly established *Globe and Mail*, bankrolled by a mining magnate and openly siding with monied interests in Canada, lashed out at union organizers and social reformers.

It was beginning to dawn on Canadians that something in their economic and social systems was fundamentally wrong, for there was plenty in a land of scarcity, affluence in the midst of great poverty. Canadians began to analyze the underlying structures of their society and their social institutions and found them wanting. Not only did compassion seem to be utterly missing from government's response to the crisis, so did answers. Clearly, the doctrine of individualism had to be replaced, or merged with, a more collective and systemic approach.

In 1933, an historic meeting of farmers, academics, social reformers, urban socialists, labour unions, and Social Gospel adherents was held in Regina at the founding convention of the Co-operative Commonwealth Federation under the leadership of J.S. Woodsworth. As much social movement as political party, the CCF condemned the failings of capitalism and called for a far-reaching program of social democracy in Canada. Horrified newspaper editorialists decried the "bolshevism" and "radicalism" of the new party; but the movement was a moderate reaction to the effects of the Depression. It rejected Communism, revolution, and violence; with the deep involvement of several churches, it was almost evangelical in character.

The CCF and its successor, the NDP, were crafted from the distinctly Canadian perspective that situates the search for social justice within a framework of deep respect for authority, community, and government. It believed that change must come about within the public order, and sought to promote that change through political office. The party was idealistic but not doctrinaire. It called for collective bargaining rights for workers and social insurance for all Canadians; and, although it advocated government ownership of the means of production, it maintained the support of farmers by guaranteeing their property rights.

The CCF made rapid headway, becoming the official opposition in British Columbia and Saskatchewan and winning seats in Manitoba, Alberta, and Ontario. It garnered 10 percent of the votes in the 1935 federal election and elected seven MPs, including future leaders M.J. Coldwell and Tommy Douglas. From the beginning, it put steady pressure for change on the government of Mackenzie King, although he saw things rather differently. He sniffed that "there is not one [CCF idea] not taken from the Liberal Party. There is not one which is not in the Liberal platform." King understood the need to incorporate limited amounts of nationalism and social reform into his party in order to prevent the CCF movement from growing.

Canadians were asking some hard questions. Were there defining characteristics of the nation that set it apart from others? In spite of our huge diversity, were there certain values that bound us as a people? If so, what should be the role of the federal government? It had played a role in economic nation-building through the creation of John A. Macdonald's National Policy in the late 1900s; should it not now focus on social nation-building through a more equitable distribution of the national income? What should be the role of government in reducing the deep disparities in opportunity between groups, regions, and classes that had become so pronounced during the Depression?

With no answers coming from government, organizations calling for economic and social reform sprang up everywhere. Women's groups were instrumental in the creation of provincial mothers' allowances, first adopted in Manitoba, and pensions for war veterans. The social gospel movement taught that Christians concerned about poverty and injustice were called to do more than set up charities; through political analysis and social action, they needed to fundamentally alter the unjust structures of society to create new, more collective, community-based institutions. The League for Social Reconstruction, with such outstanding Canadian academics as Eugene Forsey, King Gordon, Frank Underhill, and Frank Scott, became the "brains trust" of the new political formations taking shape, and would strongly influence the creation and direction of national social policy.

Change came slowly. Trans-Canada Air Lines (later Air Canada) and the Canadian Broadcasting Corporation were established in the 1930s—the result of pressure on the governments of Bennett and King from groups such as the Canadian Radio League—to assert public control in key areas of the economy and culture. CBC founder Graham Spry used to say that Canadians had the choice of "the state or the United States" to explain the role of an all-Canadian broadcasting system in nation-building. The Wheat Board was created to control the marketing of Canadian wheat exports. Also founded in the 1930s was the Bank of Canada, to promote the economic welfare of the nation and give greater stability and order to its finances. A decade later, as jobs became the government's highest priority, the Bank's mandate would include low interest rates and full employment.

A National Employment Commission set up by the Liberal government to streamline relief efforts and replace aid with jobs argued that employment was a national responsibility, and urged the federal government to take over the cost of unemployment relief. It also recommended that in times of high unemployment, the government should intervene to create jobs. Although King resisted, he was forced by public opinion to implement some proactive measures in the budget of 1938. This was an important precedent; for the first time, government spent money in the form of public works and housing to counteract a low in the business cycle.

When Canadians went to war in 1939, the full force of the Canadian state went with them. Suddenly, there was enough money to employ every able-bodied man and woman who joined the war effort. By 1943, trade union organizations reported that only 0.3 percent of their membership was unemployed, compared to 17 percent in 1939. Government's need to build a strong national war infrastructure coincided with its citizens' demands for a stable future. As the men of the relief camps, suddenly well-paid, clothed, and fed, were sent to fight for their country, government was already planning for a post-war society, one that would include a modern social security system. Much of the Liberal government's change in outlook resulted from pressure from the CCF.

Canadian support of the young party, which had dropped in the election of 1940, peaked in a Gallup poll in 1943; party membership grew from 20,000 in 1942 to 100,000 two years later. This paralleled the growth in labour-union membership, which mushroomed to 700,000 by war's end. The mainstream of Canadian political thought was moving closer to the CCF's call to "conscript wealth as well as men." In quick succession, the party won ten federal and provincial by-elections—as many as the Liberals; it formed the government in Saskatchewan in 1944 (where it held power until 1962) and became the official opposition in Ontario in 1943.

The federal Liberals could not afford to let the CCF capitalize on the public mood. King feared that losing labour's support constituted the "greatest threat to the chances of the Liberal party winning the next election." Calling the CCF the "common enemy" of Liberals and Conservatives, King told Winston Churchill "how great the necessity was for me to begin the mending of my fences, getting my party properly organized and seeing to it that I did not lose any members through the CCF." The prime minister set up a post-war reconstruction plan so progressive that Tim Buck, whose outlawed Communist Party had been reborn as the Labour-Progressive Party, declared that King's Liberals closely approached his philosophy, and called on the prime minister to join a Labour–Liberal coalition with him to campaign in the federal election of 1945.

King took no political chances. Seeing his only opposition to be the CCF, he campaigned on a theme of "building a new social order" and promised a "new Liberalism" that would provide jobs and homes for all, better labour conditions, collective-bargaining rights, guaranteed farm prices, social security, veterans' benefits, and family allowances. His opportunistic conversion saved his government; although the party's popular vote declined from 53 percent to 39 percent, and King lost his seat to the CCF, the Liberals managed to retain a bare majority in the Commons.

The CCF, although disappointed in the outcome, had doubled its national vote and won twenty-eight seats, the zenith for the party that would be reborn in 1961 as the NDP. Without doubt, however, it had an impact on the political culture of the nation and on the creation of the welfare state far beyond its electoral presence. And, of course, universal health care would be won after a showdown between the Saskatchewan medical establishment and the tenacious social pioneer Tommy Douglas.

The war effort was a deeply uniting experience for the country, and soldiers returned with great pride over having served. Social and economic nation-building was the natural next step, and it was likely that any post-war government would have had to embrace a social welfare program. Mackenzie King now turned his attention to the details.

Five major studies made up the Liberal government's post-war plan, strongly influencing the creation of social welfare in Canada.

The Rowell-Sirois Report on Dominion–Provincial Relations, published in 1940, established the principles of the modern Canadian state: federal authority over the economy and national welfare, including unemployment insurance and relief; provincial subsidies with standards for education and social services; regional equality and equalization.

The 1943 Report on Social Security for Canada made its author, Dr. Leonard Marsh, a household name. Marsh proposed pooling protection for maternity, sickness, unemployment, and old age into one universal, comprehensive social insurance plan. He called for a policy of full employment; comprehensive health insurance for all Canadians, funded by the gainfully employed and the federal and provincial governments; fully funded federal assistance programs for the unemployed; and a universal system of children's allowances. "The needs of children should be met as a special claim on the nation, not merely in periods of unemployment or on occasions of distress, but at all times." His recommendations remained the blueprint for social welfare for years to come.

The Heagerty Report of the Advisory Committee on Health Insurance, released at the same time as the Marsh report, held that the provision of adequate medical care for all Canadians was essential to the maintenance and security of a democratic state. It called for a national, compulsory system of health insurance and a comprehensive system of public health. The whole population was to be eligible for medical, dental, pharmaceutical, hospital, and nursing services.

The Curtis Report on Housing and Community Planning called for public intervention to provide affordable housing; town planning to ensure an adequate supply of accommodation; and government-assisted low-rental housing units for the one-third of the population without decent housing. Finally, the

1944 White Paper on Employment and Income committed government to full employment and would influence politicians for a generation.

Despite their popularity among Canadians, these reports were not universally accepted. Powerful forces in business and the business Liberals in government were strongly opposed to full-scale implementation. Leonard Marsh's dream was realized piecemeal, and never completely; but it established the concept of a social minimum, a crucial tenet of the just society.

The great Canadian compromise was now to be formed as the two dominant strains of social-policy thought—welfare for the "deserving poor" versus universal social rights—were to merge and compete, merge and compete, again and again.

Thus change would not come quickly. While government investment in the country's infrastructure, from highways to industry, continued to grow steadily for the next several decades; and, while the direction of social services—universal, accessible to all, and non-profit—was now clear, it would not be until the 1960s and 1970s that government investment in social welfare would again reach the level of the 1930s.

However, Liberal government policies of the 1940s did set the stage for the social programs of the 1960s. In 1945, King introduced the first universal social program—family allowances for everyone with children under age seventeen. This was the first program without a means test, and the first for which government assumed some responsibility for the well-being of all Canadian families. The principle of universality, said Leonard Marsh, "enlists the direct support of the classes most likely to benefit...at the same time as it avoids the evil of pauperization and the undemocratic influence of state philanthropy." This support was not merely symbolic: the family allowance in 1945 represented 20 percent of the average income for a family with three children.

Canadian society at war's end was ripe for change. Generous veterans' benefits enabled a remarkably smooth re-entry of service men and women into civilian society. Universities filled up, as many used their benefits to go back to school. The locus of power had shifted from the provinces to Ottawa in order to mount an effective war campaign; it was appropriate that peacetime planning for the new society should stay in the federal domain.

As well, Canadians' memories of the terrible Depression years led them to depend on the government to maintain high levels of employment: the Liberal government that had appeared so helpless during the economic crisis of the 1930s was able to finance any project it wanted during the military crisis short years later. "Almost everyone agrees," declared *Saturday Night* as early as 1941, "that health and unemployment insurance schemes, regulation of business, and a sharp limitation of profits" are all necessary to provide the individual with real security. Canada must become a country fit for returning heroes, it added, and asked if anyone would go to war to preserve the kind of society that had existed before it. Canadians demanded that their government guide a post-war nation into the modern world, with skills, confidence, and progressive social, health, and education standards.

Most important, the major political pressures and influences of this time were from the left. Capitalism was on trial, its failures there for everyone to see. Communism and socialism were on the rise, and many Canadians were giving them serious consideration as alternative systems. Real modifications were going to have to be made if capitalism were to survive. Even business leaders accepted this reality and set out to help formulate a form of welfare capitalism with which they could live. Thus Mackenzie King, who was no more progressive on social issues than is Jean Chrétien, created the foundations for the welfare state. Today, Chrétien, who grew up taking social programs for granted, is in the process of tearing them down under the economic influence of big business.

For in the 1990s, business no longer feels the need to accommodate popular demands. Capitalism, having escaped nation-state law, has triumphed almost everywhere. Former communist-bloc nations are joining the free-market countries of Central and South America in selling off state assets, privatizing social security, and embracing free trade. There exists no powerful national or global resistance to corporate capitalism; consequently, the pressure to soften the system through social redistribution is absent. Corporations can demand state governance on their own terms, and politicians are not being forced by their citizens to provide democratic counterweights. Entirely in keeping with Liberal tradition, Chrétien, like King before him, more comfortable following than leading, takes his cue from the power centres of the day.

Post-war Canada under the Liberals boomed. The gross national product doubled between 1950 and 1960. The St. Lawrence Seaway and the Trans-Canada gas and oil pipelines were built. The baby bonus and old-age pension gave families purchasing power. The birth rate grew to become one of the highest in the world, and immigration flourished.

Political activism was muted in this period. Exhausted by the brutal conflict and political dissension of the recent past, many Canadians now wanted simply to live in comfort, security, and obscurity, aspiring to the material goods that were suddenly in reach. The universities were "hotbeds of quietism," as one writer put it. For the trade union movement, it was a time to consolidate its gains and secure legal rights for its members. The Canadian Labour Congress was founded in 1956, and wages in manufacturing rose by 75 percent in its first decade.

The Liberals, like the population at large, had lost much of their crusading zeal; compromise, caution, and incremental change were all that was needed. The courtly Louis St. Laurent, who became prime minister in 1948, clearly most comfortable with the business élites, conferred a great deal of power on C.D. Howe, his minister of trade and commerce and an avowed champion of unfettered free enterprise. During the prosperous 1950s, the Liberals were largely able to rebuff calls for reform.

They did introduce the second major universal social program—old-age security for those aged seventy and older—in 1952. Many Canadian seniors were reluctant to apply for it; for them, pensions bore the stigma of charity. (My own grandmother would never cash in her cheques, which she called "dole." My more practical grandfather did, but only after he saw Prime Minister St. Laurent photographed applying for his own benefits.—*MB*) And the government introduced a limited form of hospital insurance in 1957. As well, a federal–provincial initiative, the Unemployment Assistance Act, the first legislated government responsibility for relief, set the stage for future legislation by establishing provincial eligibility conditions for federal assistance funding.

But these were not the full reforms promised after the war, and the political concerns that would dominate the next several decades were brewing. Almost half of Canada's elderly were still living in poverty. Women were entering—or refusing to leave—the workforce; soon they would be organizing for social and workplace rights. The United States had replaced Great Britain as Canada's largest trading partner, and American domination of Canadian industry was becoming a concern. Nationalism, which would become a powerful political force in the creation of national social goals, began to emerge as Canadians started to worry about maintaining control over their own culture, resources, and social structures.

A downturn in the economy and slowly rising levels of unemployment in the late 1950s reminded Canadians how vulnerable they and their families were in the absence of public health care. Demeaning public wards and means testing for medical aid compared unfavourably with the dignity of universal family allowance and old-age pensions. Calls for a national health insurance scheme strengthened. As unemployment grew, so did demands for change. Their massive election defeat in 1957–58 sent the Liberals scrambling to recreate themselves. They remembered the lesson of 1945: Liberals would do well only when seen to be progressive. The political strategy underlying the reforms of the 1960s was being laid.

In the fall of 1960, Liberal opposition leader Lester Pearson brought together the brightest young lights of the new generation of Liberals to a "thinkers' conference" at Queen's University in Kingston. Billed as a non-partisan event for "liberal-minded" Canadians, the Kingston Conference, as it came to be known in Liberal legend, moved the party sharply to the left, laying the foundation for an ambitious social security program that included pension reform and comprehensive health insurance. The gathering showcased the new talent in the party: of the 196 who attended, 48 would be named to senior appointments in the Pearson administration when the Liberals again formed a government in 1963. Among the delegates were key social reform Liberals who would go on to play major roles in what they called the "positive Liberalism" tradition: Allan MacEachen would carry social reform in the House; Walter Gordon would lead the fight for Canadian nationalism; Tom Kent would become Pearson's main social policy advisor.

The Liberals were acutely aware that a resurgent left was being formed around issues of peace, poverty, women's rights, and aboriginal justice, and that the NDP might capture the country's imagination to defeat the erratic Diefenbaker government. So far-reaching was the background paper on social policy prepared for the conference by Tom Kent that Walter Gordon enthused, "I must shake the hand that has strangled the New Party [the NDP] before it's born."

During its two minority governments, under pressure from a respectable twenty-one-member NDP presence in the House after the 1965 election, the Pearson government unleashed an unprecedented range of laws and initiatives that would define the modern Canadian state: a new flag, bilingualism in the federal civil service, a new bank act, a new labour code, liberalization of divorce laws, a new immigration act, doubling of external aid, abolition of capital punishment, collective bargaining for the public service, the Royal Commission on the Status of Women, the Order of Canada, the Company of Young Canadians, the Economic Council of Canada, the Science Council, and the National Film Board. It also declared "war on poverty" and enacted social assistance reform so broad that, by 1965, federal welfare expenditures exceeded the nation's defence bill for the first time.

Pearson's administration wove the fabric of Canada's social safety net in response to a sudden surge in populist activism. Advocacy groups—for tenants, the poor, seniors, consumers, aboriginal people, and farmers—sprang up everywhere. They demanded citizen participation and democratic involvement in the creation of programs affecting them. The notion that equality—overriding differences of region, income, age, and gender—should form a fundamental base for social policy was taking deep root.

Public participation was integral to the spirit of one of the great reforms of the time—the Canada Assistance Plan, which consolidated all federal–provincial assistance programs into one comprehensive package. In order to be eligible for matching funds, provinces would have to help people achieve and retain independence; meet financial needs regardless of cause; improve standards of public welfare; grant benefits to the working poor; and ensure national standards. Provinces could not refuse benefits on the basis of non-residency, and could not force a recipient to accept workfare. Crucial to the current debate over CAP, the preamble stated that the purpose of the legislation was to grant Ottawa the power to alleviate poverty. While this program has fallen short of its original terms of reference, largely because of uneven administration and widely varying basic rates from province to province, it did represent the right to social assistance for all Canadians in need.

Similarly, the Canada Pension Plan enshrined several key new rights: it lowered the qualifying age to sixty-five; it added a wage-related pension as a supplement to the universal pension; and it declared that Canadian seniors should receive a government pension adequate to maintaining a socially acceptable standard of living, rather than bare subsistence. Therefore, there would be an automatic increase in benefits in line with increases in the cost of living. For the first time, those who were widowed or had long-term disabilities were fully provided for.

Perhaps the most important universal program ever introduced to Canadians was launched by the Medical Care Act of 1966, which followed a Royal Commission on Health Services headed by the distinguished Emmett Hall. The commission, and Pearson's government, was influenced by a highly organized lobby of advocacy groups seeking equality of health care for all Canadians.

Conditions of federal grants for health care were clear: provinces had to deliver non-profit, comprehensive, universally available health care to their residents; and benefits had to be portable from one province to another. Medicare, which defined a social minimum in health care, transformed daily life for millions of Canadians. It was introduced together with federal funding for hospitalization and post-secondary education in the Established Programs Financing Act, which guaranteed stable financing for the services.

These major programs were joined by other innovations, some implemented in Trudeau's administration. A National Housing Act in 1964 provided loans to provincial housing corporations for public housing at reduced interest rates. A Youth Allowance extended family benefits to children up to the age of eighteen, and in 1973, a new Family Allowance Act significantly increased funding to this program. The Department of Regional and Economic Expansion addressed under-development in poorer provinces, and the new Unemployment Insurance Act of 1971 expanded benefits and access under the program, making it one of the most comprehensive in the world.

Because of these great social reforms, the gap between rich and poor Canadians would narrow (until the backlash against universality and full employment would start to reverse the trend) and Canadians would be less vulnerable to the severe recessions to come, the most notable being those at the beginning of the 1980s and the 1990s. They would also help alleviate the growing income disparity between employed and un- or underemployed during the 1980s. Although most would fall short of the original dreams of their creators because of constant funding constraints and federal–provincial squabbles, they were seen by Canadians as synonymous with the progress of a modern nation-state. (For these very reasons they would also become a target for later attacks by the resurgent strain of individualism and free enterprise in Canadian social policy thinking.) Most important, they established the principles (outlined below) that, while sometimes broken, have been key to our culture and sense of self.

Social Equality

Social programs should be based on an approach to society that includes everyone and should be universally accessible to all Canadians. Limiting them to the poor transforms them from a right to a charity; if the middle class loses the benefits of social security, it will eventually pull its support and funding.

Social security is not simply a means to relieve the conditions of the most unfortunate, nor even to establish a minimum standard of services below which no Canadian should have to fall. It is a right of citizenship, based on the fundamental notion that Canadians have equal social rights, and that it is through their institutions that equality has been denied and can be restored. The Canadian definition of social welfare addresses the well-being of the whole community. One major goal of social programs is to narrow the gap between rich and poor.

Full Employment

The cornerstone of social security is full employment. It is through employment that people are able to acquire an adequate income, develop a sense of self-worth, and participate in the building of society. When there is full employment, the tax base for public finances is enlarged and the drain on social security programs is reduced. A deliberate policy of high unemployment destroys people and harms the economy; if sustained, it will undermine the ability of the nation to fund its social programs and pursue social justice. Full employment and social security are good for the economy: a well-paid workforce, free from social insecurity, will buy and invest, creating a positive economic climate.

NATIONAL STANDARDS

Effective social programs should be based on national standards that generate a sense of shared responsibility and community. National standards guarantee every Canadian in every province intrinsic minimum rights and access to social services as a right of citizenship. Governments can give "relief" to citizens, but if it is not accompanied by strong standards, enforcement, and a national sense of purpose, it is likely to be ineffective and short-term. Universal standards give a sense of continuity and security to social funding, allowing people to plan ahead for their future. This is the great lesson of the 1930s: large sums of money were wasted in a patchwork of unplanned, inadequate, and badly managed relief measures.

NATION-BUILDING

National social programs require a strong role for the public sector, which is crucial to the maintenance of the nation-state. Our ancestors knew that living next to the biggest superpower in the world, they had to share to survive, and build on a culture of interdependence. So they created institutions—the most important of which were national social programs—to link them in ribbons of common purpose across the country. They built these ribbons through government alone or in combination with the private sector; the country was simply too big and sparsely populated to survive if left to free-market forces alone. Canada was built on a sense of community and an understanding of the need to redistribute wealth and opportunity through a strong public sector.

DEMOCRATIC PARTICIPATION

Canada's social programs were the result of years of struggle and came into being only because generations of Canadians fought, and in some cases died, for them. Canadians gained many of their rights through collective action and the formation of citizen and public advocacy groups. Governments ceded to public demand in creating social security and often sought to undermine public will by whittling away at program funding. Canadians should not be grateful for social programs; we secured them and they are our birthright.

Even though most great social reform was brought in during his administration, it would be a mistake to believe that Pearson himself was politically committed to the left. "A Liberal," he said, "is a man of the centre, moving forward." He was a pragmatist who examined each policy initiative in terms of its consequences. Although progressive Liberals liked to regard him as an ally, the business Liberals correctly perceived him as non-ideological. Like King and Chrétien, he believed that ideology merely limited one's political choices, and he had little time for philosophical debates.

Above all, Pearson could read the mood of the Canadian people: they had moved to the left, and therefore the "centre" had to move in reply. The fulfilment of the long-promised universal social security system was politically necessary. "We are well beyond the point where it is even a matter of debate whether governments should assume any responsibility...for social adjustment, for individual welfare and the basic nature of our society," he said on the eve of introducing the Canada Assistance Plan. "This is practical politics," he told C.D. Howe. "I don't intend to let the New Democrats steal the popular ground of the left. Besides, this is exactly the line Mackenzie King would have taken if he were alive today."

Pearson's cabinet and advisors were a classic combination of social and business Liberals, and the old feud continued. Paul Martin Sr., who had also served in the cabinets of King and St. Laurent, was claimed by both camps. Although he was one of the chief architects of social security, particularly national health care, he was a continentalist with no interest in limiting American economic interests in Canada.

Walter Gordon became the flashpoint for the party split. A key organizer in the revitalization of the post–St. Laurent Liberal

Party, he had chaired the Royal Commission on Canada's Economic Prospects for St. Laurent in 1955, sounding the alarm over foreign economic control and Cold War intimacy with the United States. His report was rejected by his party after bitter opposition from the business establishment. As C.D. Howe was fond of saying, "The business of America is business and the sooner Canada lives by that rule, the better off we'll all be."

Gordon was a strong critic of unfettered free enterprise, deeply concerned about the growing American control over Canadian industry and culture, and an advocate of government intervention for the repatriation of the Canadian economy. Without control of the economy, Gordon argued, the Canadian government could not maintain a commitment to full employment. The issues that preoccupied Walter Gordon are remarkably similar to those of contemporary Canada. Foreign investment was so high that Canadians owned a smaller proportion of their productive wealth than any other industrialized country in the world. Profits from natural resources, which were usually shipped unprocessed, went to foreign investors. Canadian tax law favoured the maintenance of U.S. parent-company control over Canadian branch plant operations. The U.S. was attempting to prohibit Canadian subsidiaries of American companies from trading with "enemy" countries, like Cuba. American culture dominated Canadian airwaves, and Canadians were engaged in a debate about how much domestic control over their cultural industry was necessary or desirable.

As finance minister, Gordon faced a particularly vicious personal campaign mounted by business Liberals and the business community. His successor in Finance, Mitchell Sharp, dismantled most of Gordon's nationalist policies, but Gordon teamed up with Eric Kierans to fight on. The real showdown came over the issue of medicare. Promised in the election campaign of 1963, comprehensive health insurance was introduced in 1965, to come into effect in 1967. But Sharp, backed by Prime Minister Pearson, surprised a cabinet meeting by announcing that as part of an anti-inflationary measure, there would be a one-year postponement. Walter Gordon lost face at a policy convention shortly after, was rebuked by Pearson, and openly vilified as a "Commie nut" by business Liberals inside the party and the business community in general.

How are we to assess the legacy of the Pearson Liberals to Canada's social development? Undoubtedly, the most important elements of the social safety net were put in place under Pearson's administration, and Canadians owe a great deal to social Liberals such as Walter Gordon, Tom Kent, Allan MacEachen, Jean Marchand, Eric Kierans, and Judy LaMarsh. The party that had been defined only sixty years before by rugged individualism, free enterprise, provincial rights, and free trade was now committed to full employment, universal social security, and some limited forms of cultural nationalism. Individual self-realization was wedded to the notion of community in a uniquely Canadian form of Liberalism. Liberals, explains political writer Ron Graham, now "linked the destiny of the individual to the common good, an activist state, majority rule, centralized authority, nationalism, and the will of the mass known as the people."

However, by not taking action against the growing influence of American economic interests in Canada, Pearson set the stage for the future weakening of Canada as a nation-state. He signed a joint communiqué with John F. Kennedy in 1963 that stressed "the vital importance of continental security...bilateral defence arrangements...the rational use of the continent's resources...defence production-sharing programs...cooperative development of the Columbia River...joint cabinet-level committees on trade and economic affairs and defence."

For Pearson, good relations with the U.S. were the cornerstone of foreign policy. As a former Washington diplomat, he subscribed to the Merchant-Heeney Report on Canada–U.S. relations, published during his administration. It suggested that relations between the two countries should be conducted in private by their diplomats, who should avoid public disagreements on major issues. In fact, Canada should take into account the position of the U.S. government when considering its policies on world affairs. Pearson appeared to have no difficulty in conceiving of Canada as a satellite of the U.S., and many north–south projects based on this model were undertaken during his terms.

By not backing Gordon and the social Liberals in his cabinet, Pearson strengthened the free-enterprise, pro-business, continentalist Liberal forces. They would continue to gather strength over the next decade, becoming pivotal in the campaign for free trade with the U.S. and the consequent assault on universal social programs.

Pearson's support of both social security and continental free enterprise demonstrates the central contradiction of Liberalism: the lack of a core ideology breeds inconsistency of policy. Pearson chose to support two trends that are, in the final analysis, mutually incompatible. By not taking foreign and economic policy positions independent of U.S. corporate interests, Pearson sowed the seeds for the destruction of the very universal social fabric he had woven.

Pierre Elliott Trudeau inherited strong public support for the social safety net when he took power in 1968. But social security would be under renewed assault when he retired sixteen years later. By the mid-1970s, high employment, decent wages, and social security had given working people substantially increased economic and political power. Canadians had more buying capacity and greater consumer rights. They could demand good working conditions and benefits of employers. They saw their social programs as rights and were empowered, freed from any sense of shame, in claiming services. Employers no longer had the frightened workforce that an economy of structured high unemployment produces.

Corporate leaders became convinced that Canada's social security system was hurting their profits, rendering them less competitive. They established close ties with their counterparts in the U.S., and were charged with enthusiasm for the American free-market system. Capital was going global, and Canadian corporations could see how much money could be made in countries without minimum social standards. Canadians were bombarded with negative messages about our social programs: we had grown too soft; we couldn't compete against countries with low labour rights and social standards; government wasn't the solution, it was the problem; social programs were cumbersome and too expensive.

These assertions gained wide currency in spite of the fact that, as a percentage of GDP, government spending on social security would remain constant. As well, Canada's social programs were delivered more equitably and at lower cost than comparable, market-driven programs in the U.S. In spite of all evidence to the contrary, blame for the deficit was laid at the feet of social programs, and many Canadians reluctantly started to believe that they would have to be abandoned.

The deep splits in the Liberal Party under Trudeau over the crucial issues of foreign control, social programs, and the role of the state mirrored the deep splits growing in society and help to explain the policy schizophrenia that characterized his terms in office. A sea change in political culture was taking place in Canada, and the Liberals were caught in the tide.

Trudeau's policies and public musings were all over the map. He would defend social programs and cut social programs; he would raise corporate taxes and cut corporate taxes; he would lecture the business community for being greedy and then tell Canadians that "survival of the fittest nations has become the rule of life." The man who invoked the War Measures Act in Quebec brought us the Charter of Rights and Freedoms and spent his last days in office in the pursuit of world peace.

So convinced was the business community of Trudeau's leftist tendencies that it banded together in the mid-1970s to form the corporate lobbies, right-wing think tanks and compliant media outlets that have launched a twenty-year assault on the very notions of government and social security. For the corporate community, Trudeau was an enigma. He came from money, but seemed uninterested in the acquisition of it. He was of the élite, but had little tolerance for the care and sustenance of CEOs expected of a prime minister. (They failed to notice that, always suspicious of the collective voice over that of the individual, he treated *all* "special interest" groups in this manner.)

Most important, though, it was during the latter half of his governance that the social consensus between business and citizens began to break down. The compromise that had permitted the growth of the Canadian welfare state no longer served the corporate world, which set out to destroy it. Liberalism came under assault in the U.S., Great Britain, and elsewhere. As the economy floundered and unemployment, inflation, and debt grew, political division surfaced and the middle ground disappeared.

Trudeau shared the classic Liberal distrust of ideology: "The only constant factor to be found in my thinking over the years has been opposition to accepted opinions.... Ideological systems are the true enemy of freedom." However, he believed in what he calls "counterweights" in personal life and government, which helps explain the many apparent contradictions in his policies and character.

Politically, he favoured the decentralization of power; between 1962 and 1978 Ottawa's share of public revenues dropped from 47 percent to 32 percent and constraints on how the billions in transfer payments were spent were discarded, creating the first breach of national standards. The National Energy Program, the Foreign Investment Review Agency, the Canada Development Corporation, Petro-Canada, and the Canadian Radio-Television Commission—so hated by American business interests—stemmed from practical, not ideological factors. The NDP held the balance of power in the minority government of 1972 and the nationalist forces in his own party were strong. But the measures were not anti-American in nature. For Trudeau, the NEP was less about advancing Canadian political sovereignty than asserting federal authority over provinces that had grown too independent.

Over the course of his leadership, Trudeau would grant a steady set of tax breaks to business; between 1968 and 1983, the share of corporate taxes in national revenue declined from 17 percent to under 14 percent. Unemployment Insurance coverage was substantially improved in 1971, only to be significantly reduced again in 1975. He implemented wage and price controls in 1976 after campaigning against them in 1974 and, with Finance Minister Jean Chrétien, significantly reduced the rate of growth for federal grants for health and post-secondary education in 1978.

A major social security overhaul called the Orange Paper coincided with the beginning and end of the minority government in which the NDP championed the continuation of the Pearson social reforms. The next step in the "war on poverty," it set out to promote a guaranteed annual income, a federal minimum wage, and guaranteed employment for all able-bodied Canadians. "The Parliament of Canada...has a responsibility to combat poverty by way of a fair distribution of income among people across Canada," it declared. But powerful forces in business, cabinet and the Finance Department, which had been steadily restricting growth in the tax base, were strongly opposed to any extension of social rights; indeed, they were drawing up plans to curb them.

The battle pitted Finance Minister John Turner and his deputy, Simon Reisman, against Health and Welfare Minister Marc Lalonde and his deputy, Al Johnson. A fierce animosity grew up between the deputies, who almost came to blows at one meeting. The Social Security Review was defeated with the exception of a dramatic increase in family allowances, which was wiped out in the cuts of 1978, and the government introduced the child tax credit, the first real blow to universality. Pierre Trudeau, while initially behind the project, took the side of his finance minister in the dispute, just as Jean Chrétien would do twenty years later when Lloyd Axworthy and Paul Martin clashed over a similar social security review. Deputy Minister Simon Reisman crowed, "We won the big one...we really went to the trenches on that one." After 1975, the war on poverty was dropped.

The big showdown between social and business Liberals came after the 1980 win. As always when defeated by the Tories, the Liberal Party had swung hard to the left after losing to Joe Clark in 1979, and campaigned on the need to return to small "l" liberalism. Its first budget, brought down by the new finance minister, veteran social Liberal Allan MacEachen, announced this political shift. To pay for some expensive budget items promised in the campaign and to promote social equity, the government announced that it would collect $2 billion from the rich by closing generous tax loopholes that had been granted and abused in the 1970s when Reisman convinced John Turner to load the tax system with incentives to business. Even though this medicine would be offset by reductions in direct taxes to business, the corporate community, now organized around its powerful new lobby group, the Business Council on National Issues, saw red. The old business compromises to social security were no longer on offer and the BCNI demanded reduced corporate taxes *and* the maintenance of its tax perks.

Allan MacEachen had been chosen by Trudeau for his experience, the inspirational role he played in uniting the party after the 1979 defeat, and his credentials as a social reformer. The son of a Cape Breton coal-miner, MacEachen studied at St. Francis Xavier with the great Catholic radical reformer Father Moses Coady, who inspired the young student to a life of political activism. For many years, he was the social conscience of the party and, as a key advisor and confidante to Pearson, was given responsibility for the ground-breaking Canada Assistance Plan, Canada Pension Plan, and Medical Care Act.

But for all his experience, MacEachen now misread both his party and his cabinet colleagues; he assumed they shared his views on social reform. The old left–right splits emerged. Peppered daily by angry letters and phone calls, the Liberals withdrew most of the tax measures from the budget, leaving almost nothing of its original intent.

The Trudeau government was in full retreat from reform and brought in its famous "Six & Five" legislation, capping public service wages, provincial transfers, and social security payments in 1982. An industrial policy proposed by Herb Gray that would have bolstered Canadian economic control was dropped. MacEachen was replaced in Finance by Lalonde, who, like Trudeau, was a classic Liberal of the centre. He had been comfortable representing the left in fights with John Turner on social reform a decade earlier when called to do so; now he would promise "to re-establish Finance as the main interlocutor for financial interests in the country."

Said *The Financial Post*'s Giles Gherson, "Marc Lalonde seem[s] to have wholly transformed himself in the eyes of business. No longer social-policy activist and energy-policy interventionist, he ha[s] become Ottawa's recovery architect, and arguably the most powerful finance minister the capital has seen for several decades." MacEachen's deputy minister, Ian Stewart, was replaced by Micky Cohen, a tax lawyer, disciple of Simon Reisman, and a welcome relief to the BCNI.

Trudeau took to the airwaves to convince Canadians that this turn of events was unavoidable in the new global economy, and met with a group of high-level American CEOs who were reassured by his denunciation of Canadian economic nationalism. Planned reform to fill gaps that were leaving some older women without pensions was abandoned when it ran afoul of the BCNI; the Bank Act was amended to raise the quotas on allowable assets for foreign-owned banks, and Judy Erola, Minister of Consumer and Corporate Affairs, consulted closely with the corporate lobbies to bring in a new, pro-business Competition Act.

Social Liberalism was in full retreat, its death hastened by the Royal Commission on the Economic Union and Development Prospects for Canada, chaired by former Liberal Finance Minister Donald Macdonald. Set up in late 1982 under Trudeau, the commission did not publish its report until 1985 under Mulroney, when it served as the perfect symbol of the now-shared ideology of the Liberals and Conservatives, and became the vehicle for transferring an economic platform from one government to the other. The Macdonald Commission called for the contraction of government itself in order to foster business competition. Concerned that the welfare state subverts "the genius of the market economy," the report laid the groundwork for continental free trade, planned high unemployment, and the coming assault on universal social programs.

2

THE HOSTILE
TAKEOVER

"If you really want to change the world you have to change the ideological fabric of the world."

Michael Walker, Fraser Institute director, 1974

Canada today is dramatically different from the Canada of twenty years ago. That change has not been caused primarily by uncontrollable forces beyond our borders, although they have been an important factor. It is the result of such deliberate policy decisions as deregulation, privatization, free trade, monetarism, and their many offspring. These policies are overlapping and mutually reinforcing. Their effect is cumulative and it is difficult to isolate the impact of individual policies. Viewed as a whole, however, these policies constitute a policy agenda. Even though national responses have differed widely, it is a global policy agenda. It was developed and disseminated in university economics departments and business think tanks of the New Right in the United States, Britain, Canada, and elsewhere, in global corporate clubs like the Trilateral Commission. Not coincidentally, this policy agenda closely reflects corporate priorities and is therefore referred to as a "corporate agenda." To denote its theoretical underpinnings, it is also referred to as a neo-liberal agenda. These policies produce benefits for a privileged minority, but have made life worse for the majority of the population.

The success of the corporate sector in seeing its policy agenda implemented has been driven by the growth of its power. This power rests on its resources, which include property and organization—land, real estate, plant, equipment, financial capital, information, knowledge, and technology; and "human capital"—engineers, lawyers, accountants, public relations experts, government lobbyists, scientists, technicians, and so on. It also rests on the instruments through which it exercises power—reward, punishment, and persuasion. For instance, the corporate sector's ability to persuade a government to adopt a given policy is a function of its power—the size of its production facilities and workforce, its financial resources, the tax revenue it generates, its ability to lobby political decision-makers, and its ability to punish the government by shifting production or investment to another jurisdiction. Advances in the corporate policy agenda in turn enhance corporate power. It is a self-reinforcing cycle.

Because corporate interests often conflict with those of the population at large, the corporate sector takes great pains to mask the imposition of its will—shaping prices and costs, manipulating consumers, and influencing the political process. Fully exposed, the legitimacy of corporate power in a democratic society would be questioned and pressure would mount to rein it in. That it has been able to sustain the illusion of its legitimacy is itself testimony to its overwhelming power.

When we speak of the corporate sector, we are referring to large corporations and financial institutions resident in Canada (although not necessarily owned by Canadians). We are referring to the people who own them and the executives who run them. The corporate sector includes 160 of the largest corporations, with combined assets of more than one trillion dollars, which are members of the lobby group the Business Council on National Issues. Not all big business belongs to the BCNI, however; so we might also include those companies on *The Financial Post 500* list or *The Globe and Mail's Top 1,000* list. It also includes the family empires—the Bronfmans, the Thomsons, the Irvings, Conrad Black, Paul Desmarais, etc.—with interests in the above corporate groupings. What is important is what distinguishes the corporate sector from the hundreds of thousands of small and medium-sized businesses—power: power in the market, and power to act, both as individual companies and collectively, to influence public policy.

The corporate sector dominates the myriad business organizations that seek to influence public policy—from broad-based organizations like chambers of commerce and boards of trade, to sectoral organizations from banking and insurance to forest products, chemicals, and computers. Small and medium-sized businesses are clients of the corporate sector. Though there is much overlapping of interests, they are not identical, and at times are in conflict. They do, however, provide a useful foil for the corporate sector, allowing it to hide behind the illusion of a market in which outcomes are determined by millions of every-day decisions by producers and consumers.

Two interrelated factors have been critical to the growth of corporate power and its ability to implement its political agenda, both in Canada and world-wide: concentration and globalization.

The already concentrated corporate sector has tightened its hold on the Canadian economy through successive waves of takeovers and mergers, which peaked in late 1989, and again in 1994, totalling close to $50 billion in each of these years. Between 1987 and 1993, assets passed back and forth between Canadian and foreign-owned corporations, with foreigners gaining a net $36 billion in the corporate takeover war. Ownership of economic assets, already concentrated among the very largest companies, has tightened over the last two decades. The largest twenty-five corporations increased their share from 29 percent of (non-financial) private business assets in 1975 to 34 percent in 1992. Competition laws were changed to overlook problems of excess concentration on the pretext that the North American economy rather than the national economy was now the relevant standard.

We also see corporate concentration reflected in family-based empires. The Desmarais group controls 117 companies, including Great-West Life, Investors Syndicate, and Power Corp. Edgar and Peter Bronfman control some 500, including MacMillan Bloedel, Noranda, and London Life. The Weston group has 124 corporations in its stable, including Loblaws, EB Eddy, and Holt Renfrew. The Irving family owns 168 corporations, including Irving Oil, St. John Shipyards, and Acadia Broadcasting. Conrad Black, through Hollinger Inc., controls a large chain of newspapers and magazines, including joint control of Southam and *Saturday Night*. Kenneth Thomson is another newspaper magnate with 136 companies under his control, including *The Globe and Mail*. These families are charter members of the world's billionaire club.

The second and more significant development in recent times has been the transnationalization or globalization of corporations. Major technological advances—notably computers and satellite technologies—which revolutionized transportation, communications, information, and production systems, have enabled corporations to organize their activities no longer just on a national basis, but on a continental or global basis. This integration across national borders has greatly enhanced the mobility and flexibility of corporations. It has resulted in the growth of vast networks of production, consumption, trade, distribution, and finance. The consequences are reflected in the concentration of wealth world-wide in a small group of transnational corporations headquartered in a few countries, and in a minority of the world's population that participate in or benefit from the globalized system.

Foreign direct investment boomed, as did intra-corporate trade, as corporations wove ever more intricate global webs. One-third of global cross-border trade in goods and services now takes place *within* the network of branches and subsidiaries owned by each parent corporation. (Between Canada and the

United States it now accounts for half of all trade.) What is produced and where, what is traded and at what price, are all determined by corporate managers, not on the open market.

The United Nations has identified 35,000 transnational or global corporations. The largest 300 account for one-quarter of the world's productive assets and control 70 percent of international trade and 98 percent of all foreign direct investment. Half of the 100 largest economies are now corporations. Global corporations hold proprietary rights over most of the world's technology.

Canadian-owned corporations, too, are players in this global arena—in the areas of finance, real estate, mining, petroleum, forestry, telecommunications, automotive and rail transportation, engineering, aerospace, and media. Although concentrated in the United States, their trade and investment interests straddle the globe. They borrow and lend, and move "hot money" (short-term capital) on global markets. They participate in global business forums and are present at meetings of the international financial and trade institutions.

Globalization has facilitated the concentration of income and wealth world-wide. The income gap between rich and poor countries has doubled since 1960. Countries that make up the richest 20 percent of the global population now have an average per capita income sixty times those of the poorest 20 percent. When national borders are erased, the richest 20 percent of the world's population have average per capita incomes 160 times those of the poorest 20 percent. In 1994, the combined wealth of the world's 358 billionaires (including a handful of Canadians) equalled that of the lowest 45 percent of the population of the planet.

By transcending national jurisdictions, the global corporation can avoid or resist government measures that harm its interests. For example, if a government taxes corporate profits too highly, corporate managers can artificially manipulate prices of internal imports and exports (overpricing the former or underpricing the latter) to reduce declared profits and taxes, thereby punishing that government. The global corporation can also punish an "unco-operative" government by shifting production or threatening to do so, or by locating new investment in a "friendlier" jurisdiction. The corporation can also "reward" governments and communities with, say, a new plant contingent upon lowered taxes, the granting of other incentives, or the relaxing of regulations.

Perhaps the most powerful manifestation of corporate globalization these days is the deregulation of national financial markets and their integration into a global financial market made up of banks, brokerage and investment houses, currency, bond, and stock exchanges—a global loan and bond market totalling more than $5 trillion annually. Each day $1 trillion passes through global currency markets, only 5 percent of what is needed to handle the international exchange of goods and services. Money managers move vast amounts of short-term capital from country to country in seconds, in an endless quest for rising currencies, high returns, and low risk. Governments that depend heavily on short-term foreign borrowing are vulnerable to money managers taking a run at their currencies and destabilizing their economies in response to policies they dislike. This makes a mockery of democracy, and yet the leader of the major industrialized countries refuse to take the measures necessary to curb monetary speculation.

The corporation also has power to punish "unco-operative" workers and reward those who are compliant. It can do so by threatening to relocate if its demands for wage rollbacks, reduced benefits, or increased work time are not met. Union bargaining power varies with corporations and industries, but in general globalization has reduced unions' power to negotiate wages and working conditions for its members. Democracy is diminished when wages decline and working conditions worsen, when unemployment is high, when insecurity and inequality grow. People who live in fear, preoccupied with daily survival, are not able to function as full citizens in a political community.

The social underpinning of Canadian democracy that emerged from the Second World War was as much a commitment from corporations to accept the existence of the unions and rising incomes as it was a commitment from government to maintain full employment and build a social security system for all citizens. Concluding that the social consensus had become a drag on its own interests, big business in Canada and elsewhere began to repudiate its end of the bargain in the mid-1970s. It faced a faltering economy and a squeeze on profits, which it attributed to increased external competition, ongoing demands for wage increases and social protection through the state, and an oversized and insufficiently co-operative government. Workers, bolstered by strong unions and a generous social security system, had become too powerful. An increasingly independent public sector was becoming too intrusive, both as a regulator of economic activity and as a producer encroaching on their turf. There was, they believed, an "excess of democracy" characterized by the growing political influence of groups that challenged corporate interests.

To counter this erosion of its power, big business set in motion a multifaceted effort to make its agenda the agenda of government. It revamped its arsenal of weapons to help persuade governments to adopt its agenda—the Business Council on National Issues, think tanks, the media, lobbying, party financing.

Foremost among its weapons was the Business Council on National Issues, founded in 1976 by a small group of corporate leaders. The BCNI set out to derail the just society and limit government intervention. It set out to change government's role from protector of society against the excesses of the market, to protector of a favourable climate for business; to replace the values of community and co-operation with values of individualism and competitiveness. Modelled on the U.S. Business Round Table and led since 1980 by former Liberal advisor Tom d'Aquino, the BCNI comprised the dominant players in the Canadian economy, and the main Canadian players in the global economy—banks, resource companies, and U.S.-owned firms. The Business Council sought to interact discreetly with mandarins and political leaders whose power had become more concentrated in the executive (cabinet). It focused on key issues through task forces that paralleled government departments, becoming, in the words of York University political economist David Langille, "a virtual shadow cabinet."

In a 1983 brief to the Macdonald Commission, the BCNI set out its goal "to establish a macroeconomic environment that allows Canada to achieve sustained non-inflationary economic growth and improved competitiveness." "Competitiveness" and "non-inflationary" were the key words. As its members competed in the international economy, they wanted low costs at home and access to markets abroad. They wanted low inflation. They wanted control over wages and other costs, such as transportation and communication. They also wanted to lower people's expectations, both of incomes and government social programs. To this end, the BCNI persuaded the Commission to recommend that Canada take a "leap of faith" into free trade with the U.S.

The BCNI's approach was proactive, setting out policies and proposals rather than reacting to government initiatives. In the early 1980s, the BCNI persuaded the Liberal government to give priority to fighting inflation over reducing unemployment, and shifted it from an activist to a more passive industrial strategy orientation. It also helped ensure that more business-friendly Liberals were placed in key economic portfolios, steering the government away from its nationalist propensities.

The BCNI also brokered an energy accord to finally bury the National Energy Policy. In a series of secret meetings, it brought together the oil and gas companies and utilities with the federal, Alberta, and Ontario governments. Although formally implemented by the Conservative government, the deal was negotiated during the last days of the Trudeau regime by Minister of Energy Jean Chrétien. The deal involved deregulating oil and gas prices and lowering government taxes and royalties, thus weakening the revenue capacity of the federal government.

As we discuss later, the BCNI was the driving force behind the free trade agreement. Governments have adopted its proposals, often with little amendment, on key issues such as competition policy, tax reform (including the GST), defence and social policy. Since the mid-1980s the BCNI has argued that social programs should be selective and targeted only to those who really need them.

The extent to which the BCNI has set the nation's policy, behind which government has fallen into line, is reflected in its 1994 "A Ten Point Growth and Employment Strategy for Canada." Its main points are synthesized here.

On social policy: 1) "do more with less"; 2) "assistance should be targeted to those most in need"; 3) create incentives that encourage individual self-reliance.

On unemployment: The current UI system is "badly flawed." Premiums should be kept as low as possible as they are a "tax on jobs"; incentives that encourage only short-term attachment to employment (i.e., a short qualifying period for UI) should be removed; and "[Unemployment] assistance...should be kept at levels that will not act as a disincentive to returning to work" (in other words, lower the payout).

On inflation: "After a long and costly battle against inflation waged by the central bank, a battle *that was consistently supported by the Business Council* [italics added]," the battle is won. "Non-inflationary growth must continue to be a central tenet of national economic policy."

On debt and deficit: The de facto fiscal crisis "is the one obstacle standing in the way of growth." The BCNI advocates eliminating the deficit by 1998–99, before the next recession, by cutting spending, because "the tax burden in Canada is sharply out of alignment with...[that of] the United States," and "tax fatigue" only leads to more evasion. Moreover, raising taxes would also "deter investment and kill jobs."

On trade: "the best hope for job creation." NAFTA is the centrepiece, but it should be complemented by "aggressive . . . international trade development and diversification"

On federalism: The BCNI has three priorities: 1) to eliminate all internal trade barriers; 2) to "reduce the overall burden of government in our lives"; and 3) to "create a more decentralized federation in which the government closest to the people provides the service, while at the same time the role of the central government [is reinforced] in key areas of national and international competence."

One would be hard pressed to find any part of this BCNI document that is out of sync with the current Liberal government policy.

In a 1983 speech, BCNI president Tom d'Aquino spoke about the Council's goal to "reconstruct" Canada through "fundamental change in some of the attitudes, some of the structures and some of the laws that shape our lives." Ten years later, in a *Canadian Forum* interview with Murray Dobbin, d'Aquino, surveying the transformed Canadian landscape, downplayed the role played by his immensely powerful organization. What mattered, he said, was the revolutionary power of the ideas of free trade, deregulation, and the other neo-liberal policies. These ideas were in fact very old, having been discredited only in recent times by the Depression. Their revival had more to do with the corporate money behind them than their popular appeal. Denying the enormous human cost of these policies, d'Aquino acknowledged that their effect has been revolutionary, and the revolution, as with others before it, has been "led by a small group of of people."

Policy research institutes, supported by generous corporate donations, have become another powerful tool in the arsenal of persuasion. The "think tanks" provide an intellectually legitimate framework for corporate policy priorities. The Tories abolished several government-sponsored think tanks, like the Science Council and the Economic Council, whose policy advice was not always consistent with their agenda. Since then, corporate think tanks have had greater freedom to frame the ideological boundaries of an issue. They organize conferences, seminars, retreats, and briefings; they provide forums in which élites from the media and corporate and state sectors gather, socialize, network, and share information, establishing policy consensus and joint strategies; they turn out a steady stream of reports and provide expert media commentary; they testify before parliamentary committees. Their work is read diligently and widely cited by journalists, politicians and bureaucrats. They provide an "authoritative reservoir" of knowledge that finds its way into government policy initiatives.

The C.D. Howe Institute is the oldest and most influential of the corporate-funded policy think tanks. The Howe members and sponsors, some 280 strong, are a who's who of corporate Canada: Air Canada, Alcan, American Barrick, Bank of Montreal, Bank of Nova Scotia, Peter Bronfman, Canadian Bankers Association, Canadian Pacific, John Crow, Thomas d'Aquino, Ernst & Young, Great-West Life, General Motors, Hill and Knowlton, Inco, London Life, MacMillan Bloedel, Merc Frosst, Molson, Noranda, Power Corp., Royal Bank, Southam, Shell Canada, Toronto-Dominion, George Weston, Wood Gundy, and so on. There is significant membership overlap between the C.D. Howe Institute and the BCNI. Most of the largest corporate sponsors of the Liberal and Conservative parties are Howe members. The board of directors, including its current president, are predominantly from the financial wing of the corporate sector.

In the late 1970s the Howe Institute shifted its policy positions into line with the emerging neo-liberal orthodoxy. It dropped its support of full employment and Keynesian-style demand management policies. It dropped its concern that a bilateral agreement with the U.S. could cause politically unacceptable levels of social dislocation and unemployment. In its brief to the Macdonald Commission it argued that fiscal and monetary stimulation could not restore economic growth in an interdependent world economy, as these policies delay the necessary adjustment of prices and wages to the new competitive reality. Subsidies to business also postponed this adjustment. Free trade agreements, on the other hand, would facilitate it.

By the mid-1980s the Howe's main policy priorities were deficit reduction, which had supplanted its former commitment to full employment, tax and social program reform, and bilateral free trade. It argued for a major overhaul of unemployment insurance and welfare. In 1989, it commissioned the report *Social Policy in the 1990s,* by Tom Courchene of Queen's University, which called for social changes to facilitate the restructuring and adjustment of the labour market. Courchene argued that UI was a major contributor to the deficit and a major cause of unemployment because it contained disincentives to work. (The Howe undertook a second major social policy review in 1994, which included an update of Courchene's first study. See Chapter Seven.)

Since 1986, the Howe has supported the Macdonald Commission's proposal for a universal income security program to replace UI, welfare, and child benefit programs. It has pushed for the so-called disentanglement of fiscal federalism through the transfer of tax points to provinces to provide health care and social assistance. It has advocated privatizing more of the health-care system, replacing provincial education transfers with direct transfers to students, deregulating tuition fees, and permitting private universities to enter the post-secondary education field.

With the 1985 publication of Lipsey and Smith's *"Taking the Initiative,"* free trade became a central focus of the Howe's work. Free trade—bilateral and internal—was seen as entrenching deregulation, privatization, and social program reform, thereby providing the necessary discipline to ensure a "flexible competitive cost structure."

The Howe's main competition is the Vancouver-based Fraser Institute, the brainchild of MacMillan Bloedel vice-president Patrick Boyle. Alarmed by what he perceived to be runaway government spending and pervasive intervention (the Dave Barrett–led NDP government was an immediate target), Boyle created the institute in 1973 to make the case for limited government and market solutions to economic problems, and hired Michael Walker to run it. Walker's strategy was to "change the world [by changing] the ideological fabric of the world." The Fraser is funded by large Canadian and U.S.-owned resource, financial, and manufacturing corporations, including Canadian

Pacific, Molson, Eaton's, Domtar, Imperial Oil, the five big banks, Abitibi-Price, Brascan Noranda, and many more. They are, with some exceptions, the same corporations that belong to the BCNI and finance the C.D. Howe Institute.

The Fraser has always had an explicitly right-wing agenda. (The Howe sees itself as pragmatic and non-ideological.) Originally on the outer fringe of public debate, the Fraser is now in the mainstream, a sign of how far to the right the political parameters have shifted in Canada.

Economic freedom has been a central Fraser theme. The institute argues that unrestrained democracy—the voracious demands of the public and of weak politicians preoccupied with re-election—compromises economic freedom and should be curbed by such measures as constitutional restrictions on taxation and spending. It also advocates the constitutional entrenchment of private property rights but not social rights. Economist Milton Friedman, a Fraser mentor and close friend of Walker, is quoted in the *Fraser Forum*: "I believe a free economy is a necessary condition for a democratic society. But I also believe that a democratic society, once established, destroys a free economy. So rolling back the welfare state is exceedingly difficult...."

The key to smaller government, for the Fraser Institute, is the decentralization of power to the level of local government, where services can be provided at a reasonable cost and interest groups can be more easily neutralized. If a given community does not provide cost-effective services, its citizens can move to a community that does.

The social security system is seen as a means of redistributing income to "special interest groups." Business is, of course, excluded from this category, as are its citizen front organizations such as the National Citizens' Coalition and the Canadian Taxpayers Federation. The social security system is considered both immoral and an inefficient use of taxpayers' income. In its place the Fraser advocates a mix of private charity (voluntary taxation of the wealth creators) and public charity for the deserving poor—the unfortunate, not the irresponsible. Young, single, able-bodied males who have no work are "irresponsible" and should be cut off welfare.

For the Fraser Institute, poverty results from genetic, not societal factors. Walker says: "In some cases...poverty is simply a reflection of the fact that the sufferers were dealt an unlucky physical or intellectual allocation from the roulette wheel of genetic inheritance. Others suffer physical handicaps due to no fault of their own."

The Fraser Institute also believes that the extent of poverty in Canada has been exaggerated by special interests in order to justify public "overspending" on social programs. Its 1992 publication entitled *Poverty in Canada*, by Christopher Sarlo, concludes: "Poverty is not a major problem in Canada." In order to reach this conclusion Sarlo redefines poverty as applying to those families who lack the "cost of basic necessities for absolute physical survival." The Fraser calculates the 1994 absolute poverty income for a family of four at between $14,000 and $17,000, depending on the province, far below the Statistics Canada and other measures of poverty, which are around $31,000.

Similarly, the Fraser Institute argues that the statistics greatly overstate the problem of unemployment. For most so-called unemployed, Walker claims, "idleness is no longer a sign of distress nor involuntary. It is rather a symptom of job search and a result of the fact that our unemployment insurance program encourages people to be choosy." The Fraser believes that public medical insurance should cover only catastrophic illness. It believes in replacing the UI and welfare programs with a guaranteed annual income in the form of a negative income tax at a very low level of support.

Unlike the Howe, which focuses exclusively on opinion-shapers and decision-makers, the Fraser aggressively popularizes its ideas through materials for schools and universities, and through its tax freedom day and debt watch campaigns. Its media watch division ferrets out and exposes examples of what it alleges are examples of left-wing bias in the media.

The most faithful political expression of the Fraser Institute thinking is the Reform Party. Fraser publications are the foun-tainhead of Reform Party policies. For both, the debt/deficit is the overriding obsession, both the villain and the means to destroy "the nanny state," thereby restoring the freedom of the market, the primacy of individual self-reliance, and traditional family values. (We discuss the Fraser's role in the 1994–95 deficit scare in Chapter Five.)

The third instrument of persuasion through which the corporate agenda is advanced is the media. Mass communication media, especially television, have dramatically changed how people receive information and how their opinions are formulated. The media provide the crucial means of persuasion, and since the media are market driven, the financial resources of the corporate sector give it privileged access. This is not to say, of course, that the media are a simple tool for disseminating corporate propaganda; the media contain a wide diversity of political views and opinions, many of which are critical of neo-liberal policies. Indeed, business often rails against what it perceives to be a left-leaning bias among reporters.

Nonetheless, not only does big business have privileged access to the media, but the media themselves are (with the exception of the CBC) big business. Their main goal is profit. Ownership is concentrated in a few conglomerates covering television, radio, newspapers, magazines, and cable. "The media barons are the same people who are the political barons and the corporate barons," says communications professor James Winter. As mega-mergers require mega-financing, it is unlikely that Ted Rogers would alienate his bankers by using his new acquisition, *Maclean's*, to run a campaign to lower interest rates and bank profits. The bulk of media revenues come from selling advertising space, mainly to other businesses. In 1991, three media giants, Thomson, Southam, and Conrad Black's Hollinger Inc., owned 87 percent of Canada's daily newspapers. Much to Premier Parizeau's consterna-tion, Black, Paul Desmarais, and Québécor head Pierre Péladeau control ten of the eleven daily newspapers in Quebec.

Although they rarely become directly involved in news coverage, the essential decisions—on which issues are (and are not) covered, how issues are packaged or framed, the depth and breadth of coverage, how (or if) dissenting views are handled, how the exchange of opinion is managed, who is hired and promoted, who sits on the editorial boards—are ultimately made by the owners. (See Chapter Five for the media's role in shaping opinion on the deficit.)

The ability of political parties to get their message out is determined by their ability to buy media time. They need to craft their political message in the most effective way. Their ability to win elections has come to depend more on raising money and crafting their message effectively through the media than on mobilizing people through the party organization. Political parties have become money-raising machines. Voters, reduced to consumers in the political marketplace, have become alienated from the political process.

Polling has become a staple of today's politics. Day in and day out, pollsters, like market analysts, probe the psyches of voters for their political clients. They use the results of these ongoing attitude surveys to plot their campaign strategy, to determine how best to sell their candidate. They then track how effective their campaign advertising, speeches, etc., have been each day in pushing the right buttons in the electorate. If one strategy doesn't seem to be working, they can switch gears very quickly to suit or shape public opinion. Once in power, governments use pollsters continually to identify problems in their policy initiatives and shift their communication strategies accordingly. The Liberal government, for example, commissioned almost $7 million worth of public opinion surveys in the fiscal year 1994–95. Polling is extremely powerful in identifying and manipulating voter opinions, so parties with access to it have a huge advantage. However, this immensely expensive tool, like media access, requires the kind of money that only corporations can provide.

Thus the main political parties (the NDP excepted) have become highly dependent on corporate financing. Liberals have long relied on corporate campaign donations and, with the dramatic increase in the cost of political campaigns, its dependence has grown apace. In 1993 corporations accounted for 56 percent of Party contributions. No Liberal politician these days can gain the party's leadership without the financial backing of the corporate sector. So, not only are policy priorities shaped by the need not to offend corporate backers, but the chance of leadership going to someone from the progressive wing of the party is now much more remote.

Corporate financing is neither altruistic largesse nor acknowledgment of social responsibility. Corporations expect concrete returns on their donations. They expect a Liberal government to follow policies that protect and enhance their private interests. For example, the thirteen largest contributors to the 1993 Liberal election campaign were banks and other financial corporations—Scotia McLeod, Coopers and Lybrand, Wood Gundy, Richardson Greenshields, Nesbitt Thomson, Midland Walwyn, Bank of Montreal, Royal Bank, RBC Dominion Securities Inc., Canadian Imperial Bank of Commerce, Toronto-Dominion Securities, Toronto-Dominion Bank, and the Bank of Nova Scotia. (The fourteenth was Power Corp., a conglomerate with financial interests and close business and family ties to the Liberal government.)

No one should be surprised that the Chrétien government, like its predecessor, has continued to acquiesce to the Bank of Canada's harsh monetary policy, which is so beneficial to the financial community but so damaging to the unemployed whose voice is barely audible in the corridors of power. Nor should it be surprising that no government, including this one, has limited corporate financing. Even the modest recommendations of the Mulroney-appointed Royal Commission on Electoral Reform and Party Financing have not been implemented.

The final means of political persuasion at the disposal of the corporate sector is government lobbying—paid middlemen acting on behalf of corporations out of the public eye. Political lobbying, which has greatly enhanced corporate interests at the expense of democracy, began in the 1970s and took off in the 1980s under the Mulroney Tories. In 1980, there were just a few dozen lobbyists; today more than 450 lobby firms wine and dine politicians and senior bureaucrats on behalf of their corporate clients. The Ottawa lobbying business is now estimated conservatively at $100 million annually; moreover, since corporations can deduct lobbying expenses from their taxable income, it is subsidized by the taxpayer.

When Unitel Communications wanted to pressure the federal government to open up the long-distance telephone market to competition, they hired Hill and Knowlton Ltd., for $20,000 a month, to lobby for them. When the Pharmaceutical Manufacturers Association, the organization of the transnational drug companies, wanted to have their members' drug patents extended from ten to twenty years, they hired Government Policy Consultants Inc., at $33,000 a month, to conduct their successful lobbying campaign.

Corporations acting through lobbyists have enormous influence over the direction of policy and the spending of billions of public dollars—from the approval of a project or the granting of a tax break to the waiving of an environmental regulation or the authorization of an animal hormone such as the milk production-enhancing BGH. Lobbyists are paid huge sums but are not required by law to reveal who their clients are or how much they are paid.

The business of policy formulation, the drafting of legislation and regulations now occurs largely through lobbying. Parliament has become less and less relevant; backroom brokers have reduced Commons committees to a sideshow on most issues. *Canadian Business* journalist Jenefer Curtis has described the lobbying industry as "a sort of shadow civil service. But unlike traditional bureaucrats, they push the interests of those who pay them."

A poignant example of this is the Regulatory Efficiency Act (Bill C-62), which was introduced by the Liberals in December 1994 after several years of lobbying. Touted by its sponsor, Treasury Board president Art Eggleton, as capable of saving business $3 billion a year, the legislation will give senior politicians and bureaucrats sweeping power to grant business special exemptions from health, safety, environmental, and other laws and regulations in the name of efficiency and competitiveness. Under this bill, a corporation that wants to get around a given regulation would provide the minister responsible and the Treasury Board president with an alternative means for meeting the regulation's objective. Cabinet would then give final approval and designate someone to monitor compliance. As the bill now stands, this stealth-style deregulation is beyond parliamentary accountability, contains no obligation to consult, and has no mechanism for participation by affected citizens' groups. An example of the triumph of the accountant's bottom line over the well-being of society, this legislation is certain to be a bonanza for the lobbying industry. Concerned that growing popular opposition might scuttle the bill, BCNI chief Tom d'Aquino wrote to Treasury Board president Eggleton urging him to pass it quickly into law and not to be distracted by the "campaign...of deliberate disinformation and fear mongering" of opponents.

So powerful have the lobbyists become that they have successfully resisted all efforts to regulate them. The Liberals promised in their Red Book to bring greater transparency and accountability to the industry. It was one of the cornerstones of their promise to bring integrity back to government. However, the Liberals' legislation does not require lobbyists to disclose the fees they charge their clients. Moreover, the ethics counsellor appointed to oversee the industry reports to the prime minister, not to Parliament, rendering the position susceptible to political influence. One observer described it as "more of a lap dog than a watch dog."

Most Canadians, however they identify themselves politically, want to be able to work, to earn a decent living, and to be confident that at least the same opportunities will be available for their children. They also want protection against unexpected or uncontrollable contingencies of life, such as unemployment, illness, and old age. The Canadian government has played—and most expect it to play—an important role in meeting these common priorities. Government is the only avenue through which citizens can express this will collectively. A small élite is exempted, by virtue of personal wealth, from such concerns; for the rest of us, however, the only alternatives to government are the market and the family. Recent history has taught us the hard lesson that these alone are not enough, especially in times of economic crisis. To the extent that government policies over the last two decades have ceased to meet these fundamental goals, there has been a serious erosion of confidence in government: an erosion of democracy.

Democracy presumes that power, the capacity to impose one's will, rests ultimately with the people. People delegate power, through the politicians they elect, to a sovereign state to pursue common ends. Democracy presupposes a sovereign state that sets priorities and policies reflecting these common ends. Without state sovereignty, democracy is hollow; without democracy, state sovereignty is tyranny.

Democracy also presupposes that political equality is inseparable from economic equality. Political scientist Robert Dahl poses the fundamental question connecting economic equality and democracy: "If income, wealth and economic position are political resources, and if they are distributed unequally, then how can citizens be political equals, and if citizens cannot be political equals, how is democracy to exist?" Although in practice economic inequalities exist, democracy's legitimacy in the eyes of its citizens rests on the perception that they are not extreme, and that there is an equality of opportunity that flows from access to employment, education, income, health, food, shelter, and other social and economic rights of citizenship.

Democracy is about inclusion, people being connected to one another and to their political leaders in a community. Democracy is about people having confidence that the politicians whom they vote into office will act on their behalf. It is about people feeling that their voice, whether individually or as part of an advocacy group or a local community, makes a difference. Democracy is about accountability and trust.

In the best of circumstances these ideals are approximated—there is always a gap between the ideal of democracy and its reality—but how far can a society stray from the ideal and still qualify as a democracy?

Corporate power and influence expressed through government policy has greatly altered the state in the last twenty years. Big business has seen its friends and sympathizers move into key political and bureaucratic positions. There is much intermingling of state and corporate elites, reinforcing their mutual interests. The state has been restructured so that in many areas its ability to implement policies has diminished. In other areas its sovereignty has been maintained or even enhanced. Certainly, the economic space occupied by the public sector has shrunk. There has been a major sell-off of public assets, and many previously regulated activities have been deregulated, or reregulated so as to give the market freer rein. The state has gained new power as protector of property and enforcer of market disciplines, and promoter of competitiveness.

The role of Parliament as a legislative body has been weakened, as has the influence of government committees and public consultation. In its second term, the Mulroney Conservative government instituted changes in parliamentary rules that stifled debate more often than in all previous parliaments combined. Public consultation has become less and less relevant; the Liberals have curtailed the release of a public record of committee hearings. Witnesses who testify face indifferent committee members, no media to report their testimony, and no accessible record that the session even occurred.

The availability of information is a vital pillar of democracy. The access to information law, which was supposed to usher in a new era of accountability in government, was turned into a means for withholding information from the public. The Tories abolished several important government-sponsored policy research institutes that served as a partial counterweight to the partisan barrage coming from the corporate-funded think tanks. Both Tories and Liberals have chopped Statistics Canada's budget, ending the collection of much essential information about what is happening in our society. On occasion, as with the study by two Statscan researchers on the causes of the federal debt, there has been outside meddling with its autonomy. The Liberals weakened the law requiring disclosure to the federal government of corporate financial information. The legislation harmonizes federal reporting requirements with those of New Brunswick, the province with the weakest rules, where companies like Wal-Mart have incorporated. No longer will the government or independent analysts be able to track the activities of these corporations, which vitally affect our economic life.

Regulatory and other public-sector bodies have reduced or eliminated the opportunities for public participation, while the corporate sector enhances its influence. Corporate representatives dominate advisory bodies, task forces, working groups, commissions, and regulatory boards. The corporate voice is heard most loudly in the deliberations of government while the voices of the general public have become fainter, and even when occasionally heard are usually discounted.

An international tier of government has grown rapidly over the last twenty-five years, making decisions that greatly affect our society, usually without our knowledge, participation, or consent. In this world of bureaucrats, diplomats, and corporate lobbyists, the corporate viewpoint is well represented, its interests entrenched in international agreements. The network of unaccountable institutions that make up this unofficial "world government" include the World Bank, the International Monetary Fund, and the World Trade Organization. It includes the Bank for International Settlements, where leading central bankers gather every month to co-ordinate monetary policy. It includes the Group of Seven major industrialized nations and the Organization for Economic Co-operation and Development, the industrial country club. It includes Codex Alimentarius, the obscure body that sets international food and health standards, and it includes the NAFTA commissions, secretariats, advisory bodies, working groups, and dispute resolution panels.

Civil society, the rich foliage of organizations and institutions to which people belong and in which they participate, is supposed to guard against the tyranny of government as well as the tyranny of the market. The corporate takeover of the Canadian political agenda has placed this vital pillar of our democracy under siege.

The most powerful civil-society organizations are those made up of people in their workplaces—unions. Unions represent over four million Canadians, 36 percent of the workforce. In the United States they represent only 15 percent of working Americans. The presence of stronger unions is the single biggest reason why income disparity is less in Canada than in the U.S., which has the most unequal distribution of income in the industrialized world. Neo-liberal policies of the last decade have been hard on Canadian unions. The United Nations International Labour Organization has ruled that both the Conservative and the present Liberal governments have violated federal public employees' rights of association by imposing a wage freeze and breaking negotiated contract provisions on job security. These are fundamental human rights that are being violated, as basic to the functioning of democratic society as the right to vote.

In spite of this assault and their weakened bargaining power, unions have managed to hold their membership base, and they remain important as a means of transferring income from profits to wages and providing a measure of democracy in the workplace. As such they remain the biggest threat to corporate interests.

Neo-liberal theory portrays unions as impediments to the efficient functioning of labour markets, and as creators of unemployment and inflation. In the media, union leaders are often portrayed as self-serving, at odds with their rank and file. The corporate sector, that most authoritarian of organizations, regularly exaggerates the power of unions in order to disguise its own power. Unions collect in total $1 billion each year in dues from their members, equivalent to the profits of the Royal Bank in 1994. This hardly proves a parity of power between "big labour" and big business.

The mainstream church is another important component of

civil society. The source of its power is moral, and as major political issues are ultimately moral issues, its potential as an advocate for democracy and justice is great. At times, it has been a leading force for progressive political change, notably during the 1930s. Ministers such as J.S. Woodsworth, Tommy Douglas, and Stanley Knowles, inspired by the message of the social gospel, entered politics and became prominent advocates for social justice. In the early 1980s the Catholic bishops were an outspoken moral voice against the injustices of neo-liberal policies. Strong networks within the churches, such as the Ecumenical Coalition for Economic Justice and the Inter-Faith Centre for Human Rights, do important education and advocacy work on economic and social policy issues, human rights, and international development. But these days church leadership seems unable or unwilling to speak forcefully on major political issues.

Interestingly, as former Catholic Bishops' social policy advisor Tony Clarke has observed, the vacuum created by this silence is being filled by the Christian fundamentalist movement, which is pushing hard to dismantle the social role of the state. It charges that the state has undermined personal responsibility and the role of the family, and seeks to transfer it back to the local community and the family. These conservative values, which are at the fringe of Canadian society, have found political expression in the Reform Party, whose ground troops during the last election came from the bible schools of Alberta and Saskatchewan.

Popular grassroots movements have mushroomed in recent years, reflecting a strong desire for democratic expression. Consumers, women, disabled persons, ethnic and visible minorities, anti-poverty, nationalism, human rights, gay and lesbian rights, peace, conservation, animal rights, anti-smoking, anti-pollution: these causes give voice to people and issues that have been underrepresented and undervalued in our society.

The sources and instruments of civil-society organizations' power are not great when compared with those of the corporate sector. Some leaders have gained important public profiles; some groups have built extensive organizations of volunteer activists.

Their financial capacities—whether through direct public appeals or government assistance—vary, but are on the whole precarious.

Weak sources of power translate into weak instruments with which to exercise power. Most civil-society groups don't have the power in the economy that unions have—that is, the power of withdrawing their labour. The task of drawing large numbers of people around a particular issue at election time usually requires access to major media, especially television, which is beyond their financial capacity. Besides, successful persuasion requires a concerted effort exploiting a variety of mechanisms on a scale that only the corporate sector can afford.

In the 1960s and 1970s these advocacy groups, helped by government funding, made concrete gains in making their voices heard, so strengthening the quality of our democracy. More recently, however, a right-wing backlash against these groups has blamed them for all sorts of alleged ills in society, from government overspending to welfare abuse. The funding assault that started under the Mulroney Conservatives is being vigorously pursued by the Liberals, with support from the Reform Party. Bully boys within the Liberal caucus are encouraged in their campaigns to eliminate funding and tax assistance to "special interest" groups. Indeed, Liberal funding cuts to civil-society organizations surpass those of their Conservative predecessors. (There is no similar momentum to cut government tax subsidies to business and business-sponsored lobbies like the National Citizens' Coalition). Already weak voices are being made weaker.

3

THE CORNERSTONES

"Once a nation parts with control of its currency and credit, it matters not who makes that nation's laws."

Mackenzie King, 1935

"The Bank of Canada, rather than being a servant of Parliament, has become its master. This is unacceptable in a democracy where elected representatives, not appointed officials, are supposed to govern."

Professor Duncan Cameron, before
a parliamentary committee, 1995

In May 1995, the Royal Bank of Canada released a remarkable report entitled *Why Canadian Living Standards Have Declined in the 1990s*. Its author, chief economist John McCallum, concluded that the main reason for the decline in living standards was a decline in people with jobs—higher unemployment, a collapse of youth participation in the workforce, and the levelling of female participation in the workforce. Why did this happen? The answer, from a senior bank official, was unprecedented. The main reason, according to McCallum, was "the exceptional length and depth of Canada's recession, which was itself due in large measure to the highly restrictive stance of Canadian monetary policy." McCallum went on, "Compounding the effects of this monetary shock were the US recession and industrial restructuring in response to globalization and free trade."

This explanation comes as no surprise to those who have read our work. We, and many others, have been saying this for years. The media establishment has largely excluded this analysis, ruling it outside the frame of serious debate. However, coming from the corporate inner sanctum, these ideas have suddenly acquired new weight. For the first time there is an admission that the cornerstones of the corporate agenda—free trade and harsh anti-inflationary monetary policy—have exacted a heavy toll on the country. McCallum actually identified two specific, deliberate government policies. (His reference to globalization is distracting, since the FTA/NAFTA is a concrete manifestation of this blame-absolving term.)

McCallum used a very simple methodology to measure the decline in employment: the ratio of persons employed to total population. He chose not to carry it the next step and measure the drop in employment. We extended his analysis by calculating how many people would have been employed had the employment–population ratio remained constant at its 1988 level. Our calculation revealed these policies (and the U.S. recession) as the main reason that there were, in 1994, proportionately 660,000 fewer people working than before the policies were implemented. This is not our estimate; it is a logical inference from the analysis of the chief economist of the Royal Bank of Canada. This figure does not include the hundreds of thousands (perhaps more) of people who lost their jobs and have since found other work, mostly at lower wages and inferior working conditions.

Free trade and anti-inflationary monetary policy have been the central policy tools for executing the corporate plan: crippling the fiscal capacity of the government, tying its hands, transforming the labour market, sabotaging the just society, narrowing the parameters of political choice.

The effects of free trade are intertwined with those of a tight monetary policy, which, when the free trade agreement with the U.S. was signed at the beginning of 1988, became the harshest in the industrialized world. The Tory government vigorously denied any connection, including the widely suspected side-deal with the Americans to hike the dollar. However, the resulting rise in the dollar and in borrowing costs created a huge disadvantage for Canadian producers competing with the Americans. Michael Wilson, who as finance minister from 1984 to 1992 had responsibility for monetary policy, also took control of final FTA negotiations in the fall of 1987. In a 1994 conversation with journalist Linda McQuaig, Wilson remarked that monetary policy had the hidden benefit of accelerating the pace of the hard but necessary adjustment to free trade. "It forced decisions to be taken that maybe companies, if the dollar had been low, would have put off making," said Wilson.

In any case, monetary policy dovetailed with the Americans' desire for a higher dollar to accompany the FTA, and the Tory/big business goal of zero inflation. The sky-high interest rate pushed up the value of the dollar from 75 cents to 89 cents by mid-1991, and eighteen months later squeezed the last gasp of inflation out of an immobilized Canadian economy. The combined effect of these two policies, though not their respective contributions, is not seriously disputed: a far deeper and more protracted recession than elsewhere in the industrialized world; massive business failures; a leap in unemployment, and great stress on the social security system; collapse of government revenue; and a huge increase in the debt and deficit.

The free trade campaign was a rarely revealed display of the corporate sector's political might. The main impetus for the Canada-U.S. deal came from the BCNI, which had adopted it as a priority in 1981 and began to promote it publicly in 1983. At the outset of the negotiations, d'Aquino presented chief negotiator Simon Reisman with several black binders of documents detailing what the BCNI wanted from a bilateral agreement. These became a constant reference point for Reisman.

Corporate Canada wanted two things from a trade deal. First, two hundred companies (mostly BCNI members) that accounted for 90 percent of all Canadian-U.S. trade and more than 95 percent of foreign direct investment in the two countries were very dependent on the U.S. market. More than one-third of Canada's total output of resource and manufactured goods went south of the border. Canadian-owned corporations had invested heavily in the United States. However, their U.S. interests were less than secure. American producers were launching unfair trade actions against Canadian exports, and the U.S. government, angered by Canadian policies, was threatening to toughen its trade laws and implement foreign investment controls. U.S.-owned BCNI members, for their part, wanted protection for their holdings against Canadian government interference. Thus, big business wanted greater security of access to the entire North American market than was available under the multilateral framework of trade and investment rules, the General Agreement on Tariffs and Trade. In short, it wanted preferential treatment over the corporations of other nations.

Second, big business wanted a formal economic rule-book that would force the Canadian economy—through competitive pressure if not though explicit provisions—to harmonize with the larger and more business-friendly U.S. economy. It wanted a deal that would limit Canadian governments' penchant for intervention, regulation, and spending (including social spending), and would curb workers' wage demands. The new continental market would pressure Canada to reduce social programs and lower labour and environmental standards to the U.S. level. The dislocation caused by restructuring, especially the increase in unemployment and the weakening of the tax base, would help compress wages and reduce government social spending.

Moreover, a formal agreement would constitutionalize the economic relationship so that a future government could not return to the old nationalist/interventionist ways. The Mulroney government was proceeding rapidly—cutting social programs, privatizing public assets, and removing investment controls—but business wanted these policies locked in, beyond the reach of any future democratic challenge.

Once the deal was concluded, the BCNI and the Conservative government had to discredit the arguments of the critics and to persuade Canadians that the deal would be good for them, that rejecting it would have dire consequences. Three main arguments put forward to sell the free trade deal to the Canadian public were jobs, social programs, and sovereignty.

The first argument was that a free trade agreement would bring a new era of export-driven growth, job creation, and prosperity for all Canadians in all regions of the country; it would increase living standards and reduce inequalities; it would exchange low-paid for high-paid, value-added jobs. The second was that social programs, far from being undermined, would be strengthened: a stronger economy would improve the government's capacity to deliver social programs. The third argument was that the sovereignty of government would not be undermined.

What has happened on these three fronts since 1988? First, jobs. As expected, exports grew rapidly (as did imports), accounting for a larger share of the Canadian economy; on the other hand, trade between the provinces declined. And Canadian exports became much more dependent on the United States market.

However, employment in the goods-producing sector—of which (excluding construction) almost two-fifths is exported—had dropped by 454,000 by 1994. Manufacturing accounted for 353,000 of these losses, a drop of 18 per cent of its workforce. Manufacturing employment, which had held steady throughout the 1980s, fell from 18 percent to 15 percent of total employment. So the rise in exports has not translated into a jobs bonanza. Employment fell even in the most successful export sectors. The largest export sector, motor vehicles, grew 67 percent, while employment actually fell by 3 percent. Exports of electrical equipment, etc., grew 143 percent, while employment shrank by 38 percent. Aerospace exports grew 59 percent, but employment dropped 9 percent; iron and steel exports grew 62 percent, while employment dropped 30 percent.

There was a small net increase of 183,000 jobs in the service sector, absorbing only 40 percent of the jobs displaced in the goods sector. But hundreds of thousands of new entrants have been swelling the job market each year, far in excess of those who retire. So just replacing jobs lost does not begin to absorb the ongoing demand for jobs.

Consequently, official unemployment, hidden unemployment, precarious employment (people getting by on self-employment, part-time, and temporary work), and the welfare rolls have all soared. (The estimated real rate of un/underemployment is now 25 percent.) The magnitude of the employment crisis, understated by the statistics, surfaces only when, for example, 25,000 people stand in line overnight for a chance to apply for a "good steady job" at General Motors.

What about the quality of jobs created in the free trade era? Of the nine major job categories, only "business, commercial and personal services" registered significant job growth. Its share of total employment rose from 35 percent to 38 percent. However, average earnings in this sector are the second lowest of the nine categories. (Public service jobs, a high-wage service sector, increased marginally, but with deep federal and provincial government cuts now under way at all levels, they can be expected to plummet.)

With small variations, most provinces experienced declines in their goods sectors, in line with Canada as a whole. In services, there was marginal to modest growth in most provinces, but not nearly enough to absorb the loss in the goods sector. Quebec actually lost service jobs overall. Only in British Columbia was job growth spread across every major service sector. In every province, the only service categories that consistently saw modest or significant job creation were low-wage commercial/personal services and the lowest-wage retail/wholesale trade. These two categories are dominated by restaurant and store clerk–type jobs, hardly the stuff of the new knowledge economy.

Finally, what about the job-creation performance of members

of the Business Council on National Issues, the global warriors behind free trade, whose rallying cry during the 1988
election was "more and better jobs"? We tracked a sample of
fifty (non-financial) BCNI members to assess their job creation performance during 1988–94. Thirty-nine companies in
the group shed jobs. At the beginning of free trade they
employed 765,000 workers; by 1994 their workforce had
dropped to 550,000, a destruction of 215,000 jobs. The
other eleven companies in the sample created a total of
13,000 jobs during 1988–94. The combined revenues of the
fifty BCNI corporations grew from $154 billion to $196 billion during this same period.

When confronted with this dismal employment picture most
free trade supporters resort to the circular argument that without
free trade we would be much worse off, saying in effect that their
job claims are virtually unverifiable.

Income distribution is the broadest measure of inequality in
our society, illustrating who is winning and who is losing. In the
twenty years since 1973, when inequality had fallen to a post-war
low, the top 30 percent of families gained an even greater share
of the pie (from 49.6 percent to 52.3 percent). The next 20 percent maintained their share, and the bottom half of Canadian
families lost income share (from 29.5 percent to 26.9 percent).
What does this mean in concrete terms? It means that in 1993
alone, the wealthiest 30 percent got $14 billion more of the
income pie than they would have received had their share
remained the same as it was in 1973. All of this *extra* income
came at the expense of the poorest half of Canadian families. Not
only has inequality been growing, but it has been picking up
speed, with more than half the widening disparity since 1973
occurring in the past eight years.

High-income families have benefited from the very high
interest on their savings, and from tax breaks and lower income
tax rates. Earnings of professional and managerial groups have
continued to grow, while average real wages and family
incomes have declined. The rise in unemployment, the growth

of temporary and low-paying jobs, and the decline of federal social transfers to the provinces have all played a part as well.

Social programs have been savaged. Once the trade deal was safely passed, big business resumed its relentless lobbying for cuts, now in the name of affordability—crippling deficits and global competitiveness were allegedly forcing the restructuring of the social security system in order to conform to the "realities" of the twenty-first century.

After 1988, the pace of social cuts greatly accelerated, meeting the twin aims of trimming back the social security system to more "affordable" levels and levelling the free-trade playing field. It was done precisely when the social dislocation from the neo-liberal cornerstones was at its height, when anxiety and personal hardship were climbing, and when people's need for a strong social security system was greatest. These changes (described in Chapters Six and Seven) have moved Canada much closer to the U.S. social model. The universal child benefits program and the universal retirement benefit program (Old Age Security) have been eliminated and replaced by weak, targeted programs. Unemployment insurance has been savaged to resemble its inferior U.S. counterpart. U.S. notions of workfare and charity have returned to Canada after a fifty-year absence. Health care and education are experiencing a similar fate.

The claim that FTA/NAFTA entailed only a minimal surrender of sovereignty was never credible. The agreement contains scores of provisions that directly or indirectly constrain government policy freedom. It is a masterpiece of deception, asserting in one article that a given policy is permitted while undermining or negating it in other articles.

Constitutional and trade law expert Barry Appleton, not someone prone to rhetorical excess, summed up the FTA/NAFTA straitjacket on sovereignty in his 1994 legal text, *Navigating NAFTA*. "The NAFTA represents the supremacy of a classically liberal (and United States) conception of the state with its imposition of significant restraints upon the role of government." For Canada, he says, this represents a fundamental break with tradition. "All international trade agreements entail some self-imposed limitation on government authority. However, NAFTA appears to approach an extreme. It does this by the extensiveness of its obligations which attempt to lock-in one (the American) perspective of governmental role for *all successive North American governments* [italics added]." There are many examples of how these constraints have played themselves out with regard to specific policy issues. Here we look at three that affect social policy.

While FTA/NAFTA formally retains the right of governments to maintain and expand public sector activity, in practice it deters public enterprise and systematically compresses the boundaries of the public sector. Business has a virtual veto over any decision to provide new public goods or services.

Thus, the Conservative government privatized some twenty-five Crown corporations during its nine years in office and the Liberal government is following suit. Not one new Crown corporation was created during this period. As the government continues to off-load health, education, and other social services to the private sector, the agreement will be a barrier to any future government wanting to rebuild the public social security system.

The second example of how the agreement has compressed the policy space involves drugs and health costs. In 1992, the government passed Bill C-91, extending monopoly protection for corporate drug patents from ten to twenty years, killing Canada's compulsory licensing legislation, which had kept prices low. This legislation found its way into the NAFTA intellectual property chapter and thus slipped beyond the reach of future government action. As a result, drug costs have become the fastest-growing expenditure item in provincial health plans, forcing them to cut back coverage. Drug costs are now equivalent to physician costs. Greenshield Canada, a non-profit company that administers prepaid public and private health plans, released a report that found that, from 1987 to 1993, the average cost of a drug claim increased 93 percent—far above the rise in the consumer price index of 23 percent. This was happening, it said, even though average drug prices were rising in line with inflation, because of "costly new patented drugs."

A third example involves cigarettes and health. The federal government lowered tobacco taxes to eliminate cross-border smuggling of Canadian cigarettes (and most provincial governments followed suit). Canadian manufacturers were exporting cigarettes to the U.S., not for U.S. consumption, but to smugglers who were re-importing them to Canada for sale on the black market. The tax reduction cost federal and provincial treasuries almost $1 billion in 1994. It could have been avoided with an export tax imposed at the Canadian factory gate; but export taxes were made illegal under FTA/NAFTA and the Liberal government, having just broken its election promise on NAFTA, did not want to risk a public challenge.

To compensate for the devasting health effects of the tax reduction (not to mention the costs to the health-care system), the Commons Health Committee was poised to recommend the plain packaging of all cigarettes to discourage their use, especially among youth. Appearing before the committee on behalf of U.S. tobacco giants that owned Canadian brands was Julius Katz, the chief U.S. NAFTA negotiator. The statement he carried in his accompanying brief was prepared by none other than former U.S. Trade Representative Carla Hills. The message was that any such action would violate NAFTA. Trade minister MacLaren objected weakly that health was exempted in the NAFTA text. Katz replied that the exemption did not apply to intellectual property, including trademarks. The government quickly abandoned the idea and shuffled it off for "further study."

The real face of free trade is now evident. The corporate oligarchy (with the aid of immensely powerful instruments of persuasion) sold the FTA/NAFTA to the Canadian people under false pretences. Even then, only a minority supported it, and it passed only because of our flawed electoral system. But talk of turning back is not on the political agenda these days. So confident are leading proponents of its irreversibility that they are now speaking openly about the next stages of integration: common external tariffs, a common currency, common institutions. Some are even hinting at political union. Tom d'Aquino says this will require us to "face tough political questions over the next decade."

James Tobin has been swimming against the stream for a long time. Winner of the 1981 Nobel Prize for Economics, the Yale University professor was one of the few in his profession who resisted the stampede to embrace the new dogma of international monetary deregulation. In 1971, the so-called Bretton Woods system of international monetary management broke down; it was replaced by a floating currency exchange system, and later by the lifting of controls on international capital movements. These two changes opened the door to the explosion of the "hot money" market. Tobin was one of the few to recognize the danger that these changes, particularly the latter, would wreak havoc with national policies. To mitigate this danger, he proposed a tax on international monetary transactions to discourage speculation. Seventeen years later, the global money markets are threatening national sovereignty everywhere, and James Tobin is still trying to persuade political leaders to adopt his "Tobin tax."

Following the breakdown of Bretton Woods, commodity prices (notably oil) rose, and inflation and economic slowdown became endemic throughout the industrialized world. Central bankers in most industrialized countries began to turn to monetary policy to curb price rises, even though they knew the consequence would be higher unemployment.

Anti-inflation monetary policy is essentially about using high interest rates to curb inflation. Canadians need to understand how important a tool monetary policy has been for restructuring Canadian society: for disciplining workers through high unemployment, for disciplining the social function of the state by increasing the burden on the social security system, for redistributing income from the middle class to the wealthy, and for redistributing power from government to the market. It has also been largely responsible for the emergence of deficits and the accumulated debt of twenty years, which itself—people are now painfully aware—has reinforced the drive to restructure Canadian society.

In the same way that the market serves as a veil behind which corporate power hides, monetary policy, shrouded in mystique and impenetrable to all but its own priesthood, is the ultimate tool for the undemocratic exercise of political power. The Bank of Canada governor, acting at arm's length from the government, protected by a seven-year appointment, alone wields awesome decision-making power. Although the government has the right to instruct the Bank governor, it has rarely done so, either out of fear of the financial consequences or, more commonly, because it agrees with the Bank's actions. In any case, maintaining the appearance of the Bank's "independence" and neutrality is a way to deflect political heat from an unpopular policy.

Big business, through its mouthpiece, the Business Council on National Issues, has been a staunch supporter of the Bank of Canada's harsh monetary policy, particularly John Crow's zero-inflation target. The C.D. Howe Institute provided the crucial filter, giving the policy a gloss of academic "objectivity" through several studies, from Peter Howitt's 1990 piece, *Zero Inflation: The Goal of Price Stability*, to Robson and Laidler's 1993 *The Great Canadian Disinflation*. The Howe's legitimization of the Bank's actions was then sold throughout the business media as the solution to high interest rates, sagging productivity, and a host of other economic woes. Only after we purged this demon from our midst, admittedly at some cost, could we resume the path to prosperity, claimed the Howe reports. How long it would be before we entered this better world was not specified. Nor was the immense human toll, or who would pay.

Both the Howe and the BCNI support even greater

independence for the Bank of Canada from the pressures of elected government. Both want the Bank's mandate formally changed, removing the current obligation to maintain high employment (which it no longer fulfills) and giving it one focus— price stability. They even convinced the Mulroney government to propose entrenching this role for the Bank of Canada in the last constitutional round.

The origins of the current debt/deficit crisis go back to the mid-1970s. The thirty years from the end of the war to 1975 were a time of unprecedented economic prosperity and stability. Unemployment was low; economic growth was high and steady. It was a time of expanding wages and low real interest rates, a time of great expansion of public spending on the social security system—child benefits, old age security, unemployment insurance, education, welfare, and medicare.

During the period as a whole, federal government budgets were in balance. In fact, there was a small surplus. Government debt, which stood at 138 percent of GDP in 1946, had declined to a mere 22 percent of GDP by 1975. This was possible because the revenue flow kept pace with spending. Near full employment kept the demands on the social security system manageable. Low interest payments kept government debt service payments low and encouraged business to keep investment high, which in turn kept the economy growing and employment high.

However, beginning in the early 1970s, especially after 1975, things began to change. The first turning point in government policy on the road to the debt crisis was the Liberal government's introduction of a number of tax measures, including tax breaks for business and wealthy individuals, income tax cuts, exemptions to the sales tax, reductions in oil export taxes, and more. The effect of these changes was that the revenue flow to government in relation to the economy began to fall. By 1978, revenue had dropped 20 percent, back to its 1968 level. Spending also declined, but not by nearly as much, and a gap opened up, producing a series of deficits. By 1980, the debt had climbed to 27% of GDP.

A steady flow of revenue is as essential to maintaining the social security system as a flow of food is to sustaining life. The deliberate tax measures that starved the revenue supply started unravelling the system that led to the fiscal crisis in which we now find ourselves.

Between 1975 and 1985, a period of Liberal government, federal tax revenue rose by 2.2 percent, the lowest increment in the OECD with the exception of the U.S. The average tax revenue increase in OECD countries during this period was 16 percent. Between 1985 and 1991, the Conservative years, tax revenue grew by more than 10 percent, the fourth highest increase in the OECD. The average industrialized country increase in this period was only 3 percent. By 1991, government revenue had climbed back up to 19 percent of GDP, only slightly less than in 1975. But the revenue gap that had opened up under the Liberals, compounded by the negative revenue effects of the 1981–83 recession, had produced a $200-billion federal debt by 1985, equivalent to 42 percent of GDP.

A second turning point in policy came in 1978 when the Bank of Canada, as the government's fiscal agent, turned to global financial markets. In one year the share of federal debt held by foreigners shot up from 5 percent to 13 percent. This did not happen because there was a sudden shortage of domestic savings that could have been tapped, or because there was no other source of borrowing. This was a deliberate policy choice.

Historically, when the government needed funds in a time of insufficient private savings, it borrowed from the Bank of Canada. This is what happened at the outbreak of the Second World War when unemployment was high and federal debt was high (78 percent of GDP), one-third of which was held by foreigners. The government did not throw up its hands and say, "We don't have enough private savings to finance the war effort." The result of government war spending was a big jump in debt, but it was funded largely by the Bank of Canada at extremely low interest rates. The Bank continued to hold a significant share of government debt throughout the next thirty years. In 1977, it held 21 percent of the federal debt.

However, the following year, when the government turned to private international markets, the role of the Bank began to decline. By the time the Mulroney government took over in 1984, the Bank held 10.5 percent of federal debt, and by the end of its mandate the Bank's share had dwindled to near insignificance at 6 percent of the total, mostly in the form of legal tender, the notes and coins we usually think of when we think of money. Contrary to popular myth, most money is created through the issuing of debt, not through the minting of loonies. Every time a bank issues a loan it creates money—debt money. What the Bank of Canada did was to leave the job of creating that kind of money almost entirely to private financial institutions.

So the government borrowed from the private banks at very high rates instead of from the Bank of Canada, which is constitutionally obliged to lend to the government at very low rates. The private banks made a healthy profit (as did domestic and foreign lenders). The compounding of high rates drove up the federal debt and taxpayers were stuck with a huge debt interest bill. In 1991, the Tory government abolished the requirement that private banks hold non-interest-paying cash reserves with the Bank of Canada. This was a major tool the Bank used to regulate the volume of private bank lending. The result was that the private banks were able to earn interest on this money, profiting handsomely from financial deregulation.

In addition, following advice from the international bankers' club, the Bank for International Settlements, in 1989, the Bank of Canada abolished the requirement that banks hold any of their own capital as collateral against the government bonds in their portfolios. Consequently, the banks increased their stock of government bonds 900 percent (for which they charged high interest) and the Bank of Canada reduced its (low-interest) holdings of government bonds by $4 billion. The private banks, calculates William Krehm, were in effect given a $3-billion annual subsidy, with the Canadian taxpayer picking up the extra interest bill.

The funding of federal government debt shifted to the international markets in 1978 because neo-liberal dogma counselled against its financing by the central bank, and because the market was there. This private market—the so-called Euromarket—was large, unregulated, and lucrative. It had been formed in the late 1950s as a way for governments and companies to trade their U.S. dollar holdings outside the United States. Driven by advances in communications technology, it had mushroomed in the 1970s as the vehicle for recycling surplus OPEC petrodollars. In 1978, in the middle of a lending boom, Euromarket funds were ripe for the taking, at lower rates than in domestic markets. (This global loan market grew tenfold in the ensuing years, reaching $5.2 trillion in 1991.)

Thus, the share of federal debt held by foreign creditors rose to 10.3 percent in 1985 and by the end of the Mulroney regime stood at 26 percent. But, as we have mentioned, because of the shift from low-interest Bank of Canada–funded debt to high-interest private and foreign debt, the compounding of interest on this debt was the engine driving its accumulation.

The third major policy shift came in 1980 when Bank of Canada governor Gerald Bouey, following the lead of Paul Volcker at the U.S. Federal Reserve, launched an all-out attack on inflation. Bouey hiked the nominal Bank rate up to 22 percent by August of 1981, when inflation was running at 11%. The result was the worst recession since the 1930s: massive unemployment, bankruptcy, and widespread human suffering.

Governor John Crow began his crusade to squeeze out the last digits of inflation at the beginning of 1988. Whereas Bouey could rationalize his action on the grounds that inflation had become a problem, Crow could not. When he began his assault, inflation was running at 4 percent, not a pressing problem in the eyes of most mainstream pundits. During the next two years Crow increased the nominal bank rate from 8.8 percent to 14 percent, more than double the real interest rate in the U.S.; inflation stood at 4 percent in 1990. By the spring of 1990, the recession was officially in full swing, and unemployment and bankruptcies were on the rise. Three years later the economy was still on its knees and inflation was dead. Two Quebec university economists, Diane Bellemare and Lise Poulin-Simon, calculated that the direct revenue cost to the economy of the consequent high unemployment was $109 billion in 1993 alone; the cost to all governments in lost tax revenue and higher welfare payments was $47 billion.

The Mulroney government cut program spending and raised taxes throughout its term, running a cumulative operating surplus (that is, revenue exceeded all spending except debt interest payments) of $32 billion, and still the debt kept growing. So where was all this extra revenue going? It was going to pay off interest on the debt. It comes as no surprise that average Canadians who saw their taxes rise at the same time as public services were deteriorating were not favourably disposed to further tax increases in 1995.

According to the Finance Department's own research, the growth of the debt since 1985 was due entirely to the compounding of interest on the original debt. Between 1985 and 1991, the government paid out a total of $200 billion in interest payments. Debt as a share of GDP rose from 42 percent at the start of its mandate in 1985 to 60 percent of GDP by the end of 1993. Interest payments took up 11 percent of government revenues in 1975, the equivalent of only 2 percent of GDP. By 1991, debt interest payments had soared to $43 billion and were draining one-third of government revenues, the equivalent of 6 percent of the nation's output. This was more than the combined spending on transfers for education, health, welfare, and unemployment insurance.

We know from the landmark Statistics Canada study by Mimoto and Cross that government spending, and specifically social spending, held steady from 1975 to 1991. Although the authors did not say so explicitly, it remained so in spite of major new stresses on the social security system. The authors' conclusion is very clear: "It was not the explosive growth of program spending that caused the increase in deficits after

1975, but a drop in federal revenues relative to the growth of GDP and rising debt charges." Furthermore, the study said, "Expenditures on social programs did not contribute significantly to the growth of government spending relative to GDP. Excluding the cost of unemployment insurance, which is intended to be [and is] self-financing over the business cycle, *social program spending has not increased relative to GDP over the last 16 years* [italics added]."

That other serious studies, including one by the Dominion Bond Rating Service, came to the same conclusion—namely, that program overspending did not cause the current fiscal mess—has not deterred the business-dominant media voices from continuing to propagate this myth.

Let us briefly review where the debt came from. The problem arose initially from a shortfall on the revenue side from tax reductions and a weakening economy in the second half of the 1970s. The problem grew exponentially beginning in 1980 with the sharp hike in interest rates, which compounded the debt charges, and several years of deep recession and high unemployment. This was followed by a period of lower but still high real interest rates and still high unemployment. Then came the mother of all assaults on inflation, which accelerated the compounding of debt charges, followed by an even more protracted recession, with the predictable human costs.

This is the bitter harvest of a deliberate policy to reduce inflation that created mass unemployment and put the economy in a permanent quasi-recession mode. It has occurred with the explicit or tacit approval of both Liberal and Conservative governments over the last fifteen years.

The consequences of this policy shift have been enormous. The real short-term interest rate (adjusted for inflation) for the entire thirty years between 1950 and 1980 averaged 1.1 percent. For the neo-liberal era (1980–94), real short-term interest rates climbed to an average 6.1 percent. Economic growth, which averaged 5 percent annually in the three decades to 1980, sank to an average 2.4 percent per year between 1981 and 1994.

Unemployment doubled from 5.3 percent in the period to 1980, to an average of 9.8 percent throughout the neo-liberal era. While these trends occurred with varying intensity throughout much of the industrialized world, Canada's experience has been among the worst. Behind these seemingly bloodless statistics lies a devastating upheaval in the economic and social lives of Canadians.

A debt spiral occurs when the real rate of interest (after inflation) of the stock of debt exceeds the real rate of economic growth over an extended time period. What happens is that interest payments on the debt increase faster than the growth of tax revenue (which is tied to the growth of the economy) can pay it off. This has in fact been happening since 1980. The Mulroney government tried to stabilize the debt by running operating surpluses throughout its mandate—by raising taxes and cutting public services. But the debt continued to spiral higher, especially as real interest rates soared under Crow's brutal regime and the economy went into a tailspin after 1989.

The position of the Chrétien government (and the Mulroney government before it) is that the government cannot, through its agent the Bank of Canada, do anything about the high interest rate that is driving the accumulation of debt because the rate is determined in international markets in accordance with the laws of demand for and supply of savings. The only way out, we are told, is to run an operating surplus by reducing spending (tax increases no longer being in vogue) in the hope that the markets will lower rates when they see that the government will be borrowing less. However, when real interest rates exceed real growth by as much as they do now, stabilizing the debt quickly through spending cuts would require such a huge operating surplus as to be politically unfeasible. Furthermore, it would not reach its objective if, as is likely, the cuts were to plunge the country into another deep recession. There is no historical precedent of a nation solving its debt problem this way. The only way to avoid recession, and a worsening of the debt through such a strategy, would be through a massive expansion in exports. Given our overwhelming dependence on the U.S. market and the current slowing down of the American economy, this is not likely to be successful, certainly not with the dollar at its present level.

Nor is there any empirical evidence to suggest that the government will be rewarded by the markets with lower interest rates. For example, looking at the performance of other countries, there is no correlation between the level of debt and the interest rate. Countries such as Spain or Sweden, with a much lower debt than ours, have as high, or higher, interest rates than Canada's. The same lack of a correlation applies to deficit levels. Countries with a much lower deficit than Canada's, and even countries with a budget surplus, have had greater interest rate increases than Canada's.

The debate around monetary policy comes down to a simple question: Who controls interest rates? Are they set in private international financial markets or are they controlled by the Bank of Canada? The essence of the two positions was captured in an exchange during a roundtable discussion on monetary policy organized by the Commons Finance Committee in October 1994. Professor Pierre Fortin, president of the Canadian Economics Association, stated: "The central bank controls short-term interest rates and has a marked influence on medium-term rates.... Canadian and American empirical studies say that long-term rates ease, even if the central bank does not control them directly, following the same direction as short-term interest rates." Fortin continues: "If you are telling me that the central bank cannot do anything about interest rates, what good are those people? What are we waiting for to fire them?" The response from John McCallum, chief economist of the Royal Bank, was as follows: "We both agree that in the short run the Bank of Canada can cause the short-term interest rates to go up or down... So a critical question is, if the Bank of Canada lowers the short-term rates, will the long-term rates go up or down?... [Fortin] says they'll go down. We say they'll go up."

If McCallum and his colleagues are right and our political leaders have no choice but to bow to the will of these markets, then it would seem that we are living under a dictatorship of the markets. But if this is so, no dictatorship is absolute. Sooner or later the pressure for democratic change builds up. People say enough is enough; they rise up and change the system. It is important to remind ourselves that a similar mood of resignation and paralysis prevailed in the Canada of the 1930s until a national war emergency created the political will to regain control.

It is our view that with sufficient political will the government and the Bank of Canada—in spite of the power of financial markets—do have a number of choices to lower interest rates and reduce unemployment. (Some of these are discussed in Chapter Six.) The strongest resistance to such options would come from the most powerful faction of the Canadian corporate sector—the financial faction, which is also a major supporter of this government. It is the bankers—the money managers and investment dealers who create money and credit, and control its supply—who would resist. No privileged group willingly cedes its power and the benefits that flow from it. Interest rates are not set by some magical confluence of supply and demand between millions of savers and investors. The interest rate is set through the intricate dance between the Bank of Canada and a small group of financial institutions with essentially convergent interests. The private banks have been given enormous capacity to determine the supply of money and credit far beyond their own capital base. The Bank of Canada, having ditched the goal of high employment from its mandate, has only one goal—to keep inflation very low and to protect the value of the dollar. In other words, the Bank of Canada is the guardian of wealth for those who have it. Governor Gordon Thiessen told CBC host Peter Gzowski that inflation was tantamount to thievery. Obviously the private banks also want to protect the value of their assets (that is, their loans) from erosion by inflation, and want to continue making a high profit on these loans.

Other priorities, such as full employment, a strong social security system, and reduced inequality, do not carry any weight among those who decide monetary policy. The Bank of Canada no longer acts in the public interest. In fact, so low is unemployment on the Bank of Canada's list of priorities that when the unemployment rate drops close to 9 percent, it feels justified in raising interest rates and slowing the economy in order to cool the potential inflationary pressures. The Bank has even developed a highly sophisticated rationale, complete with a complex mathematical model, to justify its action.

There is, it should be noted in conclusion, a substantial segment of the population that is positively affected by, and generally supports, these policies. This is the professional class, the technocrats and business executives, who for the most part have secure, high-paying jobs or the necessary qualifications to find such employment, and whose salaries are rising as the real wages of the average wage earner are falling. These are the savers who lend their money to banks and mutual funds, and who benefit from tax loopholes and reduced income tax brackets. These are the top 30 percent of the population whom John Kenneth Galbraith calls "the contented classes." Although they would not be so unfashionable as to openly advocate policies that deliberately inflict widespread suffering within our society, they view policy alternatives to remedy this situation as even more unpalatable.

It is worth quoting Galbraith at length on this point. "Unemployment is regretted, but less so when suffered by others unknown.... Unemployment is especially to be preferred to the measures that contend with it. Government expenditure on employment would add to the deficit, and from this could come the spectre of future tax increases. Low interest rates...are adverse to rentier income. They also lower the price that banks charge for their saleable product, namely the money they lend. Bank and central bank influence, under the shadow of seeming neutrality, is usually against what is called 'easy money.' Longer run steps to correct the adverse functional distribution of income clearly would be unwelcome to all so affected.... [Thus] for a substantial and very influential part of the industrial population, the underemployment equilibrium is much to be preferred to the relevant corrective action."

PART TWO

THE LAST BATTLE FOR THE JUST SOCIETY

4

THE BATTLEGROUND

"They've endorsed our agenda pretty well, and I'm very pleased with that. The free-trade agreement with the United States, the North American free-trade agreement, the GST, privatizations and our low-inflation policy. I was very pleased to see that those main policies have been maintained intact by the new government, and they're taking them a little further."

Brian Mulroney on Jean Chrétien's Liberals

"Tell me where the centre is and I'll tell you where I stand."

Robert Winters, on being a Liberal

In the fall of 1991, three decades after the Kingston Conference, the pivotal meeting of the proponents of social Liberalism that led to the creation of the welfare state, Liberal leader Jean Chrétien held another "thinkers' conference," in Aylmer, Quebec. Like Pearson, he wanted to create policy direction for a floundering and divided party. But unlike 1960, when political sentiment was galvanizing around the emerging

NDP, the most passionate grass-roots anger in 1990 was found in the emerging Reform Party. The Aylmer Conference was called to lay out a bold new plan for Canada in the face of globalization. Business Liberals were prominent; social Liberals notably absent.

Participants and speakers included many of those from the business community the Liberals had bitterly opposed during the fight over free trade: FTA negotiators Gordon Ritchie and Simon Reisman and right-wing political economist John Crispo; Kenneth Courtis, of Deutsche Bank Capital Markets (Asia); Peter Nicholson, senior vice-president, Bank of Nova Scotia; Guillermo de la Dehesa, chair of the High Council of Spain's Chambers of Commerce and advisor to the World Bank and International Monetary Fund on trade liberalization and foreign debt management; Dr. Martin Barkin, partner in Peat Marwick Stevenson and Kellogg International, Hershell Ezrin, senior vice-president with Molson Companies; Michael Phelps, CEO of Westcoast Energy and board member of the C.D. Howe Institute; and Guylaine Saucier, president of Le Groupe Gérard Saucier, a major Quebec-based forest-products conglomerate, and future Chrétien appointee to the presidency of the CBC.

There was a smattering of speakers with more traditional small "l" liberal views, such as Ken Battle of the National Council of Welfare; Janice Harvey, a distinguished environmentalist from Fredericton; and Rosemarie Kuptana, president of the Inuit Tapirisat; but their few voices were lost in the cheering for the "new Liberalism," based on the same principles as the "new Conservatism" of Mulroney's Tories. Lloyd Axworthy was notably absent.

The media star of the event was the keynote speaker, Lester C. Thurow, dean of the Alfred E. Sloan School of Management at the Massachusetts Institute of Technology in Boston. His speech was a random sampling of thoughts on productivity from his soon-to-be-published book, *Head to Head*. After admitting that "I haven't studied Canada," he called for a "carefully thought-out consensual strategy for economic growth" for "America" (a term that embraced both Canada and the U.S.) in its competitive fight with Japan. This was hardly the core concern of the average recession-ravaged Canadian, but participants hailed Thurow as having drawn the blueprint for the nation's future.

The real star, however, was banker Peter Nicholson, a former Liberal finance critic in the Nova Scotia legislature and a quiet but important critic of Canada's competitiveness policies in federal Liberal circles. At Aylmer, he laid out the future of the country under a Chrétien government. In a speech called "Nowhere to Hide: The Economic Implications of Globalization for Canada," Nicholson declared, "What seems beyond question is that the world has entered an era where the objectives of economic efficiency...will hold sway virtually everywhere."

Without questioning whether this reality is good for Canadians or whether anything can or should be done to halt or modify the trend, he called for a "re-appraisal of the role of the nation state." Praising the "logic of global investment," he warned, "Societies that fail to respond effectively to the market test can, at best, look forward to a life of genteel decline, and at worst, a descent into social chaos.... Today, there is no alternative and, like it or not, the world is in the thrall of global forces that cannot be defied by a relatively small, trade-dependent and massively indebted country like Canada."

He offered six "guideposts" for the future government: fiscal prudence, in the form of dramatic cuts to government spending; a social policy overhaul, based on the "wealth of specific ideas and recommendations" from the Macdonald Commission ("It is unfortunate and puzzling that the large volume of well-researched and imaginative thinking on social policy assembled by the Commission has never become part of the policy agenda of any of our major political parties"); an adjustment policy in which the "'safety net' aspects of adjustment [are] delicately balanced with incentives for the displaced to retrain and relocate to new opportunities"; economic union among the provinces; sector strategies to encourage investment, training, and research in leading-edge technologies; and the expansion of free trade, to

Latin America and to the "limitless possibilities" of Asia. "To this end, our foreign and commercial policy should be reunited with the private sector."

It came as no surprise when Nicholson was invited by Finance Minister Paul Martin in 1994 to write his cure for the debt, which came to be known as the Purple Book, or that he was seconded from the bank to be Martin's senior advisor in developing the budget of 1995.

All the pieces were there: the Chrétien government would dramatically cut government spending and the public service; it would launch the ill-fated social policy overhaul; it would allow the provinces to introduce workfare and relocate the unemployed; it would implement free trade among the provinces along the NAFTA model, based on the lowest common denominator for environmental and social-rights standards; and it would reverse its position on Mulroney's NAFTA and sign on with enthusiasm and without promised changes. Only sector strategies, a platform touted by leadership candidate Paul Martin (and the only one requiring proactive government initiatives), would be shelved.

In closing the conference, Jean Chrétien declared that the old left–right split in the party was obsolete; from now on, there was only the inevitable reality of the global economy, and Canada would have to adapt. "Globalization is not right wing or left wing. It is simply a fact of life." Chief resident Liberal free trader Roy MacLaren couldn't hide his glee. "Eat your heart out, Lloyd Axworthy."

The significance of the Aylmer Conference is only now becoming evident. Although the shift to globalization and corporate rule had started in the final years of the Trudeau government, the process had dramatically accelerated in the years the Liberals were out of office. In opposition, Liberals traded on their record as defenders of social programs and sounded like the social advocates of the party's heyday in the 1960s and early 1970s. The Tories' open espousal of right-wing economic policies gave the Liberals the opportunity to mount a strong opposition platform from the centre-left. Even John Turner, considered the candidate of business, did not stray from this pulpit for long.

As much as Pierre Trudeau was generally (and falsely) perceived to occupy the far left of his party, John Napier Turner was placed on the far right. He came from old Liberal stock (C.D. Howe was a close family friend). As finance minister, he fought poverty reforms and slashed corporate income tax. When he left politics in 1975, he served as the prominent business-Liberal-in-exile at the corporate Toronto law firm McMillan Binch. He was a friend of Ronald Reagan's secretary of state, George Shultz, for whom he wrote a position paper for the Republican Party, and who brought him onto the board of the giant engineering corporation Bechtel.

He ran as a fiscal conservative, concerned most notably with reducing the deficit in both the leadership race and the election of 1984. He "represented the longing of many Liberals to re-establish the link with the business community that St. Laurent and C.D. Howe had had and Trudeau seemed to have lost," explained Jean Chrétien, whose defeat was taken by many as a sign of the decline of social Liberalism. But those who had comfortably pigeonholed Turner were in for a shock.

John Turner's inspiration for entering politics shows him to be a classic Liberal. "I come from the mainstream of liberalism in this country. I believe in free enterprise under a mixed economy and with a heart, and I believe in a progressive, populist, reform party in the tradition of Laurier, of King, of Pearson, and of Pierre Trudeau." Above all, he held to the notion of public service to one's country in an almost courtly, old-fashioned way. For Turner, Canadian business served a role in nation-building and had a responsibility to give back to the country in equal measure what it secured from the privilege of operating here.

Invited as a peer into the inner-boardroom councils on free trade, Turner became convinced that the BCNI no longer had the best interests of the nation at heart, and that its trade deal posed a threat to the nationhood of Canada. (He was also responding to the fact that Canadians' opposition to the FTA was growing daily.) This decision altered his positions on a host of related issues, including culture, social security, the deficit, jobs, and the role of government. He was learning the lesson Pearson had not: he could not both maintain the traditional Liberal commitment to social welfare and pursue continental free trade. One would necessitate the loss of the other. Of Turner's change of heart and mind, the BCNI's d'Aquino said, "It was disturbing and sad."

The stars of the Turner government were on the left: the Rat Pack, Lloyd Axworthy, Herb Gray. There was little evidence that these and like-minded Liberals would not set the direction for the party and the country after the 1993 election. Until the Aylmer Conference, the boosters of right-wing ideology within the opposition Liberals were either careful to balance their fiscal conservatism with assurances that under Liberals social programs would be safe (Paul Martin), or were outcasts (Roy MacLaren), or had left the party to enter business (Judy Erola, Donald Macdonald).

Even after Aylmer, the party ran on a progressive platform: opposition to NAFTA, patronage, corporate power, the GST, American dominance; support for jobs, training, little people, small business, universal social programs, Canadian culture, medicare. "I don't want a...system for the rich and a system for the poor," said Jean Chrétien. Many Canadians believed him.

But the days of Liberals as defenders of the just society were over. Not one of the campaign promises would be honoured.

When the Liberals lost power in 1984, Canada was a nation-state, albeit under assault; when they regained power in 1993, the country had gone through a fundamental transformation, its economy now controlled by transnational capital and global institutions. In this new Canada no one could become leader of the Liberal Party without business's endorsement. John Turner was an aberration that the business community and business Liberals would ensure was not repeated.

The triumphant Liberals anticipated the ancient spoils of election victory. Instead they found that national governments may govern but they do not rule: Liberals had new masters. They also assumed they would govern from the familiar centre, only to find it gone, as corporate Canada pulled the plug on the welfare state compromise it had negotiated after the war. The government's marching orders were to abandon the just society, particularly the social safety net. Business Liberals, the minority who had appeared so comfortable with the policies of the Mulroney Tories, were about to call the shots.

Within two years, the party that came to power on a pledge of jobs, social security, and preserving the nation-state would gut Canada's social programs, break the collective agreement with its public sector workers, privatize its transportation system, commercialize its cultural sector, abandon its environmental obligations, endorse world-wide free trade, sever trade from human rights, promote deregulated foreign investment, yield control of the economy to global investment speculators, and become apologists for the corporate sector it had once vilified. The transition from the party's stated positions in opposition to its emergence as "Libertories," as one journalist labelled them, is not founded on an epiphany: no blinding light guided the party to a new and higher truth. The Liberal transformation was based on expedience.

The reinvention of the party did not come without pain, and some Liberals were deeply troubled about their party's new direction; indeed, a furious internal battle was about to begin. When it was over, however, social Liberals would be silenced.

Like the nation, the Liberal Party that took power in 1993 was a profoundly changed institution. It included the highest number of rookie MPs ever. (The House itself welcomed the most new members since Confederation.) Only a handful had experienced the great campaigns to establish Canada's social programs; and many of the newcomers were schooled in the anti-government politics of deficit fear and downsizing. Moreover, the heart of social Liberalism had long resided in its Quebec caucus. Because the CCF and NDP had never established a beachhead in the province, progressive Quebec politicians interested in serving at a national level identified with the Liberal Party. The formation of the Bloc Québécois, however, created a new dynamic; many Quebec social reformers chose to serve under the Bloc banner.

The composition of the House of Commons has further disenfranchised social Liberals—and the millions of Canadians who believed in the Liberal campaign platform. The NDP is almost invisible as a political presence. The Bloc has been outspoken and articulate in defence of social programs and other issues of concern to social Liberals; but the official opposition does not speak with a national voice, and in June 1995, leader Lucien Bouchard declared that the Bloc would turn its full attention to the coming referendum, ceding the role of national opposition to the Reform Party. Reform's mandate is the dismantling of the nation-state, the privatization of social security, and the redesign of government in the image of the Klein experiment—hardly a reassuring position for social Liberals.

In this political climate, no one was surprised when Chrétien appointed business Liberals to the key economic posts in cabinet—Paul Martin to Finance, John Manley to Industry and Science, Doug Young to Transport, and Roy MacLaren to International Trade—where they formed close links with other sympathetic ministers: André Ouellet in External Affairs, David Anderson in National Revenue, Marcel Massé in Intergovernmental Affairs, Art Eggleton at Treasury Board, David Dingwall in Public Works, and Anne McLellan at Natural Resources.

Social Liberalism was most visibly represented by Human Resources Development Minister Lloyd Axworthy, who had led the fight against Roy MacLaren over NAFTA when the Liberals were still in opposition. However, no coalition of social Liberals in cabinet has formed to balance the power of the right wing. Fisheries Minister Brian Tobin, although he shone in his fight to protect fish stocks, has not fought nearly so hard to maintain financial support for Atlantic fishing communities; Solicitor General Herb Gray plays the role of senior statesman and peacemaker; Citizenship and Immigration Minister Sergio Marchi, a progressive in opposition, supported the passage of the head-tax on immigrants; Heritage Minister Michel Dupuy is under constant attack by the cultural community, who consider him the worst culture minister in years.

Other social Liberals are too busy with their own battles to form an alliance: Justice Minister Allan Rock has had his plate full, with gun control and controversial Criminal Code amendments; Environment Minister Sheila Copps divides her time between standing in for Chrétien at official functions around the world, and trying to restore her department's tarnished image; Indian and Northern Affairs Minister Ron Irwin is respected in aboriginal communities but has no money to implement any substantial changes; the same applies to Agriculture Minister Ralph Goodale; Health Minister Diane Marleau, after backing down on plain cigarette packaging, is looking inept in her public battle with Ralph Klein. In any case, most have no influence over the all-important economic decisions made in Ottawa, which rest exclusively with business Liberals under the leadership of Martin.

Social Liberals in caucus who looked to Jean Chrétien to be their champion were soon to be disappointed. The prime minister leads cabinet with a business style with which he is familiar and comfortable. He listens to all sides and gives his ministers plenty of independence, even when his intervention could save some public embarrassment. He goes with the power, and the power is very clearly with his right-wing appointees in cabinet. At heart, Jean Chrétien is not the left-of-centre populist many Canadians believe him to be.

Chrétien is linked in the popular mind with the social reforms of the late 1960s and early 1970s and his years with Pierre Trudeau. He has great popular appeal and a simple, clear way of explaining himself and his policies. His personal style has been a refreshing change from the pomposity of Brian Mulroney. And, before the Liberals' return to power, he publicly championed small "l" liberalism. He reminded Canadians that "once a government begins to tamper with universality, the whole system is threatened...any deviation from the fundamental principle invites further erosion of the benefits themselves," and even looked favourably on a "movement in which progressive Liberals and populist New Democrats find themselves close enough to form an alliance." As opposition leader, he promised that, once he was in government, jobs and economic growth, not deficit cutting, would be his priorities: "As long as we have unemployment in our society and no growth, we have to use the deficit to keep the dignity of our people.... Zero deficit means zero jobs, zero growth, zero hope."

Chrétien promised "not to touch social programs" or cut transfer payments to the provinces, and declared himself opposed to clawbacks of pensions and family allowance. "The correct way to deal with that is to have a progressive tax system. If people have too much money, you tax them more. But income is income and should be treated the same way." He took a strong stand against the GST, promising to replace it, and publicly opposed both the Canada–U.S. free trade agreement and the North American free trade agreement: "One day we will be asking ourselves where are we now. It will be like walking down a corridor for 10 or 15 years and it gets narrower. Pretty soon you can't turn around."

Privately, however, as early as 1990, he was revealing a different Jean Chrétien. "Free trade is a monster," he said. "By the time we get to power, it will have had too many babies to kill." (Thus, one of his first acts as prime minister was to ratify NAFTA, in its entirety, with none of the substantive changes he had promised. Thereafter, he became such an enthusiastic booster that in Latin America he is called the "Godfather of free trade.")

He felt equally uncomfortable with his promise to axe the GST. He explained that he had not wanted to oppose the GST—he would need the money once in power—but party members talked him into taking the stand when they were low in the polls. Once it became clear that they were going to win the election, they encouraged him to distance himself from this promise, which he refused to do. (His promise has been transformed into a plan to roll the GST into the provincial sales tax, and thereby "hide" it from Canadians.)

Insiders insist that Chrétien was the leading voice in the party for fiscal restraint from the moment he became leader—witness his sponsorship of the Aylmer Conference. Witness, too, his choice of advisors: Jean Pelletier, Peter Donolo, and Eddie Goldenberg, all business-oriented Liberals who nurture their comfortable relations with the corporate community. When Chrétien became party leader, Goldenberg and Mitchell Sharp set up a series of regular policy briefings at Ottawa's prestigious club Cercle Universitaire, to which they invited key corporate leaders and business economists.

His career, inside and outside politics, indicates that Jean Chrétien was always comfortable in the business Liberal tradition of his party. "I have never been doctrinaire on issues. That is one of the great things about being a Liberal; you can base your decisions on the circumstances without having to worry about your established public image." His mentor, who "influenced me a great deal," was Mitchell Sharp, Walter Gordon's nemesis. Chrétien's wide-ranging political career (he has held almost every senior portfolio, including Finance, Justice, and External Affairs) was grounded in fiscal conservatism.

As president of the Treasury Board, Chrétien cut more than $1 billion from government spending. As finance minister, he favoured big business and private interests ("I never prepared a budget without seeking out the opinions of the Business Council on National Issues") and welcomed foreign investment ("on the whole...a good thing"). He resisted the nationalist shift in policy during the 1979 campaign and, as energy minister in the early 1980s, conciliated oil-patch executives in the wake of the unpopular National Energy Program.

He has a view of women that is, at best, old-fashioned. When Judy Erola and he first served in cabinet, he called her "la Blonde," both in person and when referring to her. He candidly admits that he had never understood the need for family allowance until his wife, Aline, explained that it gave women, even women with wealthy husbands, a little "pin money" of their own. He agreed to include a limited commitment to child care in the Red Book only when the issue was explained in terms of the welfare costs to the state when women cannot work because of inadequate child care. The argument that the equality rights of women are diminished by a lack of accessible child care was lost on him.

When he left politics, Jean Chrétien became special counsel to high-powered corporate Toronto law firm Lang Michener and special advisor to Bay Street investment house Gordon Capital; he joined Mitchell Sharp and former trade negotiator Gordon Ritchie at Strategicon, an Ottawa-based consulting firm specializing in advising corporations on how to take advantage of free trade. He sat on the boards of several powerful corporations, including the Toronto-Dominion Bank, Viceroy Resources—a Vancouver mining company with environmentally controversial interests in California's Mojave Desert—and Stone Consolidated, formerly Consolidated Bathurst.

"Connie B," as Chrétien is fond of calling the company, is where his father, Wellie, worked for most of his life. It was owned by Power Corp. of Montreal, and Chrétien was on the board both when it was sold to Stone Container of Chicago and when the company slashed the workforce from thousands to hundreds. (In 1988, Chrétien and two associates bought the company's eighteen-hole Grand-Mère golf course for $1.25 million.)

Chrétien was the perfect politician for the corporate community—he had a reputation as a social Liberal but could be counted on to carry out the business agenda. He raised $2.5 million, most of it from corporations, for his leadership bid—the most of any candidate. His chief fundraiser is the wealthy and powerful Paul Desmarais of Power Corp., a close friend (and family member through the marriage of Chrétien's daughter, France, to Desmarais's son, André, a senior executive with the company). Power's vice-president, John Rae, was Chrétien's Quebec campaign manager, and opened many corporate doors to his candidate. Chrétien graced several elegant campaign events, where invitees paid $1,000 each to rub shoulders with him. (Guests at a private dinner with Paul Martin just weeks before the 1993 election paid $3,000 each.) When confronted with criticism that this behaviour smacked of the bad old days of Tory rule, Chrétien shrugged. "Millionaires vote," he said.

Thus, it was a businessman, not a social reformer, who became prime minister in 1993. Given the gutting of Canada's social infrastructure and economic sovereignty that has taken place since, we can only assume the man who chaired the Aylmer Conference is the real Jean Chrétien, and the man who ran on a platform of jobs and social security was trading on past party glory, trolling for NDP votes, and misrepresenting his intentions to the Canadian people.

Chrétien may have been untroubled by this, but the social Liberals in the party, who were left to do battle without the support of their prime minister, were deeply concerned. The campaign promises were not abandoned without a fierce internal struggle, played out principally among three powerful contenders.

In the current Liberal Party, Lloyd Axworthy has been the standardbearer for social Liberalism. The eldest of four sons in a socially active United Church family, he grew up in the rough and tumble of North Winnipeg. He won a scholarship to the prestigious Woodrow Wilson school at Princeton where he earned a Ph.D. and became immersed in American politics. He was active in the civil rights movement, joined peace marches and campaigned for John Kennedy. Back in Winnipeg, he taught political science, worked as an urban social activist, and served in the Manitoba legislature; he entered the House of Commons in 1979 and became, almost immediately, a powerful cabinet minister in the Trudeau government, as well as the lone Western Liberal.

He made his mark right away. As manpower minister, he sounded the alarm about youth unemployment: "We could lose a whole generation of young workers who get frustrated with not being able to find a job," he warned, adding that disadvantaged young people are "raw material for social unrest." He launched an overhaul of job market policies, implemented work-sharing and on-the-job student training, and created a government–private sector training plan at the height of the

1982 recession. *The Toronto Star* called it "the runaway government success story of 1982"; *The Financial Post* praised him for helping the recession's victims at little cost to the taxpayer.

For the first time in a decade, a Liberal was talking about "full employment" everywhere he spoke. He squared off against B.C. premier Bill Bennett when, in Axworthy's words, Bennett "declared war on compassion and caring" with deep government spending cuts. "To imply there is no need for unemployment programs is to demonstrate the ultimate in wishful thinking and an unfortunate misunderstanding about the workings of the labour market.... The victims of his socially-destructive legislative programs have included tenants, minority groups, civil servants, and the sick." Lloyd Axworthy was an avowed Canadian nationalist. He was progressive on immigration policy, pro–Senate reform, and against Cruise Missile testing. He was also responsible for major improvements in maternity benefits.

On the other hand, as transport minister in 1984, he introduced airline deregulation in the name of competition, setting the stage for the major deregulation of the Mulroney years. The move deeply worried the unions, who feared non-unionized airlines could operate in Canada. And Axworthy was criticized for being "an old-style ward boss," for the unprecedented amounts of money that poured into Manitoba during his tenure. Still, as one of the hardest working of cabinet ministers, he represented, with his brother Tom, the prime minister's principal secretary, one of the few bright spots on the left of the party in the second half of Trudeau's last term.

Until a nasty public spat with Doris Anderson and the Canadian Advisory Council on the Status of Women over his suggestion she cancel a constitutional conference because it might prove embarrassing to the government, "Lord Axworthy," as he was called by *The Winnipeg Free Press*, was being touted as a possible successor to Trudeau. In 1984, Giles Gherson of *The Financial Post* called him the "hottest political property on the national scene today...a major political figure...with developed grass-roots, people-oriented political sense. One of the Liberals' most reliable sources of innovative, yet pragmatic policy ideas...a tough-minded reformer. Extremely bright and very competent...smart, imaginative and effective...increasingly revered...supremely influential." A decade later, Axworthy chose Gherson as his senior advisor on the social security review.

Once in opposition, Axworthy urged Liberals to go home and rebuild the real Liberal Party—the one that "cares." He urged members not to abandon "the middle ground" in the political stampede to the right. Axworthy was crucial to John Turner's change of heart regarding the FTA and was the acknowledged expert on its content. Not only was he fluent on the complex details of the agreement, he was able to explain the threat to Canadian sovereignty to Canadians in a way that made it completely accessible.

Lloyd Axworthy articulated some of the best analyses of the corporate-friendly policies of the Tories. "The view of the Conservative government is that the public interest is served by the accumulation of private interest. They have retreated back into a form of government that belongs in the 19th century, where all the decisions related to the needs of human beings will be decided by private decision-making and there will be no attempt to establish a public purpose. Who will hold [transnational corporations] accountable?" And he explained the threat of their policies to social security: "The social contract is the fundamental basis upon which the market system works. If you begin to unravel the social contract, if you begin to take away a sense of people's understanding that they also have a place and can be protected in that place, then the market system won't work."

He attacked Mulroney for ignoring the plight of the nation's poor children, promised to cut government subsidies and tax breaks to big business, condemned Mulroney for giving the government of China aid in the light of the Tiananmen Square massacre, and spoke out strongly against the G7 for perpetuating an international economic order that kept the Third World in poverty. He called on Canada to assert its independence from the U.S. when it joined the Organization of American States. "We can show...that there is a kind of North American gringo that doesn't walk around with a big stick," he said, stating that Canada could make major contributions in ending human rights abuses and wars, particularly in Central America.

His high profile in fighting the Tories led right-wing commentator David Frum to claim, "It's Lloyd Axworthy who's the organ-grinder of the Liberal Party. John Turner is the monkey." It came as no surprise that he decided to enter the leadership race to replace John Turner on a platform to tear up the free trade deal, scrap the Meech Lake Accord, reverse the trend to sell off Crown corporations, increase government involvement in the economy, and distance the country from U.S. economic domination—policies deeply opposed by the corporate sector and the business Liberals in ascendancy in the party.

Said fellow MP and Axworthy supporter David Walker, "His message was received enthusiastically by the people no matter where we went. It's the kind of thing that they've been waiting to hear. The trouble is that it's not the kind of thing those in the upper levels of the Liberal Party wanted, and the $1.7 million spending limit reflected that."

It came as a terrible disappointment to many Liberals and other Canadians when Lloyd Axworthy was forced to withdraw from the leadership race in early 1990 for lack of funds, leaving the contest with neither a Westerner nor a strong progressive voice. He had approached Roy MacLaren, who had close links to the business community in Toronto, to raise funds for him; but MacLaren, who would increasingly oppose social Liberals in caucus, told Axworthy there was no support for him in the corporate world and urged him not to run. Axworthy reluctantly threw his support behind Jean Chrétien, who he felt was marginally more progressive than Paul Martin. For their part, Martin's strategists, aware that Axworthy's support would have given their candidate a foothold in the West, would not forget.

Axworthy had opposed the unprecedentedly high spending limit the party had set for the leadership race, correctly pointing out that it favoured those with wealth or ties to big business, and would ensure that the Liberal Party remained a "top down" political movement. "A political reality in this country and this party...is the dominant factor of big money.... We're turning politics into a high-stakes poker game." It had become very clear to him that big business interests were now dominating the Liberal Party. Axworthy warned, "There's a debate going on for the soul of the party." He could not, in 1990, know just how prophetic those words would prove to be.

Although Roy MacLaren views himself as a classic Liberal—"start from the centre and always strive to spread ourselves like a damp fog across much of the left and right"—he has come to personify, with Paul Martin, Doug Young, and John Manley, the new right in Canadian Liberalism. He is the leading proponent of Canada's role as global free-trade booster, a key force in the de-linking of human rights concerns from trade, and a powerful advocate of federal government downsizing.

The son of Vancouver's city clerk, MacLaren studied history at UBC and Cambridge and business–government relations at Harvard. After twelve years as a Canadian diplomat serving in Vietnam, Czechoslovakia, and the United Nations, he worked as director of public affairs at Massey Ferguson, director of Leigh Instruments and president of the Toronto advertising agency Ogilvy & Mather. In 1977, with publisher Michael de Pencier and journalist Alexander Ross, he bought the pro–free-enterprise publication *Canadian Business* from the Canadian Chamber of Commerce. At *Canadian Business*, he developed extensive contacts among Toronto's corporate élite. He later became chairman and director of CB Media, president and director of his own advertising company, MacLaren Associates, and sat on the boards of, among others, Royal LePage, Deutsche Bank, and London Insurance.

In 1976, the Liberal government approached him to chair a federal task force on business–government relations. His report recommended the establishment of a national business council to give corporate Canada more clout in national affairs. The BCNI was set up soon afterward MacLaren's good friend "Tom" (d'Aquino), about whom he speaks fondly in his memoirs.

In the 1979 election, he won a seat in the blue-collar, heavily immigrant riding of Etobicoke North in Toronto, to which he "studiously avoid[ed] driving his Mercedes" from exclusive Forest Hill, where he lives. He was quickly named Parliamentary Secretary to Marc Lalonde, serving first in Energy and then in Finance. (He lost his seat in 1984 but was re-elected in 1988.) In his first term, MacLaren took middle-of-the road positions: supported Lalonde on the NEP; voiced concerns over high levels of "stultifying" foreign ownership; called for a mild form of industrial policy; spoke up for proportional representation; supported Petro-Canada. He was surprisingly cautious about Canada–U.S. free trade, calling it "a chimera or worse," and warned that Canada's social infrastructure would be eroded by it: "Pressures to make pensions, wage levels, unemployment insurance, taxation, competition, energy policy, regional development and even language policy...similar to those in the USA would soon emerge...then farewell Canada."

In his memoirs, he recalls that "at one of [Italian Ambassador] Fulci's delightful luncheons...I congratulate Tom d'Aquino for the role of the BCNI in helping to design a national productivity centre, but I chastise him for his mounting enthusiasm for free trade with the United States. My scolding, however, is without result. Tom seems to be moving steadily to the right the longer he presides over the BCNI, the days when he was an assistant to Trudeau having faded now into the mists of the recent past." But Roy MacLaren would soon follow hard on d'Aquino's political heels.

As finance minister, he was credited by Giles Gherson of *The Financial Post* for helping Marc Lalonde make the transition from social to business Liberal. To "the apparent delight" of the Canadian Bankers Association, MacLaren marshalled a favourable Finance Department response to the banks' entry into the discount brokerage business. Said then CBA president Robert MacIntosh, "He's made a real difference in the level of contact the financial institutions have had with the government."

MacLaren agreed: "I have lots of friends in the business community and from my years in government, and we bring the two groups together in a way that seems to be unusual."

MacLaren took to calling social Liberals "wets," and put out feelers to see who else wanted to discuss alternatives to universality; but, he said, tongue in cheek, "any such move—even the mere discussion of it—would be an abandonment of all that is pure and true in the Liberal Party."

It was when he served as Finance critic under Turner in 1989 that the internal confrontation began. While his party was opposing the GST and NAFTA and defending social programs, he started talking favourably about expanded free trade and the GST, and advised the Tories to reduce the federal deficit by taxing back family allowance and old-age security payments. "Every sparrow that falls is going to be blamed on free trade, even if the trade deal isn't to blame."

Short months later, MacLaren stepped down as Finance critic, leaving him free to campaign openly for the new Liberalism. With his friends in the BCNI and among the Tories, he attacked the debt and called for a fundamental overhaul of "wasteful social programs." Government must find ways to increase the competitiveness of the private sector, he said, and to "help Canadians adapt" to the global economy "whether we like it or not."

Jean Chrétien revealed his predisposition to free trade and a market approach to the economy by appointing MacLaren as chairman of the Liberal Economic Policy Committee and as Trade critic. Given free rein, MacLaren wrote a controversial party document, entitled *Wide Open,* in which he reversed his earlier stand, advising against abrogation of the FTA, and advocating expanding free trade in the hemisphere and throughout the world. "As a result of the FTA, Canada is no longer simply a market of twenty-six million, but it is now a viable springboard to a market of some two hundred and fifty million." He called on government to make Canada "a secure and competitive destination for foreign investment," by cutting down on regulations and trade rules that impede business.

In these stands, he came up against Lloyd Axworthy, who had been appointed critic for foreign affairs by Chrétien. Axworthy was not about to stand quietly by: "Globalism has become an important code word in promoting a right-wing agenda. If we fall into the trap of using that kind of language, we lose our recourse to effective democratic action. Parliament will become irrelevant. The real decisions will be made in corporate boardrooms and at economic summits. As Liberals, we have to find that repugnant."

He called for Canada to join other middle powers in setting up international economic institutions capable of holding business accountable for its actions. These might include a new international banking system, new global trade rules, a new code of commercial law, global human rights standards, and a new and effective system of environmental law to control global pollution. "Unbridled globalism," he warned, "really means that individual men and women, and the communities in which they live, are powerless to influence the forces and decisions that affect them."

Confrontation was inevitable when the party regained power in 1993: Lloyd Axworthy was given responsibility for the social security overhaul and Roy MacLaren was given international trade. (Not surprisingly, Tom d'Aquino was very pleased by MacLaren's appointment: "Roy was on the right side of history on most issues, and some of his critics were clearly on the wrong side.")

Enter Paul Martin, whose life has uncanny parallels to Brian Mulroney's. Both are bilingual Roman Catholics, born in the same year; both were devoted to their fathers; both studied law; both moved to Montreal to work for Power Corp.; both took over the presidency of a large company; both bought a mansion in upper Westmount; both entered Parliament in middle age. Martin was even a guest at his friend Brian's wedding to Mila Pivnicki.

Martin learned the political ropes from accompanying his father to pancake breakfasts and local Liberal association meetings in his Windsor riding and sliding down the Centre Block bannister while his father, who served four prime ministers and ran for the Liberal leadership three times, went about his duties in the House. After graduating in law at the University of Toronto, Martin went to work for Maurice Strong, then president of Power Corp. of Montreal. Soon afterward, Paul Desmarais—friend, confidant, and financial backer of Brian Mulroney, Pierre Trudeau, and Jean Chrétien—replaced Strong at Power and in 1973, gave Paul Martin, then thirty-four, responsibility for the company's giant transportation subsidiary, Canada Steamship Lines (CSL).

Eight years later, Martin and a partner, whom he later bought out, acquired CSL, and turned it into the largest Great Lakes shipping fleet, a Canadian multinational with its own subsidiaries, including shipbuilding yards, a corporate realty arm, and Voyageur, North America's third-largest bus company. His assets, which he filed when he ran successfully for office in 1988 and again when he became finance minister, include multimillion-dollar transport and shipping companies, a 400-acre farm in the Eastern Townships, a home in Westmount (in his wife's name) valued at over $2 million, a condominium in his riding of LaSalle-Emard, a condominium in Ottawa, and a personal fortune of $30 million.

Although he placed his corporate assets in a blind trust for the duration of his political career, the disclosures of his assets led to concern about his ability to make impartial financial decisions in areas affecting his holdings. Pierre Lecomte, a special advisor to the federal government on the conflict code, said it presents "the most complex case ever faced in terms of the diversity of the companies involved, their size and their interrelationships." Senior officials have been instructed by the agency responsible for monitoring the conduct of cabinet ministers not to involve Martin in any discussions related to his private interests, including shipbuilding, marine transport, and VIA Rail (because of possible conflict of interest with Voyageur), and to take special care in any Quebec financial dealings as Martin is also minister responsible for the Federal Office of Regional Development-Quebec.

Further complicating this delicate situation is the fact that Martin's companies are currently involved in three lawsuits against the federal government for losses incurred during closings and strikes on the St. Lawrence Seaway. As well, CSL is a member of a private consortium attempting to take advantage of the Liberal government's privatization plans for the St. Lawrence Seaway. The Seaway is the lifeline of central Canada's economy, bringing in $3 billion in economic benefits annually. CSL and the other companies stand to make a great deal of profit from the government's plans if their bid is successful.

Like MacLaren, Martin chose to represent a blue-collar riding; unlike MacLaren, he moved there, renting out his Westmount home. His desire to represent the many unemployed of LaSalle-Emard reflected Martin the politician. "I wanted to run in a riding that reflected the problems I hope to deal with in government." Paul Martin, the politician and son of a social reformer, was often in conflict with Paul Martin, the powerful businessman. "I really loved business, but I never felt that you make the contribution in business that you could in public life." As a result, he made promises in opposition in order to satisfy social and business interests in the party and the country that would come back to haunt him as finance minister. Explained Peter Maser of Southam News, "His company means boats, boats mean trade, trade means new markets, markets mean competing, competing means new policies, and new policies means rethinking everything from day care to full employment to re-education."

In opposition, Martin the politician spoke passionately about the need to preserve and expand social programs, even campaigning in 1988 for a national child-care program and extended benefits to seniors. "The fact is that 25 per cent of the people on social assistance in this country are mothers under the age of 28 with one or two or more children and less than grade 8 education. How are those mothers going to get off social assistance? How are they going to be trained? How are they going to get jobs if we don't have an adequate daycare system? The 1990s problem is that one out of five poor people in this country is a child under the age of 10. That is the real problem we face."

The opposition politician was opposed to cruise missile testing and the GST and supported the screening of American investment through the Foreign Investment Review Agency. He considered the Bank of Canada's high-interest-rate policy to be damaging to the poor and to small business, and held that government should directly set interest levels. As Environment critic, he presented a strong case for enforceable national environmental regulations and standards. He proposed an "ecological union for Canada," called for stiff fines for corporate polluters, and said Canada should take the lead in imposing international environmental standards.

Martin the opposition politician also attacked Mulroney's preoccupation with the deficit ("I believe the way you reduce the deficit is by increasing revenue") and his budget cuts, which were "ripping the heart out of democracy." He called the Tory claw-backs to seniors' pensions and family allowances "theft" and railed against government retreat from unemployment insurance. "We need a new social contract in this nation, one that recognizes that a dollar spent today reduces poverty and despair and gives us much more in the future."

"I am a very strong economic nationalist," Paul Martin, the opposition politician, said often. In a fiery speech to the Council of Canadians in 1989 he described his humiliation at the hands of American business interests. As a young lawyer working for Dominion Glass, trying to negotiate a deal for Canadian research, Martin was told by the American head office that they weren't in business to promote Canadian interests. It was a turning point in his life. "I walked out of that office humiliated, disillusioned and angry. And I swore to myself that my children and grandchildren would never have to go to a foreign country and be treated like puppets who have to jump when somebody else pulls the string."

But Martin the businessman is another matter. In 1989, CSL, of which Martin remains the sole shareholder, registered some of the company's ships under foreign flags and announced that the shift to deep-sea routes would result in new vessels being built in foreign shipyards. (The firm now runs its deep-sea operation out of Boston.) This practice allows the company to avoid Canadian taxes through loopholes and write-offs. Canadian marine safety standards do not apply to these ships. Crews under foreign registry do not pay Canadian taxes and are not eligible for Canadian social programs. Operating costs are cut by as much as half because of the lower salaries paid to foreign crewmen who have taken the jobs of hundreds of Canadian seamen. One of the reflagged ships, now under Bahamian registry, was renamed the *Atlantic Erie*; the ship was originally named the *Paul Martin*, for his beloved father.

The two Paul Martins said different things to different audiences. To a York University student audience in early 1990, the opposition politician deplored the "tragedy" of the takeover of Connaught Laboratories by a French firm: "We must never again see this nation debate whether a Canadian company should be taken over by foreign interests or whether it should be allowed to stay a small Canadian company." Months earlier, however, Martin the businessman told a corporate audience that the spate of corporate takeovers by foreign companies would have happened with or without free trade and that they were "not necessarily a bad thing." In 1988, "Current government industrial policy is geared to encouraging foreign multinationals to come here and I have nothing against that," Martin the businessman said.

On the Canada–U.S. free trade agreement Martin the opposition politician toed the party line, calling it "unilateral trade disarmament...a terrible, terrible deal that is in the process of coming apart at the seams." At the same time, however, Martin the businessman publicly promoted renegotiation of the most objectionable parts of the deal while assuring the business community that he would not touch its core. (Eventually, Martin the government politician would support NAFTA without any renegotiation.) In attempting to explain how this position was not at odds with his party's opposition to free trade, Martin said that the Liberal promise to rip up the deal had been the right one at the time to ensure that the NDP did not claim the allegiance of people opposed to the deal.

As the 1993 election approached, with the NDP clearly in trouble, and knowing the centre-left constituency was not going to vote Tory or Reform, Martin and the Liberals felt safe assuring the corporate community it would prosper under a Liberal government.

Martin started quoting Ted Gaebler and David Osborne's *Reinventing Government.* (The bestselling book on privatizing government and social security is also cited frequently by Ralph Klein and Newt Gingrich.) Of its entrepreneurial proselytizing to public servants, Martin said, it's "what I want to do in spades." He started to promote government–private sector partnerships for universities and public institutions that would be "helpful in attracting multinationals," and talked about leading a "culture shift" in the nation. By the time Chrétien appointed Martin co-chair of the party's election platform, Tom d'Aquino noted with relief that Martin had "picked up a lot of the language the Liberals have resisted.... I think they have crossed the divide."

When they took power in 1993, many Liberals reached for the old compromise between their social and business wings. For a short while, buoyed by their huge majority, Liberals navigated a wild river of political change in two canoes. Paul Martin steered one, his mandate to put Canada's fiscal house in order; Lloyd Axworthy guided the other, with a major overhaul of Canada's ageing social security system. Together, they were to forge the political consensus for the third great goal—national unity.

The decision to let Axworthy's initiative go first was tactical; Martin knew that if he were to win concessions on the fiscal side, the party would have to show its human face. The social security review was to be completed in the spring of 1994. By that fall, the second big debate would be launched, showing that Liberals take their fiscal and social security obligations equally seriously.

Very soon, however, the canoes were moving in different directions. There may have been consensus on process, but there was major disagreement about the mandate of the Axworthy review, known as the Green Paper. Axworthy and his department saw it as a genuine examination of Canada's social programs and believed that any money saved from one would be allocated to another: intended changes to UI, for instance, were earmarked for fighting child poverty. For Paul Martin and the Finance Department, however, the social security review was a cost-cutting measure, period. Almost from the beginning, public statements from the two departments reflected this split.

Finance and the Prime Minister's Office never intended the review to be as extensive as the one Human Resources Development undertook. Axworthy's adventure into changing the funding of post-secondary education was his own, not agreed to by the other players. The polls showed clearly that Canadians might be willing to cut aid to the unemployed, but education and health care were sacred cows. Finance officials knew that any changes to the funding of these programs would have to come through general cuts to transfer payments, not openly targeted as Axworthy was suggesting. They knew from the beginning that they were dealing with cuts, not reallocation of funds, and they would have to take the money by stealth. Moreover, Axworthy, strongly committed to the student loan reforms, spoke of them as if they were policy rather than merely talking points and trial balloons.

During the summer of 1994, positions hardened. Pitched battles in cabinet were being reported, and by the fall, Axworthy and Martin were not on speaking terms. When the Green Paper was released in October 1994, it was already moribund. The national political debate had been overtaken by debt hysteria, and intended cuts of $7.5 billion to Axworthy's budget had been leaked to the press. The Social Policy Committee MPs dutifully travelled across the country listening to the views of Canadians, enduring the fury of those who felt betrayed by this apparently futile and diversionary process. But there was talk of a "motherlode transfer" being cooked up in Finance. Fearing that the hearings, indeed the whole process, had been a sham, they waged a fierce campaign in caucus to protect the integrity of their report and took it to the public fearing that it would be buried otherwise.

Axworthy put up an angry public defence as his reforms were

greeted with hostility by the progressive groups he needed on side; moreover, he was clearly losing the support of the PMO, particularly of Eddie Goldenberg, who was aggressively monitoring his every move and word. He became combative in public, yelled at university students, and attacked Ontario's education minister for disagreeing with his proposed education reforms, calling his criticisms "the big lie."

Early in 1995, he created a rift that damaged the whole government. Insiders say he was desperate, that he "had fought with everything he had" and knew he was losing. Catching his parliamentary committee totally off guard, he announced to reporters that the review had been shelved and would take a back seat to Martin's fiscal program. Martin was furious. Axworthy had met with him the day before and had not mentioned his intention of speaking to the press. His comments had totally undermined the original two-part plan. Chrétien was "apoplectic," according to one close source, and immediately rearranged his schedule to fly with Axworthy to Toronto, where Axworthy issued a denial to the press.

Up to the day of the budget, the Social Policy Committee did not know if any reforms—theirs or those in the Green Paper—would be included. They and other social Liberals were disillusioned over the depth and breadth of the cuts in the budget. They say that on budget day, Lloyd Axworthy closed rank with his cabinet colleagues. "I have no role in transfer payments now...I can't tell anyone what to think," Axworthy said. He now gives the best defence of block funding and the social transfer of any minister. He is moving ahead with deep cuts to UI (which have been ringingly endorsed by Tom d'Aquino) and old age pensions, the only real jurisdictions left in his portfolio. A sympathetic associate noted that he looked like he had gone ten rounds with Mike Tyson; but another was less charitable, saying, "he buried his heart."

A few weeks after the budget, Axworthy gave an interview to Ed Greenspon of *The Globe and Mail*. During this "withering critique," he put most of the blame for problems with social-program delivery on his department. "You won't believe the sort of barnacles I have." Senior bureaucrats in HRD were angry and hurt at this public slight, which was all the more painful because Axworthy had just announced that they would have to cut 5,000 employees. (Axworthy had been the only minister to refuse to cut his department voluntarily; his 5,000 staff cuts were imposed.) Said one senior member of the department, "This is the worst thing he could have done. It is unheard of to think you can attack your own department and win."

What had brought Lloyd Axworthy, so buoyant and charged with power in the fall of 1993, to this defeat? Why is he staying in a game he is so clearly losing? If he has debated about giving up his power over this policy conflict, it is not the first time. He has agonized before—over cruise missile testing, the party's position on the Gulf War, and its change of heart on free trade—but each time he has chosen to stay the course.

Some say that, at heart, he is a man who likes power. He is remembered from his days as Trudeau's only Western minister as a powerful regional boss, a man who could be arrogant and didn't like to be crossed. Although his political heroes stood for great principle, he knew a politician could be hardnosed, too. As he told Giles Gherson, "Remember, the Kennedys were known for their activist politics—but they were also known in Massachusetts to break kneecaps to get elected."

A more sympathetic reading is that Axworthy knew that the business Liberals in Cabinet had won and he stayed on to try to soften the blow of the inevitable changes they would bring. Angry that social advocacy groups did not support him, he told them that the cuts would have been worse if the right wing of the party or Reform had been in charge of the social security overhaul. A third possibility is that he became convinced, like so many of his former allies, that there was no alternative. One department member describes feeling like a "hostage to the white-hot debt fear" that was swirling around in the early months of 1995, fanned by Chrétien's office. The demand for cabinet solidarity exerts pressure; to disagree on any issue is almost impossible.

Whatever his motive, it is generally acknowledged that Lloyd

Axworthy took poor political advice. Insiders, business and social Liberals alike, agree that HRD's political promotion was a disaster. Axworthy did not lay the groundwork with his colleagues in cabinet or caucus, refusing to "shmooze or hold hands" as one observer puts it. He did not see the need for a "team" such as Martin had developed, and is not close to potential political allies, such as Sheila Copps. He would not admit that Finance and the PMO saw his review as a way to save, rather than allocate, money, even though that had been made clear in the 1994 budget, and lost credibility because of it. His consultation process was generally regarded in the party as a diversion, the hearings a "circus." The committee members were seen to have been captured by "special interest groups" who did not reflect the opinions of average Canadians. When they returned to Ottawa after their cross-country tour, they felt discounted by all sides, including Axworthy and the department.

In the absence of a concerted strategy on this undertaking from the PMO, consultants and pollsters, working independently, gave Axworthy conflicting advice. Brought in to lead the campaign was a political neophyte, *Globe and Mail* editorialist Giles Gherson, who, as a reporter for *The Financial Post*, had heaped praise on Axworthy a decade earlier. Described by one insider as "breathtakingly naive," Gherson upset almost everyone and, of course, he drew the wrath of the press gallery for seeming to favour *The Globe and Mail* by arranging exclusive interviews with the boss.

The flawed media strategy landed Axworthy in hot water and left him vulnerable to attack. The minister went public with his anger over the sidelining of his review in order to win sympathy and get Chrétien's attention; and he put down his own department to deflect criticism from himself. The idea was to make Axworthy look like a victim of Finance; but, in the end, it looked contrived, and Axworthy was further hurt.

For every mistake by Axworthy, Martin further consolidated power inside his department. Jean Chrétien, who gives his ministers enormous autonomy, sees Martin as the government's intellectual leader. Although he was slow to become involved in the dispute between Martin and Axworthy, he clearly sided with Martin. Not only is he more comfortable with Martin's agenda, he remembers how, in 1978, Trudeau went on television to announce deep spending cuts without having first informed his finance minister. Chrétien says Trudeau almost destroyed his career: "I was made to look like a fool." Chrétien would back *his* finance minister all the way.

The PMO abolished all but two cabinet committees, thereby eliminating competing power centres and cementing Finance's authority. Every government department has been enlisted to serve Martin's budget-cutting agenda: Marcel Massé must undertake massive layoffs in the public service; Ralph Goodale has to wind down farm subsidies; Doug Young is selling off transportation services; Art Eggleton must put infrastructure plans on hold. In spite of the hoopla and publicity around the social security review, the real mandate for change—the big money issues—has been handed to Finance.

Through budget slashing, Finance has captured the government agenda for the foreseeable future. Deputy Minister David Dodge worked hand-in-hand with Tory Finance Minister Michael Wilson to implement his attack on government structures, and stayed on to help Paul Martin finish the job. It was David Dodge who set out the big spending issues that the Chrétien government would have to confront, months before the Liberals took office: pensions, transfers to the provinces, unemployment insurance, welfare, and farm and business subsidies. And it was David Dodge who put the nation on notice that the 1995 budget cuts were just the beginning; next would come major reforms of Old Age Security, the Canada Pension Plan, and medicare. And Dodge reminds us who is dictating this agenda: "Companies that operate internationally and move their people around are telling us there's a problem." Martin heard

Dodge loud and clear: "Nothing so wonderfully concentrates your mind as the feeling that the Department of Finance is breathing down your neck."

Martin turned to Peter Nicholson as his key policy advisor for both the Purple Book and the budget. Nicholson, on leave from the bank, was brought into the Department of Finance as Clifford Clark Visiting Economist, an innocuous title that hardly describes the power he was given or the influence he exerted. (He has recently been hired by BCE for his extensive government contacts to head up the company's government relations strategy.) He and Martin talked almost every day, and he served as point man throughout the struggle with HRD. Unlike Gherson, Nicholson has great credibility in the party; his Liberal roots go deep, and as an organizer and policy guru to the Aylmer Conference he had earned the respect of the powers-that-be. As the battles between Axworthy and Martin heated up, Nicholson had the credibility that Gherson did not.

For strategy, Martin and Finance chose Earnscliffe Research and Communications, a consulting and polling firm with close ties to Martin. The principals of the company are Tories Bill Fox and Harry Near; Liberal-turned-Tory Bruce Anderson (brother of Liberal-turned-Reformer Rick Anderson); and Liberal Mike Robinson (Martin's campaign manager). The core PR strategists for the budget, however, are newcomers David Herle, a key Martin advisor, and Elly Alboim, former Ottawa bureau chief for the CBC. On a $180,000 contract, they were given exclusive control over all polling and communications research for the department, and undertook the most intensive pre-budget consultations in Finance history. Using polling and focus groups they came up with a tight and disciplined strategy that Martin and Dodge followed to the letter.

In mid-October, Martin went before the Commons Finance Committee to warn of impending financial ruin if the country didn't turn its attention immediately to the debt. Armed with charts, statistics, and reports, Martin gave a brilliant performance. "We are in hock up to our eyeballs," he admonished. He knew better than to lead with warnings of cuts; they could come later. For the next several months, he hit the road to tell Canadians of our need to get our house in order. Martin used two techniques: he drove home the message that there is no choice but decisive action; and he played on Canadians' fear of taxes. Headlines carried the message: "Martin stresses 'equity' in taxes"; "Martin says Canada can stand more tax"; "Martin to take more in taxes"; "Tax rise needed, Martin asserts"; "Rich will lose tax breaks, Martin says"; "Martin vows to make the rich share burden.... No Canadian will be spared."

In fact, what the focus groups showed was that Canadians were prepared to allow cuts, because they had come to believe they had no choice; but they wouldn't stomach increased taxes. The strategy was to allow tax hysteria to grow, so that, with every tax revolt meeting in Canada's heartland, the tide turned in Martin's favour; for, of course, there were no significant tax hikes in the 1995 budget. In that one brilliant move, Martin took the wind out of Reform's sails, made himself look responsive to ordinary people, and made the harshest budget in Canadian history appear moderate. Frightened Canadians, who expected to have their programs slashed *and* their taxes raised, let out a countrywide sigh of relief, telling themselves it could have been so much worse.

The only group that Herle and Alboim found Canadians willing to see taxed higher were the big banks, so they were singled out by Martin for a capital-assets tax. Even though the tax will be lifted at the end of 1996, the government knew the banking community would not be happy; on budget day, Jean Chrétien personally called the nation's bank presidents and asked them not to put his deficit-fighting budget in jeopardy by speaking out publicly. He reassured them that the tax would be of short duration. The bank presidents held their tongues.

The struggle was over.

The business community, the big winner, has shown its appreciation to another big winner, the Liberal Party (to "Welcome [it] back from the wilderness," as Tom d'Aquino explains). At a recent Vancouver dinner featuring Martin, businessmen showed their support of his budget by raising $85,000 (after expenses) for the party. A Chrétien dinner in Toronto brought out 1,600 people, who paid $500 each, raising a total (before expenses) of $800,000. In 1993, the party raised over $20 million, more than it has ever received in an election year. In 1994, it collected $9 million, more than it has ever raised in a non-election year and more than twice as much as the Conservatives ever raised.

The Department of Finance was also a winner. Responsibility for the sick, the poor, and the unemployed has been handed to a lower level of government, which does not have the power to set monetary policy or borrow as much capital. As Paul Martin explained it to a New York audience, his budget "sheltered" the federal government from the next economic downturn; when it comes, Finance won't have to take the heat.

It was also a sweet victory for Roy MacLaren, who backed Martin all the way, entrenching the international side of the agenda. Canada is now firmly ensconced in the global economy, playing by the rules of the International Monetary Fund and the World Bank. He was also the winner when Axworthy promoted the idea of taxing domestic and international electronic currency speculation to pay for social initiatives (the Tobin tax). Even Chrétien seemed ready to discuss the idea at the G7 in Halifax; but it was trounced by business editorialists, the business community, Martin, and MacLaren, so the prime minister backed off.

Two big losers were Axworthy and the social Liberals in caucus. So complete was the rout that even Marcel Massé, who supported Martin, felt safe in admitting that the Liberals were cutting social programs faster and deeper than Mulroney's Tories: "It's the first time that we've managed to do a Neilsen exercise," he said, referring to the extensive review of all government funding undertaken by the former Tory house leader, but never implemented.

Backbenchers were losers, too. In the words of one, they are "nobodies" in the Chrétien government; their voices have been largely silenced. Chrétien has reacted strongly against dissenters, threatening that he might refuse to sign their nomination papers in the next election as punishment.

The biggest losers, however, are Canadians. The years ahead will be painful, indeed, as we struggle to survive the gutting of the just society. The current political players will be replaced by others, and largely forgotten; but they will have destroyed, in just a few years, what it took generations to build. In the wake of quickly retreating government, Canadians are left to fight corporate rule alone.

5

THE REVERSAL

*"There are times in the progress of a people when funda-
mental challenges must be faced, fundamental choices
made—a new course charted. We can take the path—too
well trodden—of minimal change, of least resistance, of
leadership lost. Or we can set out on a new road of fundamental reform, of renewal, of hope restored. Today we
have made our choice."*

Thus, Paul Martin began his budget speech in the House
of Commons at 4:30 p.m. on the next-to-last day of
February 1995, as a winter storm was raging outside.
Thanks to orchestrated leaks and trial balloons, many of the budget's contentious elements were expected—the elimination of
40,000-plus public service jobs, the withdrawal of federal economic and political responsibility for social programs, the emphasis on program spending cuts over tax measures, the privatization
of transportation services.

Despite the government's campaign to soften up the public
for the harsh cuts now being announced, and despite the fact
that these measures were signalled by Martin's strategy document released five months earlier—the so-called Purple Book—
there was a sense of shock and disbelief in the scene unfolding.

A mere fifteen months after the Canadian electorate swept the Liberals to power on a platform that flatly rejected the "neo-conservative" path, the government was embracing Tory policies on a scale their predecessors would not have dared to implement. Through changes to the fiscal structure, they were dismantling government and decentralizing the federation well beyond what was proposed in the Meech Lake Accord. This dramatic divorce from Liberal tradition must have had Liberals across the country pinching themselves in disbelief.

The Liberals were withdrawing the federal government as a major player in the social lives of Canadians. Provinces would be left to go their own way on social assistance, post-secondary education, and health care. Without a strong national presence the system would cease to be national. A political scientist, the late Donald Smiley, described Canada as a political federation: "The bonds of Canadian nationhood are primarily in the sphere of government and in activities decisively shaped by government." Foremost among these were the national social bonds forged by the federal government using the leverage of provincial transfer payments. Smiley was worried that "free trade" would exert great pressure to weaken these structures. Now the former opponents of the FTA were simply abandoning them, without any concern for the effects on the cohesion of the nation. Canada was becoming a federation of ten sovereignties.

The political distance travelled from Martin's pledge, as he was sworn in as finance minister, to give top priority to growth and jobs—"the root cause of the deficit and the root cause of unemployment are one and the same, and that is an ailing economy"— to his budget speech, in which all else was subordinated to the one overriding imperative of cutting spending, seemed unfathomable.

The single-minded preoccupation with spending cuts and laissez-faire policies, for which the Liberals had so vehemently attacked the Conservative government when in opposition, had quickly become their own obsession. Strange irony that the Liberals would deliver a budget that would, like no other before it, diminish the ability of the federal government to be an active force for economic and social development in Canada. When asked about turning his back on half a century of Liberal tradition, Martin replied simply: "the greatest strength of the Liberal Party is its ability to change."

The budget took some $25 billion and 45,000 jobs out of the government sector over a three-year period—a net loss of 80,000 jobs to the economy as a whole in the first year alone, according to the forecasting firm Informetrica. This was fourteen times the cuts planned in the Red Book. Federal spending was to be rolled back forty years in relation to the size of the economy. Social program cash transfers to the provinces would fall by almost two-fifths in three years; in fourteen years they would be gone completely. The savaging of social programs would move Canada to the bottom of the industrialized country standings, neck and neck with the United States, in social spending.

The budget cut the infrastructure program in half and cancelled the promised child-care program. The only component of spending projected to grow was interest payments on the debt, expected to jump by $9 billion to $51 billion by 1996–97. Budget expectations of continued high real interest rates, slowing growth, and high unemployment signalled that monetary policy would remain tight. Gone was the government's former commitment to jobs and growth.

Why the chasm between the political agenda laid out months ago in the Red Book, and the budget? Paul Martin was the architect of both documents. Did events change his mind? Or was the Red Book merely a decoy, obscuring his real political agenda with vague and conflicting assertions to give voters, weary of economic and social turmoil, what they wanted to hear? In tracing Mr. Martin's journey as finance minister, we start with the Red Book.

The Red Book criticized the Conservative government's economic policy on three fronts. First, its obsession with the deficit or inflation, while ignoring the costs of the "cure" in job losses and poverty. This, said the Red Book, was what most distinguished the Tories from the "balanced" Liberal approach. Second, it restated the Liberal commitment to a mixed economy, including an active role for government, criticizing the Tories for over-reliance on market solutions. Third, it stressed that the solution for Canada's economic woes was not "another five years of cutbacks, job loss and diminished expectations," but rather, "immediate measures to make our economy grow and create jobs."

Liberals would address the five major problems facing the economy: "lack of growth, high unemployment, high long-term real interest rates, too high levels of foreign indebtedness, and excessive government debt and deficits." It would do so through a two-track policy. The first, jobs and growth, involved spending on infrastructure and housing, incentives to small business, spending on training and R&D, and trade promotion. The second, fiscal responsibility, involved holding the line on spending and financing new initiatives by reallocating existing spending. With a view to eventually eliminating the deficit, the Red Book set an interim deficit reduction target of 3 percent of GDP by 1996–97, a level "compatible with putting Canadians back to work. Unless Canadians get back to work, the cost of lost production, unemployment and welfare will inevitably increase the deficit as it has in the course of the Conservative mandate." It went on to warn that "Faster economic growth and reduction of unemployment is a prerequisite for sustained deficit reduction."

These fiscal measures, it said, "will make possible a monetary policy that produces lower real interest rates and keeps inflation low...." Other than to criticize the Tory preoccupation with high interest rates and zero inflation, the Red Book suggested no specific monetary policy measures. (It is interesting, in light of both Martin's and Chrétien's calls in opposition for the government to instruct the Bank of Canada to lower interest rates, that an easing of monetary policy was not prescribed in the Red Book.)

The Liberal plan would cut spending over the four years, 1994–95 to 1997–98, by $1.8 billion beyond what the 1993–94 Tory budget had projected. This would be achieved through cuts to existing Tory programs of $7.1 billion and new spending initiatives of $5.3 billion—mainly on infrastructure, R&D, training, and child care. There was no mention of tax measures apart from

a vague reference to examining tax expenditures to reduce ineffi-
ciency and promote growth. Regarding the co-ordination of federal and provincial economic policies, the Red Book criticized the
Tories for their "unilateral decisions...to cut transfer payments to
the provinces." The Liberals would, they claimed, ensure maxi-
mum stability and predictability in financial arrangements.

In the days following the 1993 election, a Chrétien aide gave
the first hint, in a conversation with *Globe and Mail* reporter Ed
Greenspon, of what appeared to be a hidden Liberal agenda. The
aide said, "You have to remember we were not elected on the
deficit in any way, shape, or form. So he [Chrétien] has to bring
everyone on side—caucus, cabinet, everyone." If the party's election campaign—explicitly focused on a policy document that
people were encouraged to refer to to keep the government hon-
est—had in fact been a lie, then the basis on which the Liberals
were elected was fraudulent.

Yet, shortly after the Liberals assumed power, Chrétien
appeared on a special CBC *Prime Time News* "town hall" to field
questions from "ordinary Canadians." Peter Mansbridge asked
him if, having had a chance to look at the government books,
things were worse than expected. He replied, "I knew the deficit
would be bad, though not quite this bad." "Nothing changes in
the Red Book promises?" Mansbridge prodded. Chrétien was
very clear in his response. "Nothing!"

In early December 1993, the newly sworn-in finance minister,
Paul Martin, assembled what the media called "Canada's leading
economists" to advise him on preparing his first budget. They
gathered, forty-strong, in the Ottawa Conference Centre to offer
expert advice for six hours before a national television audience.
This event is worth examining in some detail for two reasons. It
provides an important clue to where the Department of Finance,
if not the minister, wanted the government to go. It also provides insight into the process by which the public is conditioned
to accept unpopular government policy measures.

Who were these forty individuals? Why did Martin choose

this particular group? And what advice did they give? Many were regular media commentators: the "authoritative voices" that reporters turn to when they require commentary on the news of the day. Eighteen were from business—banks, investment houses, brokerage houses, management consultants, business-funded think tanks, and business lobbies. Eleven were academics, nine of them adherents of the neo-liberal orthodoxy. Three were from hybrid business/government policy think tanks, purveyors of the same orthodoxy. Six were from independent consulting companies. Of these, two were neo-liberals, two were Keynesian economists, and two fell somewhere in between. Finally, two were political economists employed by unions.

It seemed an odd mix of advisors to an activist government embarking on a program of employment-driven growth. All but four or five were neo-liberal exponents. Close to two-thirds supported Bank of Canada governor John Crow's harsh monetary policies, which the Liberals had so vigorously opposed. These advisors talked about deficit reduction solely in terms of program spending cuts, differing only on depth and speed. They did not call for reductions in corporate tax expenditures or tax increases for the well-to-do. They believed that deficit cutting and government downsizing had to come before job creation as policy priorities. In contrast, only a handful of so-called progressives—the Keynesians and the political economists—would be inclined to support the Liberal Red Book policies.

Only within the parameters defined by the invitation list did debate take place. Framing the political discussion in this way allowed the organizers to set the parameters of the debate and convey to the public a number of convenient myths about economic and political reality, the relationship between government and society, the range of choices, and what could not be changed. Five such myths emerged in the course of the consultation.

The first myth is the notion, stated by speaker after speaker, that government is inherently inefficient, unproductive and an obstruction to the creation of wealth. The "marketplace" is, by definition, good, efficient, etc., and hence, market solutions are always to be preferred. The current economic problems, viewers were told again and again, stem from government being too big. The debt crisis, most agreed, provides the opportunity to downsize government through social spending cuts and privatization.

This negative view of government was, of course, selectively applied. The military, the police, the judiciary, the penal system—these property- and privilege-protecting functions of government escaped the general public-sector bashing.

The second myth is that people have become too dependent on government and must learn to stand on their own. According to Michael Walker of the Fraser Institute, our idleness-inducing unemployment insurance system is why our unemployment rate is so much higher than that of the U.S. The debate was limited to deficit hawks and deficit doves—rapid draconian cuts *vs.* gradual and not-so-deep cuts. They talked about "reinventing" social programs to cope with the realities of the 1990s: ending universality and delivering programs to those most in need (targeting).

Training was evoked as an antidote to the unemployment problem. This view assumes that much of the unemployment that does not result from such labour market "distortions" as unemployment insurance and minimum wages is caused by a mismatch of jobs and skills. Hundreds of thousands of jobs, it would seem, are unfilled because people are improperly or inadequately trained. (In other words, the public education system has failed.)

That there might be something deeply wrong with an economic system that does not produce enough jobs for those who want to work was shrugged off: such "structural imbalances" must play themselves out in the market. There is little that government can do.

The closely related third myth is that Canadians have been living beyond their means, and the chickens are coming home to roost. "There is no choice, no way out." Consequently, the market is forcing Canadians to pay the price for their sins. What is this price? Greater insecurity, lower living standards, weaker social supports, and high unemployment. Steve Tanny of Ernst & Young talked biblically about fat years and lean, and the inexorable correction of an "overconsumed, overlevered and overemployed" economy—too many people in relation to the ability of the economy to produce efficiently. Restoring the equilibrium demands lowering wages and expectations. This was echoed by Leo de Bever of Nomura Securities, who said that competitiveness and growth can be restored only by a fall in wages and greater labour market "flexibility" (standard code for gutting unemployment insurance, minimum wages, unions, and other impediments to "the bottom line").

The fourth myth concerns globalization, the impersonal, technology-driven forces against which it is fruitless to struggle: events, we are told, are beyond our control. We can't protect ourselves or our communities from the global market. The best governments can do is to promote free trade, deregulation, and competitiveness. The best people can do is to adjust to the new reality and ride the wave, bearing in mind that responsibility for adapting lies with the individual. That there may be fundamentally different ways of defining the problems and the choices in this era of globalization was "beyond the frame" of serious debate.

The last myth is that there can be too much democracy. According to Gail Cook Bennett of Bennecon Ltd., the fiscal mess has been caused by the social demands of "special interest groups," which have forced government to "spend beyond its means." This is code for blaming our problems on the irritating voices of social advocacy groups, which élites find it fashionable to scapegoat. This "excess of democracy" notion is mirrored by the attitude that "we, the experts, know what is best for society." Though people may not like their bitter medicine, it's for their own good. Free trade advocate Richard Lipsey countered criticism that those prescribing social cuts might act differently had they first-hand experience of these programs, saying such experience wasn't necessary to provide "creative solutions." Michael Walker urged the finance minister to "exercise leadership" in making spending cuts, as the majority would always support retaining government "handouts."

The context of the debate made the few progressive voices

sound far more radical than they were. Calling for a reduction in unemployment to 8 percent over a three-year period seemed to stretch the bounds of "responsible thought." The message of the exercise was that there were no alternatives to program cutting: the only question was how much and how fast. Election promises of job creation as the first order of business were, at best, naive, and had to give way to tough political decisions.

The advisors were not going to have first-hand experience of the prescribed economic austerity. Most earned upwards of $100,000, putting them in the top 1 percent of the income hierarchy. Canadian governments have provided such high income earners with some of the most generous pension and other tax breaks in the industrialized world. These are people with stable incomes and secure futures; they have no need of social assistance or unemployment insurance or old age security, and no kinship with the victims of austerity.

The Finance Department spent close to a million dollars putting together this meeting of leading economic lights, and other conferences—from Halifax to Vancouver—during the weeks leading up to the first Liberal budget. In the cross-country consultations, an effort was made to get representation from labour and social groups; however, as Concordia University economist Margie Mendell, who chaired one of the working groups at the Montreal conference, said, organizers exercised tight control over the content of conference reports to ensure they toed the official line. (For example, Montreal conference co-chair Michel Belanger reported to Martin that "there's a real consensus against a rise in taxes as a solution to the deficit problem." There was, in fact, no such consensus in the working groups.)

Martin's first budget did not stray too far from the "balanced" approach of the Red Book. Despite the revised accounting, which showed a deficit $10 billion higher than that forecast by the outgoing government, spending cuts were modest, except those to unemployment insurance, which took a brutal three-year hit of $5.5 billion, and provincial transfers for welfare and education, which were cut by $1.5 billion. It included such Red Book initiatives as the infrastructure and social housing programs.

Several weeks after the budget, Chrétien told an Edmonton radio audience that there would be no more spending cuts in the effort to reach the Liberals' 3 percent of GDP deficit target. He was assuming that the government would meet its targets for economic growth and interest rates; moreover, he had not ruled out the possibility of cuts beyond 1996–97. Martin, on the other hand, told an April 1994 meeting of the Aerospace Industries Association that the next budget would contain "major, major cuts, which are going to affect every segment of our society," including "massive cuts" to provincial social transfers in a major restructuring of fiscal federalism. His message was that these cuts were in addition to those already announced. This speech marked the beginning of his campaign to prepare the public for a 1995 budget that would change the face of the country.

By June 1994, the interest rate was two points higher than expected, putting an extra burden on the government's debt interest bill. On the other hand, the economy and employment were growing faster than predicted, putting enough additional revenue in government coffers to more than neutralize the adverse effect of interest rates. The media were reporting heated deficit battles within cabinet between the so-called economic hardliners, led by Martin, MacLaren, Young, Manley, and Massé; and the doves, led by Axworthy, Copps, and Tobin. Still, it appeared that social security reform remained a top priority, to the extent that there would be no further cuts in the social envelope beyond those announced in February.

By the fall, the balance had clearly tilted. Axworthy, who wanted the savings on social programs reinvested in other social initiatives, had lost to Martin: a huge chunk of the savings from the social security review would be used for deficit reduction. Cuts would also be made to pensions and to medicare transfers.

Social programs were not the only area where big cuts would be made. Away from public view, Marcel Massé was heading a review of $60 billion worth of government program and operations spending (everything except the $40 billion under review by Axworthy, and $20 billion in old age security programs, which were being examined by a separate Department of Finance task force). It was originally directed to find savings to be phased in over five years. Now they would be squeezed into three years. A cabinet committee, dubbed the Star Chamber, was conducting intense and highly secret deliberations with a mandate to cut or even eliminate entire areas of government considered no longer relevant.

By late fall, word was filtering out of a massive hatchet job: the Department of Transport would lose half its employees and three-quarters of its functions would be privatized; half of the Industry Department's subsidy and regional development budget would be axed; Agriculture would lose its grain transportation subsidies and other farm support programs; Fisheries, Defence, and Heritage would also be hit. As many as 50,000 employees would be let go.

It was clear that Martin's view of the relationship between the debt/deficit and jobs/growth had reversed itself. In a speech to the International Monetary Fund, he said deficit reduction was "a *precondition* [italics added] for sustained economic growth and job creation," not the other way around. He had said exactly the opposite a year earlier.

According to a long-time Martin advisor, Martin's switch was due to his taking on responsibility for a debt/deficit that was spiralling out of control. Environics pollster Michael Adams was less charitable. Martin, he said, had become a captive of the Finance Department. Tom d'Aquino seemed to attribute the rearrangement of Martin's deficit priorities and the Axworthy Green Paper's approach to social reform to an epiphany: "The Liberal government is now in the camp of correct economic thinking...it's an historic position for the Liberals," he glowed.

Along the road from the Red Book to Budget II, Martin's apparent conversion was formalized in the October 1994 Finance Department document *A New Framework For Economic Policy*, drafted by Peter Nicholson, and known as the Purple Book. The Red Book approach—jobs/growth and fiscal responsibility—

became a single track in the Purple Book: fiscal responsibility first and foremost, then jobs/growth. It stated that "returning Canada to fiscal health (i.e., deficit reduction) is a prerequisite to achieving all of the other elements of the economic strategy." The Red Book had put it the other way around: growth and job creation would lead to deficit reduction.

The Purple Book set out to "reinvent government"—that is, have it "withdraw from those things that are no longer essential to the public interest or that can be better accomplished by provincial or local government"; in other words, make government smaller. To "reform" social security was to help get people back to work by putting the squeeze on their unemployment insurance and welfare cheques. Although Martin was careful not to blame social spending for the current dilemma, the government in his view had no choice but to undertake massive cuts if it wanted to preserve the social system.

The Red Book had slammed the Conservatives for their fixation on inflation at the expense of jobs and poverty; the Purple Book focused on deficit/debt reduction as the hope upon which all prosperity and jobs rested. The Tories had promised that once inflation was smothered, interest rates would come down, thereby creating the conditions for growth and job creation. The Purple Book promised that, even though inflation was conquered, a massive effort to wrestle the debt/deficit tiger to the ground must precede lower interest rates, and, after that, sustained growth and jobs. Jobs would have to wait.

In order to accomplish the Purple Book's "fiscal adjustment," spending had to be cut or taxes had to be raised. But since "the scope for higher taxes is extremely limited," lower deficits would be reached only by cutting spending by whatever amount necessary—in Martin's words, "come hell or high water." Only when this was accomplished would it be possible to provide "more and better jobs."

The chosen colour of Martin's economic strategy document was a fitting reflection of the change in orientation. The addition of blue to red makes purple.

Through the fall of 1994 and the first months of 1995, the deficit scare grew to hurricane force: Axworthy, Martin, and other government spokespersons warned that, if Canada didn't take the hard fiscal medicine, the international financial markets and the International Monetary Fund would force even harder medicine upon us. The C.D. Howe Institute, the Fraser Institute, *The Globe and Mail,* and other "authoritative voices" blanketed the media with this message. Preston Manning shouted from his parliamentary pulpit that financial markets were poised to punish us unless we wiped out the deficit in three years.

The Howe published a pamplet called *The Courage to Act,* which urged the government to speed up its deficit reduction timetable, wiping it out over three years. It recommended eliminating the $17-billion cash transfer for health, education, and social assistance, and cutting another $5.5 billion out of unemployment insurance to break the vicious circle of "dysfunctional fiscal and social policy." Shortly thereafter, *Globe and Mail* editorial writer Andrew Coyne published his prescription for balancing the budget through massive spending cuts—$24 billion over three years, half of which would come from social programs.

The chorus in support of deficit slashing was nothing new. What was new was that the spectre of international debt terrorism forcing us to our knees had been brought to the top of the political agenda. The argument went as follows: Foreign creditors were reaching the limit of their tolerance for Canadian government debt. We had become so bad a risk that we were fast approaching a "debt wall." Unless we got our debt under control through deep spending cuts, foreign lenders would pull their money out. The converging horrors of a debt wall and an imminent tax revolt left no alternative but to cut government spending. This was the theme of a Fraser Institute conference held in Toronto in late November called "Hitting the Wall: Is Canada Bankrupt?" Major corporate sponsors of the event included Loblaws, Toronto-Dominion Bank, MacMillan Bloedel, and Sun Life.

Interest rates were beyond national control, according to the authoritative voices, therefore direct government action to lower interest rates and thereby reduce the $45-billion federal interest burden was not an option. Interest rates were set in the global markets; it was not possible for the Bank of Canada to intervene to lower rates.

Moreover, even if the Bank could lower interest rates, complained Paul Martin, "I cannot tell the Bank of Canada governor what to do." This was a different Paul Martin from the Liberal leadership candidate who stated that "It is incumbent on the minister of finance to lay in front of the governor a deficit reduction plan that is credible. At that point I think one is entitled to say to the governor, 'we would like over the next 12 to 14 months for you to get interest rates down to their traditional [levels].' And the governor has his choice of accepting or resigning." (Chrétien, as opposition leader, had also called for the Bank to lower interest rates. But he shrugged off the possibility during a televised town hall on the first anniversary of his government, saying, The government's credit card is full. I can't ask the Bank of Canada to print more money.)

The Commons Finance Committee held a special roundtable session to discuss interest rate policy. Despite expert testimony that the Bank of Canada could indeed lower both short-term and long-term interest rates to the benefit of the Canadian economy, especially job creation, its final report sided with the private bankers, Bank of Canada officials, and other neo-liberal economists who argued that any attempt to impose a made-in-Canada interest rate policy would precipitate a flight of capital, an interest rate hike, and inflation. (Interestingly, the Bank of Canada was not perceived by financial markets as being irresponsible when it deliberately engineered a huge increase in interest rates in John Crow's war on inflation.)

Two events fuelled the pre-budget debt hysteria. The first was the December 20 collapse of the Mexican peso, which sent shock waves through global financial markets. Within weeks of the Mexican central bank's announcing that it was letting the peso float (its reserves were almost exhausted), it had lost almost half its value. The rush of speculators to get out of Mexico destabilized financial markets throughout the Americas, Europe, and the Far East. The Canadian dollar fell and the Bank of Canada raised interest rates in an effort to stem the tide. Nor did they settle after a $US50-billion bailout package for Mexico organized by the United States administration and the International Monetary Fund.

Nervous currency traders gave the debt warriors the perfect opportunity to up the ante in their campaign. A *Wall Street Journal* editorial on January 12 warned that Canada, like Mexico, was on the edge of the financial abyss: Canada, it warned, "has now become an honorary member of the third world in the unmanageability of its debt problem.... If dramatic action isn't taken in next month's federal budget...Canada could hit the debt wall...and have to call in the International Monetary Fund."

The next day, *The Globe and Mail* enthusiastically reprinted the editorial under the headline "Bankrupt Canada." It turned out that the author, John Fund, had attended the Fraser Institute conference on Canada's hitting the debt wall. Mr. Fund was also pals with the *Globe*'s Andrew Coyne. In fact, Coyne had provided him with information for his piece. Coyne then used the *Journal* editorial as a springboard for a typical harangue against rampant government overspending.

Interviewed by the television networks and radio phone-in shows, Mr. Fund gave viewers advice on how to avoid hitting the debt wall and a tax revolt: legislated tax and spending limits, dramatic government cuts, elimination of all social transfers to the top half of income earners, and the transfer of services such as welfare to the charitable sector.

A week later a Toronto currency speculator, Albert Friedberg, set off another run at the dollar with the prediction that Canada, bloated with government debt, was on the verge of a major currency collapse. This was echoed by Patrick Paradiso of Deutsche Bank Capital Corp., who warned, "They [the politicians] better come across this time." Peter Plaut, of New York–based Salomon Brothers, weighed in with a more measured assessment of Canada's debt woes, but said that big cuts were needed to calm financial markets. Alan Frane, director of Barings International, said Canada is a "wonderful country [with] everything going for it...but the federal government has not really got to grips with the social spending issues...." (Unknown to Mr. Frane, Barings also had a few problems with which it had failed to come to grips.)

The Canadian population was being besieged. The faces and words of the "authoritative voices" from the financial lobby were all over the media, warning that the country was in grave danger and the government had to turn it around—*without* raising taxes, they said, or the markets would not respond favourably.

Toronto-Dominion Bank chairman Richard Thomson, in a widely reported speech to shareholders, warned that Canada was in danger of a Mexico-like crash unless it did something about its debt, which threatened the well-being of Canadians. Each man, woman, and child in Canada owed $29,000 of the public debt, and it was growing larger by the minute. Ironically, in spite of his aversion to government debt, the TD had doubled its holdings of government bonds in the previous year, a banner year for bank profits.

Bank of Canada governor Thiessen, in a Montreal speech, renewed his commitment to controlling inflation and protecting the dollar, and urged the government to "put the deficits and debt on a more sustainable track." A research article in the winter 1995 issue of the *Bank of Canada Review*, blaming the debt for the drop in Canadian living standards, also received media coverage. It recommended accelerating the rate of deficit reduction beyond the government's current target. What was not picked up by journalists covering the article was its projection that lowering the ratio of debt to GDP by 20 percentage points would raise growth by only 0.4 percent and job creation by 0.2 percent, and reduce the risk premium on Canadian interest rates by less than one-fifth of a percentage point. In other words, all this sacrifice was not going to produce much in the way of results.

As the panic mounted through January, the speculation

against the dollar threatened to push it through the 70-cent barrier. The Bank of Canada continued to raise its prime rate in an effort to halt the slide. Real interest rates climbed to the levels immediately preceding the last two recessions. As the day of reckoning was apparently approaching, Paul Martin was making his pitch to cabinet on his budget package. Discussion around the table was regularly interrupted by officials bringing news of the dollar in markets around the world. Quieting the few dissenting voices, the budget was approved unanimously.

The second event that fanned the deficit panic was the very public warning by the New York bond rating agency Moody's, only eleven days before the budget. It was putting the federal government's debt on a credit watch, a signal that it was about to lower the government's coveted triple A rating. This sent a new round of shock waves through the markets and the media. The dollar tumbled half a cent; the Bank of Canada raised its interest rates by half a percentage point. Martin reacted with surprise and dismay at Moody's announcement. "Moody's certainly could have waited until this government brought down its budget," he told Canadian Press.

Deficit fever was reaching its peak. An Angus Reid poll showed that for the first time in its history the deficit was the top priority for a plurality of Canadians. The message that we had all resisted for so long was finally sinking in. Why did Moody's time its announcement so close to the budget? Was Moody's acting on its own, or was it acting as a stalking horse for domestic interests: lenders who wanted to keep the value of their investments high? Business leaders who wanted to force the government to downsize? A government that wanted to scare the public into supporting the harshest cutbacks in fifty years?

Moody's senior Canada analyst, Vincent Truglia, told author Linda McQuaig in the summer of 1994 that Canadian analysts were continually harassing him to downgrade his ratings of Canadian debt. "It's the only country I handle where usually nationals want the country downgraded on a regular basis." Why? Truglia told *Toronto Star* journalist Susan Kastner, "I can't answer that one, but that is invariably the case. Most times we're yelled at and screamed at for downgrading, but [not] in Canada."

The answer to the questions on what and who was behind the Moody's action is, to some extent, all of the possibilities proposed above. Truglia no doubt felt the heat from the Bay Street heavies. The fallout from the orchestrated *Wall Street Journal* article and the continuing jitteriness in the markets also contributed.

Moody's, which communicates weekly with senior Finance officials, had signalled its intention to put the government on a credit watch. It was understood by both parties that the selling of the budget would be helped by Moody's making public its intention before, rather than after, Martin brought down the budget.

On the day of the Moody's announcement, several newspapers also reported the latest deficit numbers released by the Finance Department. For the first nine months of the fiscal year the deficit was a whopping $6 billion less than the $39.7-billion target projected in Martin's last budget. An economy growing at 4.5 percent—the highest of the major G7 nations—job creation at well over 400,000 for 1994, and declining unemployment insurance payments, had brought in an extra $7 billion. While interest payments were $2 billion higher than forecast, program spending was down $1.3 billion. Such good news should have mitigated the doom and gloom from Moody's, but it was out of sync with the cresting wave of deficit frenzy. It didn't fit into the context that had been created and, therefore, when it was announced, it didn't resonate. It didn't have weight, so the media buried it in the back pages. It was also in Martin's interest to play up the doom-and-gloom news from Moody's to bolster his case for a tough budget.

The budget came and went. Targets were met. Cuts were massive. Taxes were kept down. The dollar fell briefly, then rose, then settled back. Most Canadians applauded; they said Martin was "on the right track." Six weeks later Moody's announced that it had downgraded the federal debt a notch. This was prominent news, but the reaction was very different. Financial analysts were calm; the hysteria had subsided. No surprise, they said; the markets had already factored it in. Martin was in Asia. He did not come rushing back to reassure investors. The dollar was rising and interest rates were heading down. The time for panic was over.

Didn't the Moody's downgrade mean that Canadian debt was now riskier to hold? Shouldn't the dollar have fallen as a result, and shouldn't Governor Thiessen have had to raise interest rates? Apparently not. It seems that even after the downgrade, the risk of Canada's defaulting was still negligible. According to an official of a major debt rating agency, it would appear that the Fraser Institute types crying "debt wall" were wrong all along: "It's not a question that Canada's not going to be able to finance itself. That's ridiculous." Perhaps *New York Times* columnist Thomas Friedman had overstated the case when he claimed that Moody's could destroy a country by downgrading its bonds. "It's all voodoo economics," said Peter Dungan, an economist at the University of Toronto. The chance of Canada's defaulting is about as great as "a [nuclear] meltdown at Pickering at the very same hour that there is an earthquake that breaks the containment building and a tornado that carries the stuff to Ottawa."

Meanwhile, the Department of Finance is preparing for more big cuts in next year's budget. Assistant deputy minister for fiscal policy Don Drummond told a Queen's University conference in April that Finance is planning for a balanced budget by 1998–99. This would shrink federal program spending to 10 percent of GDP, the lowest level since 1948—the lowest of any central government in the industrialized world.

Paul Martin's budget rolled back the Canadian state with such force that even Preston Manning seemed at a loss on budget day. It was, as the finance minister himself noted, the most radical reduction in government since demobilization from a wartime to a peacetime economy.

The budget "ripped the guts out of liberalism as a governing political idea in Canada," crowed David Frum. "Pretty much everything accomplished by the Liberal party between 1968 and 1984 now stands condemned."

At the Empire Club, Martin told a Bay Street audience that the Canadian public was solidly behind him. The government's polling revealed that 69 percent of respondents believed the budget was "on the right track"; 83 percent of high-income respondents felt "it was on the right track."

The Globe and Mail ran a story the day after the budget profiling the reaction from a supposedly middle-class Calgary family. The Calverts have an income of $120,000, considerably above the median family income of $45,000. They were pleased with the budget. Said Mr. Calvert, "We've had the benefits of Canada.... Now is the time for our generation to suffer a bit." Mrs. Calvert was pleased that the budget did not "hack away at the middle classes." The $25-billion public-spending cuts were a step in the right direction. If government didn't knuckle down and live within its means, the Calverts warned, their children would have to pay. Neither seemed troubled by the contradiction that both their jobs were financed by public funds, or that they might end up casualties of the chain reaction set off by this budget.

The irony of the smug suburbanite Calverts of Canada was noted by Public Service Alliance president Daryl Bean in *The Ottawa Citizen:* "These well-meaning but gullible crowds cried out for a permanent moratorium on taxing the wealthy and corporations, while demanding cuts in public services that are their only return on a disproportionate tax burden."

By the normal rules of politics, the popularity of the Liberal government should have fallen in the wake of the budget. The echo of Chrétien's words—that Canadians could come to him, the Red Book in hand, and say, "Look, Mr. Chrétien, you did not keep your promise"—should have started coming back to haunt him. But Mr. Chrétien's (and the government's) popularity remained extraordinarily high in the weeks and months following the budget's release.

In light of a masterful propaganda campaign, which created a context in which what little criticism found its way into the media proved to be weightless, it was not surprising that public opinion responded favourably. Martin said the government had met its deficit target and that there were few tax increases. He said the budget was fair, and that the rich and the corporations were bearing their share of the pain. He went unchallenged—the magnitude of the cuts was still an abstraction. He said the markets were happy and the dollar was rising. People wanted to believe the budget was "on the right track." The media managers gave little room to those who would challenge the dramatic change of direction.

Nova Scotia journalist Parker Barss-Donham, surveying economic stories from the Canadian Press wire service over the last year, found that the Fraser and Howe Institutes were quoted four times more frequently than centre and left think tanks. Indeed, the Fraser was quoted in 140 news stories, while the Canadian Centre for Policy Alternatives was quoted in 16. Barss-Donham believes that "a staccato drumbeat of hectoring commentary on the deficit" has been used to manipulate public opinion. Unfortunately, such media self-criticism is rare.

The Liberal government's confidence in incessant pre-budget and post-budget polling may not have been totally warranted. In late March, one-third of the respondents to a Compass poll gave Martin's budget a failing grade and another third gave it only a C/D grade—hardly a ringing endorsement. One-third of respondents who professed to vote Liberal gave the budget an F on fairness to low-income Canadians.

Perhaps, in the intervening month, wrote columnist Dalton Camp, Canadians were feeling a little sheepish about having been rattled by the deficit frenzy. "It effectively separated Canadians from their collective sense as citizens so they could dispassionately accept the sacking of 45,000 of their public servants, agree to the further traducement of their government's support of the arts and public broadcasting, and to the odious nickle-and-diming of the pensioned and the poor."

More significant was an elaborate study of Canadians' attitudes and values carried out by Ekos Research, made public several weeks after the budget. The study, conducted throughout 1994, provides a more reliable picture because it sought to uncover attitudes and values, which are more stable over time than the gyrations of the typical opinion poll.

The study found that, although Canadians are deeply dissatisfied with the performance of their governments, they strongly support the things that government does and the services it provides, and do not support the new-found Liberal zeal for limited government. They continue to see a top priority for government to be training and job creation, regardless of the fiscal pressures. The study also found that the high approval for the Chrétien government is superficial and that anger against governments is still bubbling just below the surface.

Perhaps the most significant finding of the study was a marked accentuation of social class divisions in the country. It found that the large middle class is splitting by access to knowledge and level of economic security. It also found a widening gulf between the attitudes and values of the élites and the general public. Elites were overwhelmingly preoccupied with the deficit, while the general public's concerns were for issues such as employment and social and cultural issues that are central concerns of the just society. Elites wanted government to focus far more on "competitiveness, prosperity, and minimal government." The general public ranked these goals at the bottom of their list. The study also found a growing distrust of the élites by the average citizen: fully half the people surveyed believe the deficit crisis has been manufactured by government and big business.

The survey also found that differences about whether the government should maintain its current commitment to the unemployed also run along class lines, with high-income earners far more likely to want a reduction of this commitment.

The study uncovered major ambiguities in people's attitudes toward the deficit. On the one hand, most would rather live with reduced services than pay higher taxes; on the other hand, the general public's support for spending cuts is much more equivocal than would appear from their responses to standard opinion polls—in other words, once they are made aware of the consequences of deficit reduction. When poll respondents were asked to pretend that they were decision-makers and rank spending priorities among ten randomly selected pairings, deficit reduction was way down the list. With one exception, the preferred alternatives all involved job creation or training, indicating a strong desire for a hands-on government.

It may be a sign that, as the reality of the budget sinks in over the coming months and years, Canadians will turn on this government with the same ferocity that they turned on its predecessor.

6

BARBARIANS AT
THE GATE

"Bluntly put, the proposed Canada Health and Social Transfer is the worst social policy initiative undertaken by the federal government in more than a generation."

National Council of Welfare,
government advisory body

Challenged by a *Maclean's* interviewer who said that, with a few broad budget strokes, he was turning his back on the social legacy of his father and the Liberal Party, Paul Martin became quite impassioned: "I've seen what's happened to my father's legacy over the past ten years, and the Canada my father built was not a Canada where the largest income group—the fastest growing—was the working poor. My father's legacy was not a Canada replete with food banks. It was not a Canada whose health care system was deteriorating. If you look at Canada today, by God, it's nuts that we have food banks and shut hospitals." While accurate as a description of the country's social deterioration, this was a remarkable rationalization of his Canada Health and Social Transfer (CHST), which would dramatically increase the number of food banks and shut more hospitals.

Described by Martin as an example of flexible federalism, it would roll back fifty years of federal leadership in creating the Canadian social state. Federal-provincial transfers were introduced in the 1960s as a means of creating nation-wide social citizenship rights in post-secondary education, health care, and social assistance—in areas of provincial jurisdiction. (Unemployment insurance had been transferred to federal jurisdiction by a 1941 constitutional amendment.) Federal dollars formed a powerful incentive for provinces to follow the federal lead, as all three were originally cost-shared programs—that is, federal money matched each dollar of provincial spending. In 1977, health and education transfers were combined into a block grant called the Established Programs Financing (EPF). The block was to grow according to an agreed formula tied to the growth in the economy and population. Under the EPF, the federal government transferred some of its taxing authority to the provinces so that they would actually collect some of the money themselves. (For example, the federal personal income tax was dropped by 13.5 percentage points and the provincial income tax was raised by the same amount. The grant had therefore been split into a cash portion and a tax point portion.)

The Liberal government of 1982 first tinkered with this formula, but four Mulroney budgets, dating from 1986, rejigged the formula to take vast amounts out of health and education and introduce the virus that would eventually destroy national medicare and post-secondary education. First it reduced the growth in the transfer to GDP growth minus two percentage points, then, GDP minus three points. Then it froze the transfer completely, first for a year, then for five years. Since the tax-point portion automatically grew as tax revenues grew in line with the economy, it was the cash portion that would shrink, eventually to zero early in the next century to keep the total transfer in line. The National Council of Welfare calculated that the Mulroney cuts would take $98 billion out of health and education by 2000, even if the Liberal government made no further changes.

Mulroney planted another virus in the social security system in 1990, just as the recession was beginning, by putting a 5 percent ceiling on the growth of social assistance transfers to the three wealthiest provinces, Alberta, British Columbia, and Ontario. The so-called cap on the Canada Assistance Plan (CAP) marked a shift from a 50–50 cost-shared program to a block-funded program. Alberta used the reduced federal transfer as an excuse to cut back provincial funding roughly to the level of federal contributions. Ontario and British Columbia chose to maintain their provincial programs intact, as the demand for social assistance was soaring. Consequently the federal CAP contribution represented less than one-third of the total cost of these programs. The federal government saved itself billions by this measure: the Ontario government estimated that it was fleeced of nearly $8 billion over four years by the cap on CAP. A study published in the *Canadian Tax Journal* estimated the total cost of the Mulroney social transfer cuts (EPF and CAP) from 1986 to 1994 at a staggering $37 billion. (Moreover, Mulroney's cuts to unemployment insurance further increased the pressure on the provincial welfare system.)

If Mulroney planted the virus of social disintegration, Martin's Canada Health and Social Transfer represented the full-blown disease. The CHST combined transfers to the provinces for health, education, and social assistance into a single, smaller block grant to come into effect on April 1, 1996. At $26.9 billion, it would be $2.8 billion less than the $29.7 billion in transfers in the previous year. In its second year the CHST would fall to $25.1 billion, the first time ever a government would cut the absolute dollar amount of these programs. (The Mulroney government cuts simply reduced the transfers below their planned rate of growth in line with a growing economy and population.) However, the extent of the federal withdrawal was even greater than it appeared, because, as mentioned, part of the transfer was in tax points. The cash portion of the CHST would drop from the $17.3-billion level of the year before it was introduced to $12.9 billion in its first year and $10.3 billion in its second (1997). This represents a 40 percent funding cut in just two years.

It would continue to shrink to nothing in the subsequent ten years, a little faster for some provinces than others, depending on projected growth in tax-point revenue, though its value as a lever to enforce standards would by then be long gone. This represents a huge speed-up of the federal government's abdication of responsibility for the social underpinnings of the nation. (Mulroney, in two terms, had cut federal spending on health, education, and welfare from 20 percent to 15 percent of provincial spending. The Chrétien Liberals intend to cut it to 9 percent by the fourth year of their first mandate.)

By withdrawing its direct financial commitment, the federal government is surrendering its capacity to maintain national standards. For two of the three transfer programs—health and welfare—federal money enforced standards specified in acts of Parliament. The lack of legislated standards for the post-secondary education transfer allowed provinces to use the money for other things if they wished. The Canada Health Act and the Canada Assistance Plan Act are history. With dwindling enforcement authority, the vague commitment to health care is hollow, because the capacity to enforce standards disappears with the funding. The elimination of CAP means the end of all but one of the standards for providing social-assistance funding.

Individual provinces can still bring in progressive child-care or other social policies, but there is no longer any likelihood of these programs becoming national. Without federal leadership, medicare, which was originally introduced by Saskatchewan, would never have expanded nation-wide. Creating a social Canada was the single most important act of nation-building in the last half century. It is now rapidly unravelling.

The Canada Assistance Plan, despite its many flaws, was a landmark when it was introduced in 1966. The legislation helped to consolidate a patchwork of provincial programs and ensure common principles. Foremost among them was the principle of need. Everyone was entitled to assistance, provided they could demonstrate they needed it. Before CAP (and still the norm south of the border), the distinction was made between deserving and undeserving poor. Under CAP, it was immaterial whether need was because of a disability or because one could not find work and could not access unemployment insurance.

CAP also preserved a modicum of dignity for poor people caught in the welfare system by ensuring that they would not be forced to do menial make-work jobs in exchange for their welfare cheques. Workfare forces people onto the job market in direct competition with "regular" workers, at far below the minimum wage—and herein lies the crux of this morally repugnant policy. The object is to put downward pressure on the whole wage structure. (It is not surprising, therefore, that the strongest proponents of workfare are also calling for the elimination of the minimum wage.)

The CHST opened the door to the wholesale return of workfare. Before, the federal government looked the other way as several provinces—Quebec, New Brunswick, and Alberta—violated the prohibition against workfare under CAP. With its announced intention to repeal the act, the march to workfare has become a stampede. Testifying before a parliamentary committee, Bob White, president of the Canadian Labour Congress, did not mince words in describing the corrosiveness of workfare on social cohesion: he called it "a social sickness that afflicts societies that are about to devour themselves." The only standard retained from the wreckage of CAP was the requirement that people could not be denied welfare because they had recently arrived from another province.

Although CAP did not create uniformity among provincial welfare programs, it did place limits on the differences. The fact that it was a shared-cost program, that the federal government matched every dollar that the provinces spent, meant that in times of recession the burden of expanding welfare would be borne equally by the provinces and the federal government. The

Tories ended the cost-sharing principle for three provinces; Martin's CHST ended welfare-cost sharing altogether. Come the next recession, provinces will be on their own, and the federal government has recession-proofed its deficit target. As a consequence, the most vulnerable people in our society have lost their safety net of last resort. In the grab for shares of the single shrinking pot of money, health and education programs, which have a much larger political constituency, will get the lion's share. Welfare will get only the scraps, if there are any.

Cutting welfare adrift from the national standards of CAP encourages a "race to the bottom." The Klein government, which had been somewhat restricted in what it could do with its welfare system, now has carte blanche to cut off the "undeserving." Even provinces that do not want to penalize the most vulnerable are being forced to "compete" with Alberta. The Harris Conservatives in Ontario will follow enthusiastically in Alberta's footsteps.

The repeal of the Canada Assistance Plan Act also doomed a wide range of social services: community assistance for people with disabilities, homemaker and meals-on-wheels services for the elderly, child-care support for low-income families, start-up assistance for the self-employed, support for women and/or children fleeing abusive spouses, and many others.

Martin's social transfer cuts and the repeal of CAP are the ethical equivalent of bringing back capital punishment and have brought enduring shame to the party that once aspired to creating a just society. Sheri Torjman of the Caledon Institute put her finger on the rot at the core of the CHST when she called it the "let-them-eat-cake law." Richard Splane, who headed the 1965 committee that drew up the national standards of CAP, predicted a return to a stigmatize-the-poor welfare system.

The Martin budget dismantled the financial foundations of social security. It promised negotiation with the provinces to determine "shared principles and objectives"—a far cry from national standards. Moreover, to create an omnibus block fund with the goal of off-loading program responsibility while putting conditions on individual programs would defeat the purpose. Paul

Martin, to reinforce this point, pledged to the Bloc Québécois "that the government has no intent to impose anything on the provinces. There is no intent to meddle into the business of the provinces."

Tom Kent, former advisor to Prime Minister Pearson and one of the architects of the social security system, doubted the provinces could agree, even on vague principles for a national framework of social programs, when the federal government is pulling out. The consequence, according to Kent, will be a broadening of social divisions within our society.

Only the unconditional equalization transfer was not directly affected by the Martin budget. This transfer, managed by the federal government, is paid by the three richest provinces—Alberta, British Columbia, and Ontario—to the eight "have not" provinces. The principle of equalization, though not the amount, is enshrined in the Constitution; but the "have" provinces will be increasingly unable, and perhaps unwilling, to maintain the current level of equalization transfers when they come up for renegotiation.

Most people simply do not yet understand what the Canada Health and Social Transfer represents—largely because of the absence of a national political opposition and an effective press. An Angus Reid poll conducted a month after the budget found that 80 percent of Canadians felt that it was "very essential" to have national standards for health care; 56 percent said it was "very essential" to have national educational standards. Even for welfare, which tends to have less support, 36 percent of respondents said that it was "very essential" to have national standards, and another 42 percent said national standards were "somewhat essential" for this program.

Another reason for the lack of public outrage over the federal government's actions is that it is difficult to grasp in the abstract the magnitude of the federal cuts. When they come, the actual dirty work of implementing them will be done by the provinces; the federal government will not be directly in the line of fire. Matt Sanger, a researcher at the Canadian Union of Public Employees, has examined the cuts on a province-by-province basis, and projected what the shrinking CHST money would mean in terms of cuts to specific health, education, and social services in 1996, its first year of operation. Here are some examples of what is to come in 1996 alone:

- Newfoundland will lose $73 million in 1996. This amounts to 85 percent of the provincial operating grant for school boards, or more than half of all payments to physicians.
- PEI will lose $17 million in 1996. This amounts to the total funding for six of the nine public nursing homes in the province, or almost half of total spending on post-secondary education.
- Nova Scotia will lose $118 million in 1996. This amounts to more than all provincial grants to public libraries and museums, or twice the provincial spending on mental health services.
- New Brunswick will lose $94 million in 1996. This amounts to almost half of the total cost of the provincial medicare program, or more than the total operating grant to municipalities.
- Quebec will lose $1.1 billion in 1996. This amounts to twice the cost of the provincial drug plan for the elderly, or half of all payments for doctors' services.
- Ontario will lose $1.4 billion in 1996. This amounts to twenty times the amount spent on community health centres, or almost three-quarters of the budget for universities.
- Manitoba will lose $139 million in 1996. This amounts to the entire budget to operate the province's sixty-five smaller hospitals, or two and a half times the child-care budget.
- Saskatchewan will lose $123 million in 1996. This amounts to half the budget for long-term care services, or more than twice the budget for community living services for the disabled.
- Alberta will lose $330 million in 1996. This amounts to more than five times the cost of cancer diagnostic and treatment centres, or more than twice provincial spending on student assistance.
- British Columbia will lose $471 million in 1996. This amounts to four times the cost of ambulance services, or one-fifth of the budget for all acute care and extended care hospitals.

The federal government's two main programs providing social security directly to individuals are the $20-billion Old Age Security Program (the Canada Pension Plan is a separate fund financed entirely out of premiums that cannot be used for any other purpose, and is therefore not included in the government accounts as program spending) and the Unemployment Insurance Program. Old Age Security got a temporary reprieve in the budget, apparently because Chrétien, fearing the same kind of seniors' backlash that occurred when the Tories tried to de-index pensions, wanted to make sure they were consulted. But the budget left no doubt that it would be cut in 1996, through tighter targeting (this is code for cutting off some of the 3 million Canadians who now get the benefit), and through calculating eligibility on the basis of family income rather than individual income. Details of the reform will be revealed in the fall of 1995 in a paper being prepared jointly by the Finance and Human Resources departments.

The first two Martin budgets cut the Unemployment Insurance program by $3.5 billion per year beginning in 1996, more than one-fifth of the $16 billion the UI fund paid out in 1994. Martin set the fiscal parameters of the social security reform—a 10 percent reduction overall and a transfer of money from areas that "create dependence" into "investments in people which make them more employable." The cuts will likely mirror earlier cuts, with an increase in the work period required before qualifying for benefits, a reduction in the amount of the benefit, and a shortening of the period during which benefits can be collected. The Liberals' UI changes were, despite their opposition to earlier Tory cuts, much greater than any the Tories had made. They were carried out in spite of the fact that the UI program, supported by worker and employer contributions, is self-financing over the business cycle. The Finance Department now expects payouts to continue to fall and the UI fund to have a $5-billion surplus by the end of 1996.

In line with a scaled-back, "Americanized" UI system, the

budget outlined the likelihood of major reductions in employer premiums. UI premiums are a social security payroll tax, the largest single source of tax revenue next to personal income tax. Mr. Martin described these premiums as "job killers," although most economists, and even recent OECD studies, find that the impact on job creation of lowering them would be minuscule. Undeterred by the facts, Martin told a Montreal audience: "We have made it very clear that, as far as we're concerned, payroll taxes are a cancer on job creation, and that for a government that wants to create jobs there is nothing more asinine than to impose increasing costs that make it impossible for entrepreneurs to hire young Canadians." These were fighting words from a government that had simultaneously chopped its job-creating infrastructure program and decimated public sector jobs.

Ironically, the Canadian government collects less social security payroll taxes than do most other industrialized countries, including those that have maintained very low unemployment for most of the last fifteen years. The research clearly shows that the burden of the payroll taxes is eventually passed on from employer to workers in the form of lower wages. The Ontario Fair Tax Commission concluded that "it is possible to sustain much higher rates of payroll taxes than are typical in Canada without adverse economic impact."

Conservative and Liberal governments have slowly starved the unemployment insurance system, making it more difficult for individuals to qualify, lowering payments, and shortening the duration of benefits, submitting claimants to means testing and disqualifying people who quit their jobs "voluntarily." The Mulroney government withdrew completely its contribution to the system; money from the UI fund was diverted to training. As a result, the proportion of unemployed people actually collecting unemployment insurance dropped from 87 percent in 1990 to under 50 percent by mid-1995. A mere 40 percent of unemployed Canadian workers will be able to draw UI after the next round of slashing proposed by Axworthy. Moreover, all this has been done deliberately during a period of high unemployment and high insecurity, when people were most in need; and it has been done by a government that claimed to be acting in the name of fairness.

Martin justified the social revolution embedded in his budget to the *Maclean's* interviewer by appealing to the realities of the times: "a party that is not reinventing itself is brain dead." This is consistent with the ethos of power that guides the Liberal Party. The leadership of the Liberal Party has had the "brains" to do what was necessary to retain power. If, with the corporate agenda on the rise, this means taking apart what they built up over forty years, so be it. What the Liberal Party has lacked is a set of core beliefs on which to ground its policies.

"The budget is fair." Fairness was a high priority for Canadians and a message the Liberal government wanted to get out. Martin, Chrétien, and other spokespersons bombarded the airwaves with the F word in the days and weeks before and after the budget's release. "A great deal of effort has gone into making sure the budget is fair," Martin told the House of Commons.

Fairness was one of the four principles, according to his budget speech, that purported to guide the making of the budget. "We must never ever lose sight of the need to be fair. Fair among our regions and fair among individual Canadians," he said. Over and over, Canadians heard: "The budget is tough but fair.... Canadians said to me, make sure the budget is fair, make sure our neighbours are not getting off scot-free; that is what we have done...."

In his first post-budget interview with CBC's *Prime Time News*, Martin repeated the claim made by the "authoritative voices" in the lead-up to the budget—there is not much revenue to be had from closing tax breaks, since most have already been closed. "If I could close some more [tax] loopholes, I'd close them," Martin said, apparently with a straight face. He was telling us that wealthy Canadians just don't have a lot of money. Therefore, deficit reduction has to concentrate on the big money—and for the Liberals that means social programs.

Let's see if government claims of fairness stand up to

scrutiny. Although the vast majority of Canadians make regular use of one or more components of the social security system—particularly education and health care—other elements, such as welfare and unemployment, are used disproportionately by lower-income individuals. Therefore, they bear the biggest burden of the budget cuts.

Most people would be surprised to learn that a large chunk of federal social programs are delivered through the tax system in the form of exemptions, deductions, and credits. Some are income-tested, some are not. Unlike direct social spending, this part of the federal social budget is hidden. Although it was outside the mandate of the Commons committee reviewing social security, the committee's final report, which came out two weeks before the budget, provided a list of thirty tax-based social spending programs for 1992, the latest year for which statistics were available. These cost the government an estimated $36 billion, roughly equivalent to the $40 billion in direct social spending that the committee was mandated to review.

Those of us who fill out tax forms recognize many of these programs, though we probably do not think of them as social spending. They include deductions for pension payments and child-care expenses; credits based on age, married or equivalent to married status, dependent children, education; Canada or Quebec Pension Plan; and employer-paid UI benefits and workers' compensation payments. As the list implies, tax-delivered programs were put in place to deal with many of the same social issues as their direct spending counterparts: assistance for child care, for retirement planning, for people with disabilities, for single-parent families, for working mothers, assistance to encourage the transition from welfare to work, assistance for low-income consumers. Some go mainly to high-income earners, some are widely distributed, and some go primarily to low-income individuals or families. In most cases, very little is known about how they work and whether they meet their objectives—whether they are fair. There is very little public scrutiny even of what programs exist.

Spending through the tax system differs from direct spending on social programs only in that the government says: rather than give the recipient an outright cheque—for example a UI cheque—let the recipient deduct the money from what she or he owes the government in taxes. Either way the recipient gets the money. Unfortunately, most people think of reducing this kind of spending (collecting the money owed) as tax increases and the anti-tax people are conveniently uninterested in correcting this misperception.

The biggest item by far on this list is pensions. Deductions claimed for private pension schemes—RRSPs and RPPs—cost the federal treasury $10 billion in 1992. (They cost provincial treasuries another $5 billion.) The only budget cut to tax-based social spending was to pensions. Saying that "we must ensure that the benefits of [pension] tax assistance are shared fairly in these times of restraint," Martin outlined the cut. The ceiling on subsidized contributions to these plans was lowered from $14,500 to $13,500 for the next two years. Thereafter it will be raised back up to the previously planned ceiling of $15,500. What pain did this inflict on those who benefit from these programs? Martin's changes saved the treasury a puny $260 million over the next two years, then it will be handed back. Not only was it a token amount, but it was also temporary, to give the illusion of fairness.

Although many Canadians use the RRSP and RPP program, it overwhelmingly benefits the rich; 50 percent of the benefits end up in the hands of the top 10 percent of income earners. One reason for this is that it is delivered as a deduction instead of a credit. Thus a person earning $75,000 gets a $500 subsidy for every thousand dollars put into an RRSP: someone who earns $30,000 gets a subsidy of only $80 for every thousand dollars placed in an RRSP.

Furthermore, few middle-income earners are able to save anything close to the $13,500 RRSP maximum. Only those with incomes over $150,000 tend to put away that much. People making $30,000 to $40,000 put about $2,000 per year on average into their RRSP. Had Martin lowered the ceiling to $8,000, he would have saved the government $1.4 billion per year in forgone revenue without affecting taxpayers earning $60,000 or less. (Even a "middle class" family with two $60,000 salaries would not have been affected.) Only tax filers with taxable income of more than $100,000 put more than $8,000 into their RRSPs, on average.

Thus, as Martin cut $9 billion from direct social spending—health care, education, social assistance, unemployment—with such fanfare, he left virtually untouched almost $40 billion of tax-delivered social spending. Worse, while the government announced reviews of health care, pensions, and other public services, with the clear intent to shrink the money that goes into them, no review of tax-based social spending is planned. Such policies fail the test of fairness miserably.

What about tax-based government spending in general, not just social spending? When we think of federal government spending we think of direct government programs (and interest payments to service the government debt). When business critics and the Reform Party call for government cutbacks, this is what they are referring to. But there is a tax-based spending budget almost as large as the program spending budget, and also largely hidden from view.

The Department of Finance published a document in 1993 that provided estimates of personal and corporate tax spending, commonly known as "tax breaks" or "loopholes." Finance estimated that there were $90 billion in such expenditures; however, the estimate is not complete. It listed fifty tax-spending programs for which the department was unable to evaluate the revenue lost. As well, 100 spending programs under $2.5 million were not included. Thus, tax-spending programs were at least three-quarters of, but more likely closer to, the $120 billion worth of direct program spending by the federal government. Martin's budget cut direct program spending by $25 billion over three years. It cut less than $1 billion from the tax-based spending budget over three years.

Why is direct spending on public programs and services considered inferior, inefficient, and unaffordable, yet public spending delivered through the tax system into the pockets of the well-off considered efficient, affordable, and untouchable? Why is there not a whisper of "getting its fiscal house in order" or "living within its means" when it comes to this kind of government spending? What has happened to fairness?

Martin had many corporate loopholes to plug, but he chose to leave them wide open. Here are just a few:

Businesses are still permitted to deduct from the money they owe in taxes 20 percent of their expenses for meals and entertainment—such as luxury boxes at the SkyDome and escort services—from their taxable income. As Liberal MP George Baker put it, "The government is subsidizing wine, sex and song for the corporations." Closing this loophole would have yielded the treasury as much as $500 million a year.

Lobbying has become a booming business in Ottawa—estimated at $100 million a year. Corporations are allowed to deduct from their taxable income the costs for hiring lobbyists to influence policy to their advantage. The Liberals promised to restore integrity and democracy to government by reining in the lobbyists; however, neither the budget nor subsequent legislation requires lobbyists to disclose their fees or eliminates this tax subsidy, which is costing the treasury at least $50 million a year.

One-quarter of all capital gains can be deducted from a corporation's taxable income. This produces a drain on government coffers of more than $400 million a year. The same tax break for individuals costs another $700 million a year. Generous tax subsidies to oil and gas companies for their exploration and development costs could be cut back to save the treasury $500 million. The research and development tax credit, which the large banks regularly abuse, could be tightened up to save taxpayers at least $200 million per year.

So many tax loopholes are available to corporations that each year tens of thousands of profitable companies pay not a penny in income taxes. The result is that corporate income tax paid in Canada is one of the lowest in the industrialized world. A corporate minimum tax of 13 percent of profits would have brought in an extra $500 million per year.

If, in the name of fairness, Mr. Martin had closed these six corporate loopholes, as well as pension and capital-gains breaks for high-income Canadians, he would have cut tax spending by as much as $11 billion over three years. This would have been more than enough to make up for the $9 billion cut from health, education, social assistance, and unemployment insurance programs.

Canada has the second worst record in the industrialized world (after Australia) for taxing wealth, making it a tax haven for wealthy individuals. If the government had introduced a modest tax on inheritances (exempting the first million dollars of the estate and exempting all transfers between spouses), it could have raised $2.5 billion per year. This would be more than enough to pay for a child-poverty tax credit for low-income families. It would also allow the government to maintain international development aid, as well as federal health, housing, native, and immigrant assistance programs at current levels.

Martin did not touch personal income tax rates, even for the well-to-do. If he had increased slightly the 29 percent federal income tax rates for individuals with a taxable income of more than $75,000 by adding a 31 percent bracket between $75,000 and $100,000, and a 33 percent bracket above $100,000, he would have brought in an extra $850 million. This would be more than enough to eliminate the 3 percent surtax on the basic federal tax for individuals earning less than $20,000.

Martin increased slightly the large corporations tax and the corporate surtax. He also put a small temporary tax on financial institutions—a mere $100 million on $4-billion profits in 1994. Osgoode Hall tax expert Neil Brooks summed up how the budget spread the pain to the wealthy: "They said they were going to hit the rich with their tax changes, but all they have done is nudged and winked."

In the early fall of 1994, quite a different budget process was taking shape. A group of researchers, activists, and academics at the Canadian Centre for Policy Alternatives and CHO!CES, a Winnipeg-based social justice coalition, began work on an alternative federal budget, which would reflect priorities quite different from those driving the government's budgetary process. With financial assistance from the Canadian Labour Congress and its major affiliates and the energy of scores of volunteers across the country, committees and policy working groups were formed, contacts were made with national and community organizations, and discussion papers were prepared. The guiding principles included full employment, greater equality of income and wealth, fair taxation, elimination of poverty, strengthening of public services, and environmental and human rights protection. The budget would also be guided by a number of fiscal constraints, notably a commitment to meet the government's deficit target of 3 percent of GDP by 1996–97.

After months of consultation and compromise, a final budget emerged that reflected the principles, priorities, and fiscal criteria set for the project, and that all participants could support. It was then submitted to the independent economic forecasting company Informetrica, which certified that the alternative budget's deficit-reduction plan was achievable. Some fifty university economists, including a former Macdonald commissioner, also certified that the alternative budget's monetary and fiscal plan was viable.

The point of departure of the CCPA/CHO!CES budget was that the root of the fiscal dilemma was not government overspending but an excessively tight monetary policy, which was strangling the economy, keeping unemployment high and tax revenue low. Indeed, the alternative budget approach was similar in many ways to that promised by the Liberals in the Red Book. It sought to reduce the deficit through employment and growth, rather than seeking to reduce the deficit through spending cuts, as a prerequisite to growth and job creation.

The first step, according to the alternative budget, was for the Bank of Canada to lower the interest rate. The work of many economists—notably Pierre Fortin—confirmed that the Bank did indeed have the power to lower both short-term and long-term interest rates. The Ontario government's macroeconomic model and federal Department of Finance calculations demonstrated that a reduction in interest rates would quickly raise employment and revenue, and shrink the deficit. A modest easing of interest rates would allow the alternative budget to meet Martin's deficit target without any spending cuts or tax increases whatsoever.

The government and the corporate financial establishment's rationale for deficit reduction through massive spending cuts was based on the premise that the Bank of Canada could *not* control interest rates, that they were set in financial markets. If the Bank reduced its short-term interest rate, they argued, financial markets, expecting inflation or a lower dollar, would force up long-term rates. The difference in the path to deficit reduction that flowed from this crucial assumption about the power of the Bank of Canada over interest rates was truly astounding.

There were other revealing differences as well. The alternative budget sought to create jobs also through direct public investment, to reduce inequality, and to begin to rebuild the social security system, turning around years of cuts in transfers to health, education, and welfare. It also included rebuilding the unemployment insurance system, introducing a national child-care program, a generous low-income family tax credit, and income-tax relief for low-income earners. Overall, government spending would grow a modest 2.5 percent per year over three years, less than the expected growth of the economy.

How would this spending be financed? A stronger, more fully employed economy would bring in most of the needed revenues and make fewer demands on the social system. As well, a tax package placing a greater burden of deficit reduction on corporations and the wealthiest members of society would close tax loopholes and introduce new measures as suggested above. This, too, departed from the government line. Deputy Finance Minister David Dodge claims that there is no room to raise such taxes because many wealthy individuals would move to the U.S., and companies would move capital and jobs there. Apart from a bump in tax level in the first year of the alternative budget, the level would thereafter move in line with GDP growth, well below the average tax burden of industrialized nations.

The alternative budget demonstrated something quite remarkable in the current climate of slash and burn. It showed that there were in fact choices—credible choices—to be made in reducing the deficit. The government claims cutting spending was the only possibility. This is simply not so. It made a choice. That choice reflected its priorities, and its priorities echoed the priorities of the big corporations, big banks, and big bondholders.

The media also had a choice, and they chose by and large to disregard the alternative budget. They chose to pump out the message that any credible budget had to have deep spending cuts, had to hold the line on taxes, and we could only hope that the money markets would reward spending cuts with lower interest rates. The alternative budget was outside the framework of serious debate as defined by the mainstream media.

7

SLIDING THROUGH GETHSEMANE

*"Social security has become accepted as one of the things
for which the peoples of the world are fighting. It is one
of the concrete expressions of a better world."*

Leonard Marsh, 1943

*"I never envisioned I would be here, in this position, at
my age.... I have nothing; I own nothing.... I now know
it's not realistic to dream any more. All I want in life
is to find work."*

unemployed bank clerk on welfare, 1995

In May 1994, sixteen social-action groups went before the
United Nations to charge that Canada had violated its obligations under the 1966 UN Covenant on Social, Economic
and Cultural Rights. Canada had ratified the UN Covenant in
1976, along with every other industrialized nation except the
United States. Article 6 of the Covenant asserts the "right of
everyone to the opportunity to gain his living by work which he

freely [italics added] chooses or accepts, and will take appropriate steps to safeguard this right." The Canadian government, under its compliance obligations, always cited CAP as evidence of its adherence to the Covenant, especially its prohibition on forcing people to work for welfare and its guarantee of financial assistance based on need. According to University of Toronto law professor Craig Scott, the Canada Health and Social Transfer legislation (C-76) repealing CAP "will place Canada in a position of breaching international human rights law."

The committee monitoring compliance with the UN Social, Economic and Cultural Covenant will ask the Canadian government to justify this measure in its report due in the fall of 1995. To underline the seriousness of the matter, the committee wrote to the federal government immediately after the appeal, questioning its suspension of CAP, which, as committee member Virginia Bonoan-Dondan said, implements Canadian obligations under the covenant.

The UN covenant is a remarkable document that came into being under the leadership of the Pearson Liberals. Representing internationalism at its best, it was the value of the just society writ large. That the Chrétien government was now accused of violating this international treaty commitment by abolishing the Canada Assistance Plan symbolized how far the Liberals had moved from the heyday of just society optimism.

In the heat of the 1993 election campaign, information was leaked about a secret Conservative policy document outlining major cuts to social programs. Kim Campbell backpedalled furiously, protesting that social policy reform was too complicated to discuss during an election campaign. Chrétien attacked her apparent cover-up, waving the Red Book as he had done many times during the campaign. "The social safety net that we have in Canada will remain," he promised. This pledge that the Liberals were planning no major changes to the social security system was important because, although there was no mention of a social security review in the Red Book, Chrétien had stirred the waters on a swing through New Brunswick by musing that welfare recipients might be forced to work for their benefits.

The Red Book noted that social spending cuts by the Tories had "set us on the path to becoming a polarized society, divided into rich and poor, educated and uneducated, with a shrinking middle class. This is not the kind of country most Canadians want to live in." Those seeking further information on the likely Liberal direction on social policy could have looked at a caucus task-force report on income security released in the pit of the 1991 recession. It advised against using UI funds for training purposes while slashing post-secondary education transfers. It also cautioned against making social policy reform subservient to deficit reduction and noted that social reform "will fail unless accompanied by comprehensive tax reform to ensure that the wealthy individuals and profitable corporations pay their fair share."

Barely three months after the election, Lloyd Axworthy, now in charge of the new Human Resources Development super-ministry, rose in the House of Commons to announce a fundamental review of the social security system. The review would focus on unemployment insurance, welfare, education, and training. Health would be dealt with separately and, as it turned out, so would pensions. The goal, said Axworthy, was to create a new, "re-tooled" social system for the twenty-first century that "rewards effort and offers incentives for work"; one that "ends the cycle of dependency." He challenged potential critics to free themselves of obsolescent ideas. The problem with existing programs was that they were created decades ago for an economy that no longer exists. They contained too many "disincentives" preventing people from getting into the workforce. The core of a remodelled system would be a series of measures "to enable people to move from income support to meaningful employment."

Later that day, Chrétien told a receptive Toronto Board of Trade audience that the government was going to "reinvent" social programs to bring back the "dignity of work," an oft-repeated Chrétien campaign slogan. That, most Canadians assumed, would be achieved through the creation of jobs, not through the reinvention of social programs. Repeating his campaign musings about workfare, he hinted that those who didn't enrol in training programs or who refused work might be denied welfare or UI. Several months later he again raised the subject of workfare, in a tone that suggested something less than restoring the dignity of work: "It's better to have them at 50 percent of productivity than to be sitting at home drinking beer at zero percent of productivity."

Few would disagree that social programs should be improved, and that reform was overdue. Many social policy analysts consider the system uneven, demeaning, and badly frayed; indeed, the government's own advisory body, the National Council of Welfare, had issued a report in 1987 saying that the safety net was in need of major repair. What was surprising was that a government elected to create jobs was focusing on restructuring welfare and unemployment insurance programs as if they were a major cause of unemployment. The neo-liberal orthodoxy—that these "rigidities" in the labour market kept the "natural" rate of unemployment artificially high—was not thought to hold much sway within Liberal policy circles.

Just a week before Axworthy's announcement, *The Globe and Mail,* the most prominent standardbearer of this doctrine, editorialized that the problem was "not so much that social programs are costly because unemployment is high, as it is that unemployment is high because social programs are costly." Noting that UI alone was thought to add two points to the unemployment rate, the *Globe* concluded (as had Axworthy) that the goal of social program reform should be to "restore incentives to work, train and if necessary move to find a job."

What had caused the Liberals to switch from blaming the economy for failing to provide jobs and straining the social safety net, to seeing the social security system itself as the problem? What had caused them to see social programs rather than a serious shortage of skilled, stable, full-time, decent-paying jobs as the real disincentive to work?

Axworthy was careful to emphasize that the goal of the social security review was not to "slash and trash," but rather to "renew and revitalize." After all, the Red Book had promised new commitments to child care, apprenticeship training, and a youth service corps. However, the first Liberal budget contradicted the reform-as-renewal approach. It stated that social policy reform would be conscripted to help reduce the deficit. To reinforce the point, it executed a three-year, $5.5-billion cut from unemployment insurance, and carved $2 billion from post-secondary education and welfare transfers. Despite evidence to the contrary, Axworthy continued to deny that deficit reduction was the motivation for the review. "I am not doing this as a stand-in for the Finance Minister," he told a *Maclean's* reporter.

As the months passed, the language of restraint became harsher. What was initially supposed to run parallel to deficit reduction was increasingly becoming the vehicle for deficit reduction. By May 1994, Axworthy was saying, "There is no point in pretending that we can spend additional sums now on our social programs—we cannot...." By October, he was warning, "If we do not...make the changes in the social security system that we want, it will be the bond dealers in New York and London who will make those decisions for us."

Prominent Liberals and advisors close to the review process expressed concern about the the review's shift to deficit cutting. Judith Maxwell, a member of Axworthy's independent advisory group and Liberal appointee to the Bank of Canada board, warned, "The danger...of cutting expenditures to reduce the fiscal deficit...[is that] we will destroy the good part of public services and make the social deficit even worse than it is now." Marc Lalonde, the former Minister of Health and Welfare who had tried unsuccessfully to introduce major social security reform in the early 1970s, cautioned that the costs of reform would actually increase the fiscal deficit in the short run, and savings in terms of deficit reduction could be expected only after five to ten years.

Further evidence that this was primarily a deficit-cutting exercise for which the mould had already been cast came on the eve of the release of Axworthy's *Improving Social Security in Canada*, the so-called Green Paper. A secret Treasury Board memo obtained by *The Toronto Star*'s Derek Ferguson revealed that Axworthy and Martin had agreed to the "fiscal parameters" of the social security review—an additional $7.5 billion would be cut from UI, welfare, and post-secondary education programs by the end of the Liberal mandate—throwing into question the legitimacy of the consultation that would follow. The savings, according to the document, would be achieved through "structural changes to UI," extending the freeze on CAP, and phasing out educational transfers. The last, warned the memo, is expected to cause college tuition fees to double by 1997 and could trigger "explosive political fallout." Axworthy denied that the document represented a final cabinet decision. He also denied that the savings would go to deficit reduction. However, the cuts outlined in the secret memo were close to those that appeared five months later in the Martin budget.

Coinciding with the announcement of the social security review in January 1994, the C.D. Howe Institute launched a fourteen-part series of studies on reforming social policy. The series' co-editors were William Watson, professor of economics at McGill, and John Richards, professor of business at Simon Fraser University. Richards, a former NDP member of the Saskatchewan legislature, represented the left, although he would not be recognized by many, apart from the Howe, as having such an orientation. Watson, a *Financial Post* columnist, carried the banner of the right. Leaving aside the question of why the Howe chose economists rather than social policy experts for the job, the co-editors spanned the narrow boundaries of "responsible" policy differences acceptable to the Howe.

Thomas Kierans, president of the Institute, wrote a foreword to the first study that set out four reasons why social policy re-examination was needed. First and foremost, social programs must be enlisted in the fight for debt/deficit control, given the "perilous" fiscal situation. Second, average, middle-of-the-road Canadians were no longer willing to finance "the apparently unending expansion of the welfare state." Third, social programs were not good for the people they were supposed to help, as they created dependency. And fourth, Clinton's promise to reform welfare in the U.S. had legitimized a rethinking of the Canadian welfare state.

Several weeks before the release of the Green Paper, the C.D. Howe Institute published a study, *Social Canada in the Millennium*, by Tom Courchene which bore striking similarities to the government's paper. Courchene warned that our social security system was no longer affordable. If we didn't redesign it, international financial markets would do it for us. What this meant was that we Canadians had to "filter our long-standing values of fairness, sharing and equity through the new realities of fiscal restraint, globalization and the information revolution."

What was wrong with the existing system, in Courchene's view? It trapped people in poverty, throwing up barriers to their getting into the workforce. Education and training programs were not providing skills for the new information age. Overly generous unemployment insurance kept unemployment in some areas higher than it would be if wages were allowed to fall to a market-clearing level, that is, where demand and supply balanced; it also discouraged people from moving to where the jobs are.

What kind of social overhaul did Professor Courchene have in mind? Eliminate cash transfers to the provinces for education, and replace them with student vouchers. Eliminate health-care cash transfers and hand over new tax powers to the provinces. Double or triple the qualifying period and increase the period worked as preconditions for receiving full unemployment insurance benefits. Replace the minimum wage with wage subsidies. Cancel the Canada Assistance Plan and hand responsibility for welfare to the provinces. Reintroduce workfare. Courchene's vision of a twenty-first-century social Canada was closer to the social Canada of the early twentieth century.

Delayed by months of provincial opposition, anxiety over the coming referendum in Quebec, and wrangling within the cabinet, Axworthy finally released *Improving Social Security in Canada*. It contained no real surprises. The major proposals, framed as options, and the cuts that would shape the review had already been leaked; moreover, Axworthy had already revealed much of the new Liberal thinking on social policy.

The Green Paper was only a partial review of social security; major components of the system—pensions and medicare—were left out. Social programs delivered through the tax system were also ignored. It defined the purpose of social security as "taking care of society's most vulnerable members." This is a radical departure from the goal of social security as spelled out in Liberal policy documents since the 1930s: to protect *all* citizens from life- and work-related contingencies through the pooling of risk. Social security was no longer a right for which society bore collective responsibility, but a contract of "mutual responsibility" between the individual and the state. This was a halfway house to the "personal responsibility" approach to social security espoused by the Reform Party. Individuals would now have to bear a bigger share of the burden of their security, and public security would be provided only conditionally.

For the post-war social architects, a strong social security system and a full-employment economy were inseparable. If people had a sense of economic security and optimism about the future, they would spend, businesses would invest, employment would be created, and the economy would grow. Beginning in the mid-1970s, as discussed in Chapter Three, the government began to cut back the revenue flow needed to support the social security system. As the economy faltered and unemployment grew, putting more stress on the system, the declining revenue stream caused a fiscal deficit to open up and grow.

The Green Paper accepted the radically altered labour market of the 1990s—permanent mass unemployment and a preponderance of unstable, low-paid and part-time work—less as a problem than as a given. A return to full employment was simply not feasible; therefore, the focus was on employability. To this end it proposed a leaner social security system, targeting only the most destitute. The role of social security was no longer to prevent poverty, but rather to care for those in deepest poverty. For example, the enhanced child benefit would be targeted to families in severe poverty; families at the poverty line or just above it would not be eligible. Money would be taken from one vulnerable group—the unemployed—and given to a more desperate group. This approach fosters division rather than social solidarity, pitting one sector against another in competition for shrinking resources.

At the very time the labour market was weakest, the Green Paper would force people to increase their dependence on the market, their families, and private charity. It stigmatized the vulnerable as "dysfunctional," in need of "incentives" to upgrade their labour skills and kick their dependence on public supports. With economic insecurity at its height, the Green Paper proposed increasing that insecurity by further shrinking the federal government's role in an already deteriorating system. It absolved the government of responsibility for restructuring the economy to counter now widespread "Wal-Mart" workplace conditions and help create good stable jobs.

The Green Paper's key proposals were the following: a scaled-back UI system, possibly a two-tier system with a smaller benefit for frequent users; elimination of most of the educational transfer to the provinces, possibly turning what was left into a loan fund for students; a shift from a cost-sharing to a (smaller) block-funded social assistance transfer, with the possible removal of national standards, notably that prohibiting workfare; an effort to reduce child poverty, including an enriched but more tightly targeted child tax credit and the expansion of child-care spaces; and enhanced funding for training financed through UI. However, the leaked fiscal parameters—which were not specified in the Green Paper—left little room to implement the new training and child poverty initiatives.

The Globe and Mail called the Green Paper proposals "admirably ambitious" and urged Axworthy to move quickly to persuade the public of the "distortions, disincentives and discrepancies in social programs," and of the need for reform. It called UI a "deeply distorted social entitlement...a corrosive subsidy for business and an unnecessary supplement for individuals...it has become a tax on jobs. Most damning, it has helped to establish a culture of dependence." The "inefficient" welfare system, it claimed, "did not serve the interest of those that most need it."

BCNI head Tom d'Aquino, who had been arguing that Canada's social programs were no longer affordable ever since he stopped claiming that free trade would strengthen government's capacity to provide social programs, was also pleased with the Green Paper as it "called for sweeping reforms that essentially embrace the principles I have outlined." D'Aquino has been in high spirits over the Liberal performance now that, as he puts it, they have finally shaken free from "the clutches of the economic nationalists."

The Green Paper's view of the employment problem closely paralleled the *OECD Jobs Study* released earlier in the year. The cure for unemployment, the report said, was to make labour markets more flexible. The way to move the 35 million unemployed in the industrialized countries back to work was to enable them "to price themselves into jobs"—that is, force them to accept lower wages. How to make labour markets more flexible? The study recommended "giving more weight to the market-clearing role of wages." In other words, loosen the "rigidities" in the labour market that prevent the balancing of labour supply and demand. Once these rigidities—too-generous unemployment insurance programs, too-high minimum wages, too-high employer contributions to pension and health care—are dealt with, people will be forced to offer their labour at a lower wage, and employers will be more willing to hire them.

Recent Canadian experience does not support this theory. Ten years ago social and labour market standards were stronger, and wages and benefits were higher than they are today. Successive measures to reduce these protections and increase flexibility in the labour market have not reduced unemployment. In *The Wage Curve* (1994), the most rigorous cross-country survey ever undertaken, involving 3.5 million people in 12 industrialized countries, British economists David Blanchflower and Andrew Oswald found that nowhere has the lowering of wages led to a lowering of unemployment. Lawrence Katz of Harvard and Alan Kreuger and David Card of Princeton found that increasing the minimum wage up to a point actually had "a positive effect on employment." Such facts, however, did little to dampen the Liberal government's eagerness to incorporate the recommendations of the OECD report into the Green Paper.

The Green Paper's contention that the "too-generous" UI system was "destroying the incentive to work" was countered in a study by Miles Corak of Statistics Canada, commissioned for Axworthy's department. It found that people were using UI more frequently, not because they were losing their incentive to work, but rather because employers were losing the incentive to create full-time permanent jobs. Instead, they have been relying on a rapidly growing pool of contingent workers to whom they have no obligations.

Training, a major pillar of the Green Paper, presupposed that unemployment was caused by an inadequate skill base, or a mismatch of skills. (Strangely, for all that the study rested so heavily on this assumption, it was not able to specify how many jobs are going unfilled because applicants did not have the right skills.) The demands of the new knowledge economy required workers to continually upgrade their skills; hence the need for a "learning culture." The key to getting back to work was therefore training, which could be financed by transferring money in the UI fund from passive income support to active training support. In this, of course, it betrayed a certain blindness to the obvious fact that the proposal would create poverty, the biggest impediment to making the transition from one job to another.

The Green Paper did exactly what the 1991 Liberal caucus report on income security vowed the Liberals would never do: as it shuffled funds from the UI fund into training, it proposed reducing the education transfer to the provinces that helped fund colleges and universities. It thereby transferred the cost of education from the federal to provincial governments, and thence to the individual or family. The increased debt burden—the reduced education transfer would double tuition costs—would make education less, not more, accessible to students from the increasingly strapped middle- and low-income families—the opposite of its stated goal. The federal government initiated the educational transfers thirty years ago to ensure that university education was within reach of virtually anyone with the qualifications and desire to go. This proposal would move higher learning toward the privileged few.

The basic message of the Green Paper on unemployment and social security is that most people on UI and welfare have become "addicted" to these programs. The challenge, therefore, is how to get people to kick their habit and move into the job market. The "cure" is a combination of incentives, such as training and child care, and disincentives, such as less generous UI or welfare benefits and workfare. The logic behind this approach is that the increased supply and quality of labour will increase competition for existing jobs (unless one accepts the questionable assumption of a mismatch between job vacancies and workers' skills). This competition will push down the price of labour and push up the employers' willingness to hire, because wages are lower and workers have needed skills. Thus is labour market supply and demand brought into balance and dependence on government reduced.

Although training is a motherhood issue that virtually no one opposes in principle, it is not the cure, for the fact is that the economy is not creating enough jobs. Welfare advocates and food-bank volunteers can attest that their ranks are full of educated people who have trained, got counselling, and moved—and are still unemployed. The solution then lies, first and foremost, in improving the functioning and structure of the economy to create enough jobs to go around. This, of course, requires a very different prescription to deal with unemployment. But the Green Paper is less about improving our social security system to reduce unemployment than it is a strategy to compress wages.

The social security system envisaged by the Green Paper is, we have said, a conditional system. Benefits are conditional upon compulsory work or training, or on disincentives so onerous that they create the same result—workfare, which previous Liberal governments had made illegal through the 1966 Canada Assistance Plan. Workfare—"community service" work or training in return for a government welfare or UI cheque—represents a return to a past when desperate people were humiliated before receiving meagre income support.

Three provinces—Alberta, New Brunswick, and Quebec—currently conduct workfare programs in violation of CAP. Not only has the federal government turned a blind eye to the practice, but the Green Paper (while skirting mandatory workfare) encouraged the use of "incentives" and "disincentives" that make it almost impossible not to participate. The budget also eliminated CAP, and with it the sanction against workfare.

Workfare is a threat to all working people. It sends the message that a government whose duty it is to enforce laws protecting workers against exploitative employers is itself going to force people to work for compensation far below the legal minimum wage. It undermines not only wage levels but jobs and working conditions as well.

Here's how it works. At the Red Deer Regional Hospital the number of $12/hour nursing assistants was radically cut back. Workfare nursing assistant jobs were then posted at $6 an hour. No new jobs were created, but above-the-line jobs were replaced by working-poverty jobs. In Alberta, recipients are told to apply to the Alberta Community Employment Program or be cut off welfare.

In Quebec, welfare recipients who do twenty hours' "work" per month get a $2/hour bonus on their welfare cheques. Employers are not required to provide training; nor are they obliged to hire the workers at the end of their six-month work period. Only 2 percent of welfare recipients have got real jobs as a result of this program. Employers can employ one workfare candidate after another, thereby not having to hire a real worker at a legal wage.

New Brunswick has the lowest welfare rate in the country; for a single "employable" male, it is about two-thirds below the poverty line. Its workfare program offers people up to $12,000 a year for doing community work, such as replanting forests, without losing their welfare, drug, and dental benefits. If they refuse, their rock-bottom welfare benefit is reduced. This program therefore creates a labour pool that undercuts minimum-wage jobs, replacing them with workfare jobs.

The Human Resources Department sponsored—and Lloyd Axworthy participated in—a Queen's University forum on social policy. A small group of academics and politicians from Europe, North America, and New Zealand discussed policy challenges and shared experiences. The event, held in a fifteenth-century British castle bequeathed to Queen's, was filmed by a CBC crew and broadcast on Newsworld. From Axworthy's interventions during the conference we can distill his thinking on social policy reform in a way that the Green Paper—a bureaucratic document—cannot.

Axworthy believes that the transition from an industrial economy to a knowledge or information economy has left a huge mismatch of skills. This, he believes, is at the root of the employment problem. Employers need all kinds of skilled jobs in this new economy, but those looking for work do not, by and large, have those skills. His job, therefore, is to restructure the social security system to address this new economic reality.

He believes that the traditonal role of the state as a provider of entitlements and security is obsolete, and that universal social programs are no longer feasible. Security must be redefined as having ongoing access to the means for skills development, because access to skills means access to the jobs required by the new economy. The new role of the state is to facilitate access to the training and education that create the new foundation for security.

Part of the reform, Axworthy claimed, is to remove barriers in the current social security system that impede personal "retooling"; for example, penalties in the current welfare system discourage people from entering the workforce by reducing their welfare benefits dollar-for-dollar from part-time wages: as well, moving from welfare into a low-paying job means losing drug benefits and subsidized housing. Single unemployed women are penalized for, say, volunteering at a women's resource centre, because they are required to be available and looking for "real work." This valuable work should not be penalized by withdrawal of benefits; rather, unemployed people should be encouraged by the UI system to do this kind of work. Whether this work is valuable enough to pay a regular wage rather than the less-than-market UI rate is unclear.

In addition, some new features are required to facilitate personal retooling: enhanced child-care support to enable women to enter a training program or get a job, and new funds that people can tap into in the form of low-interest or income-contingent loans.

Axworthy talks about innovative training experiments involving his department, notably sectoral labour–management council training funds. These set training priorities and curricula, and create internship programs for youth to facilitate their entry into the workplace.

He also sees an important role for the non-profit and non-government sector in job creation and training. Much valuable work gets done in this "third" sector, but because of the way work is currently organized and compensated, there is no pay for much of this work. Thus, new mechanisms of compensation must be developed. He envisages partnerships between government and the third sector to provide young people with training and entry-level work experience in the transition to a market job—for example, providing security in parks, or tree planting. Similarly, the unemployed fisherman, instead of sitting at home collecting his extended unemployment, would receive a bonus in return for participating in a meaningful conservation program to restore the fishery. Apart from the obvious dangers of such initiatives being coercive, very low-paid, and a means of job dumping from the public sector, many of Axworthy's ideas are laudable.

Looking back, Lloyd Axworthy's strategy for reforming the social security system in the fall of 1994 was not only a gamble, but an impossible juggling act. First, the idea that the unemployment problem is primarily a mismatch of skills is at best a leap of faith. There is no evidence of a skills shortage. This is a political device to mask the real shortage: jobs. Therefore, putting all the emphasis on training for new economy jobs that do not exist in nearly sufficient numbers to meet the demand is a formula for immense frustration down the road.

Second, creating a system geared to continuous training is a very expensive undertaking. Axworthy proposed to do it by transferring a few billion dollars from UI into training initiatives and other supports such as child care, low-interest loans. To assume that reallocating those funds could be done without damaging the existing system ignores the crucial role the system still has to play in providing "old-fashioned" security.

The present system has been gored repeatedly during the last ten years; yet if people don't have a basic income support level they cannot engage in the training activities Axworthy is pushing for. UI provides a barely satisfactory basic level of income support; welfare does not. Cutting UI forces more and more people onto welfare, where poverty is the biggest barrier to successful training. Even if he were able to accomplish this without weakening the social security system, the few billion dollars that Axworthy was allocated for his reforms would not be sufficient; the reform would require additional government revenues, which were not forthcoming. Finally, the political momentum for deficit reduction meant that the money squeezed from UI was applied to deficit reduction, not redirected into training.

This is the worst of all worlds. The cuts to welfare and unemployment insurance have made conditions for recipients intolerable, and hope for escape from poverty is more remote. Axworthy, like his counterpart, U.S. Labour Secretary Robert Reich, has seen his proposed financial incentives to get people back into the labour market rejected, while his disincentives, such as welfare sanctions, are tightly embraced.

Lloyd Axworthy made it clear that the Green Paper was just a discussion paper. Unlike the Tories, who conducted their social policy by stealth, the Liberals wanted to consult with "Canadians" on their proposals. Axworthy sees labour and social-advocacy groups as protecting entrenched special interests, and therefore resistant to his reforms. "Canadians," however, are much more receptive to what he is trying to do. In order to circumvent these "special interest groups" and reach ordinary citizens, his department distributed a few hundred thousand "workbooks" on the Green Paper, an interactive questionnaire-type device through which people could respond to the proposals by mailing back the completed workbook to the government. Axworthy saw it as a kind of public legitimation of his reform. "Once this is done they can put their signatures on the reform which then becomes a new contract."

More than 25,000 Canadians sent in their workbooks, but the only publicly available summary of their reaction is brief and incomplete. What we do know is that, while there was widespread support for the concept of more targeting of social programs, when it came to specific programs, more than two-thirds of the respondents opposed the two-tier UI proposal and an even greater number opposed tampering with the program's eligibility and benefit levels. There was widespread support for increased training and more child-care assistance; a majority supported an income-contingent student loan program, although there was also concern about what happens to those unable to find a well-paying job after graduation.

What emerges is that people approved of the parts of the reform that involved new initiatives and opposed those parts that cut back the existing social security system. What they got in the Martin budget was the opposite—cutbacks without new initiatives.

In the fall of 1994, a Commons committee travelled across the country consulting on the Green Paper in more traditional parliamentary fashion. The public response was very large: more than 600 people appeared before the committee, as individuals or as representatives of groups; hundreds more were turned away. The committee received another 1,200 written or taped submissions. People also held protests, vigils, and counter-hearings, and official hearings were often disrupted as anger boiled over.

Who were these people who came to tell parliamentarians what they thought of the proposed changes to the social security system? They represented people with disabilities, aboriginals, and immigrant groups. They were child poverty advocates and seniors. They represented local social service organizations, volunteer groups, community development groups, and municipal councils. They represented social justice coalitions, social planning councils, labour councils, and churches. They came on behalf of teachers, academics, students, and research organizations. They spoke on behalf of women, gays and lesbians, and visible minorities. They represented chambers of commerce, boards of trade, and service clubs. They spoke for steelworkers, autoworkers, communications workers, public and private service workers, physicians, nurses, and construction workers. They represented farmers and fishers and forest workers. They came from community health centres, housing co-ops, and food banks.

They were also individuals concerned about their future, the future of their families and friends, the future of their communities, and the future of their country. They came as mothers and fathers, job-seekers and welfare recipients, students and retirees, community and national leaders, and policy experts. They came as concerned citizens, who cared deeply about a social system that expressed their values as a civilized society, which they saw slipping away—collateral damage from the "war on the deficit." Many had helped to build the system or were the sons and daughters of pioneers in the struggle for labour and social rights. Most held a vision of moving toward a society in which children could grow up in nurturing families free of deprivation; in which those who found themselves without a job had enough income to enable them to find another job without poverty and anxiety about their future; in which all seniors could live comfortably in retirement; in which there was equal access to education and training, and an ample pool of job opportunities; in which people on low incomes had a solid floor of income support and access to affordable housing and medical care.

Together they comprised a society struggling to find ways of building a common future. These were not "special interest lobbies" narrowly focused on personal gain, as they have been disparagingly portrayed by the media and politicians. These were citizens actively exercising their responsibilities. Such active engagement in the political process, not public opinion polling, is the essence of democracy.

Among the hundreds of people who appeared before the Commons Social Security Review Committee was Bob Bossin, folk singer, of Gabriola Island, a small island off the coast of British Columbia. Bossin's insights go to the heart of the debate on social security, the issue of values and choices.

For the first time in his life, Bossin told the committee, the legacy of Canada as a decent, caring society is being fundamentally threatened. The vast majority of the experts on *Morningside* or *Prime Time News,* he says, tell us we're broke and can no longer afford the programs that define who we are. Bossin turns the issue around and asks, "Can we afford not to?" Put this way, affording social programs is no longer an objective barrier, but rather one of several choices, each having its own costs and benefits. "We can have a choice of the kind of social safety net we have, or we can increase the cost of policing, the cost of prisons... we can pay with the kind of insecurity in our daily lives that people south of the border feel, that we did not feel as I was growing up. I think that's far too great a price to pay."

Why, he goes on, are we asking whether we can afford health care and not asking, for example, whether we can afford the multi-channel universe? Bossin's choice is clear. "We want these social programs and we are going to *have* to pay...because that's the kind of people we are and that's the kind of values we have."

The loudest message from these hearings was a rejection of key Green Paper assumptions and proposals: the social security system, flawed as it is, represents a fundamental element of our heritage, and must be maintained and improved. Don't cut the deficit by sacrificing this valuable heritage. Look instead to reforms of the tax system, specifically tax breaks for corporations and well-off citizens, and measures to lower interest rates and create jobs. Training is very important, but it cannot be a substitute for job creation. A strong federal presence in the social security system is essential, especially to ensure national standards. Don't reform UI by cutting back access or the level of benefits, or by making it a two-tier system. There are many ways to reform CAP other than by reducing or eliminating the funding, and abolishing such national standards as those prohibiting workfare. Don't cut higher education funding and transfer the cost, and hence the indebtedness, to individuals from low- and middle-income families. This valuable public good should be financed collectively.

To the committee's credit, it reported these themes in its final report and, to the dismay of the architects of the Green Paper, incorporated some in its recommendations. It opposed workfare and a two-tier UI system. It stressed the overriding need for jobs. Uncharacteristically, it went beyond its terms of reference and flagged social spending through the tax system as integral to social security reform, as many witnesses pressed it to do, and as an area needing further examination.

Most important, although the Commons committee report made many concessions to the Green Paper, it rejected its underlying premises. It defined social programs as a vehicle for promoting the "values of security...through mutual caring and collective compassion for each other." It went on: "*All* individuals in society need to feel that the country and their governments care about their well-being." While it accepted that workers must adapt to the current global realities, it concluded that "Canadians want to see us adjust to new realities and undertake new initiatives in light of our enduring values." This differs profoundly from the Green Paper's vision of a targeted social system whose defining value is caring for the most vulnerable.

Despite the rising pre-budget deficit panic whipped up by the media, the financial lobby, and "highly placed government sources" that the budget would contain radical cuts to social programs, Axworthy doggedly insisted that his social security reform was on track. However, three weeks before the budget, in an interview with Edward Greenspon of *The Globe and Mail*, Axworthy said that reforms would be put on hold until the government had got its deficit under control. The next day he told *The Ottawa Citizen*'s Mark Kennedy that the government had to go through the "Garden of Gethsemane" to test its resolve on the deficit. "There's a reality there that even the most committed social philosopher and proponent has to take into account.... You may not like it. And I don't like it. And you may not feel that it's fair. And it's not fair. But it's a reality." Unless the international markets are soothed with clear action on the deficit, Canada could "hit the wall," as New Zealand did a decade ago, he told Kennedy, and foreign lenders could force drastic social program cuts.

Looking back on Lloyd Axworthy's social reform initiative of 1994, it was naive to expect that it would renew and revitalize the social security system. From Axworthy's perspective the review was more likely a way to limit the inevitable fallout from the government's fiscal woes and target remaining funds to key programs. At worst it was a cynical attempt to provide a cover for continued dismembering of the social system. The corporate die had already been cast, the political space narrowed, the choices predetermined. The Liberal Party had acquiesced to that mould, having made the predictable political bargain with the corporate oligarchy that would secure its hold on government. Genuine progressive social reform was never in the cards.

Radical social changes were, however, in the works; but they were being built on another foundation. The bureaucrats at the Department of Finance were preparing to combine the provincial transfer programs for welfare, health, and post-secondary education into one block transfer. There would be billions less in the fund, but the provinces would have few restrictions on how they spent it. As its leverage diminished, the federal government would become a marginal player in social policy. National standards would go, provinces would increasingly go their own way, and the social face of Canada would be transformed.

PART THREE

TOM D'AQUINO: HAPPY AT LAST

8

PUNISHING THE INNOCENT

"I don't want a medical system in Canada where there
will be a system for the rich and a system for the poor....
We will keep it as it is, and nobody will touch it as long
as the Liberal Party is there."

Jean Chrétien, 1993 federal election campaign

Several days after Paul Martin released his budget, Jean Chrétien told CBC's *Morningside* that a fundamental rethinking of medicare would be necessary in light of the current fiscal reality. He mused that $10 billion should be cut out of health-care spending to get it down to European levels of 8 to 9 percent of GDP.

Chrétien said that the original intention of medicare was to cover only catastrophic illness and major surgery, to ensure that "nobody would lose his home because somebody is sick in the family"—apparently repudiating two basic medicare principles: accessibility based on need and comprehensiveness of coverage. Indeed, the 1966 legislation establishing medicare stated that all in-patient and diagnostic services and hospital prescriptions were to be free. In fact, the original recommendation of the Hall Royal Commission exploring national medicare was that medical coverage be extended to include all prescription drugs as well as dental care.

Chrétien also surprised many with his observation that when the federal government introduced medicare in 1966, its involvement was intended only to kick-start the system. "I remember, too, at the time," Chrétien said, "we would say to the provinces, 'we were helping you to get organized.' It was to be temporary in nature...because it's provincial jurisdiction." Now that it was well established, Chrétien went on to suggest, it was time to return the responsibility to the provinces. This is not, of course, a perception that is widely shared, and there was certainly nothing in the original act that even hinted that the federal role was to be temporary.

Chrétien was noticeably defensive when Gzowski pointed out that several provincial finance ministers had charged that the federal cuts amounted to off-loading and would result in fundamental changes to health care. He countered that the provinces were already preparing for the federal cuts by restructuring their own health services. This was an odd response, given that he had promised during the campaign that he would not reward provincial restructuring, as the Tories had done, by further federal cutbacks.

The budget cuts to medicare and other social programs not only directly contradicted what the Liberals promised in the Red Book, but also broke commitments Chrétien made after becoming prime minister. In December 1993, shortly after the Liberals assumed power, Chretien appeared on a special CBC *Prime Time News* "town hall" to field questions from "ordinary Canadians." To a questioner who asked if he intended to reverse the Tory cuts to health and education transfers, he replied that his government would offer the provinces a stable five-year financing framework. He did not promise to increase federal funding, but did say unequivocally: "Transfer payments will not be cut."

The budget cuts and Chrétien's post-budget musings on medicare gave new meaning to the word pragmatic. It set off alarm bells, not only because of Chrétien's hands-on approach to health-care issues, but also because he had made integrity a cornerstone of his campaign to an electorate weary of broken promises. Keith Banting, director of the School of Policy Studies at Queen's University, pointed out that although "Canadians would not stand for the open and explicit repeal of the Canada Health Act...the [Liberal government's] quiet erosion of the cash transfer is achieving the same political end by stealth."

Chrétien's ruminations were at odds with the image that he cultivated as the public champion of medicare. In the lead-up to the 1990 Liberal leadership convention, he told *Winnipeg Free Press* columnist Frances Russell, "In principle, I believe that medical services for all Canadians is a right." In *Straight from the Heart*, Chrétien attempted to position himself to the left of John Turner in the 1984 leadership race, as a populist defending the Liberal heritage and appealing to Main Street, not Bay Street. That heritage, according to Chrétien, included a social vision rooted in the universality of social benefits. He wrote: "social benefits are given to every Canadian citizen as a right. They can be taxed back from the rich because the rich should pay more taxes than the poor, but to extend the social safety net to some, and not others, makes it charity and not a right. Any deviation from the fundamental principle invites further erosion of the benefits themselves." To illustrate his point, he raised the issue of medicare user fees: "To charge an additional $2 opens the door to charging $20 or $200 or $2,000 because the principle has been destroyed. " He went on: "Ultimately the rich would have access to medical services and the poor would not."

The federal role in health care has changed in the last ten to fifteen years. The national medicare system was introduced in 1968 over the objections of provinces such as Ontario, which, supported by the medical and business establishment, wanted a limited U.S.-style catastrophic-illness plan. Many provinces went along with medicare grudgingly, and only because of the federal funding for it. The medicare transfer, lumped with the federal education transfer into Established Programs Financing (EPF), was delivered on a 50–50 cost-shared basis.

That arrangement changed in 1977 to a block grant (see Chapter Six), setting the stage for federal backsliding. It was, however, Tory budgets that brought massive cutbacks through changes to the funding formula. During the ten years to 1993, successive budgets removed almost $41 billion from federal health-care transfers to the provinces, forcing them into a radical restructuring that has reduced the accessibility, scope, and quality of medical services: closing hospital beds; de-listing and de-insuring services and drugs; laying off workers; contracting out to for-profit companies of management, laboratories, nursing, and other services; privatizing services; and off-loading to the voluntary sector and to families (i.e., women). The federal government share of public health spending plummeted to less than one-quarter at the end of the Mulroney era. The Martin budget ensures that this trend will continue.

During the 1988 free trade debate, Monique Bégin, former Liberal health minister and architect of the 1983 Canada Health Act, warned Canadians that medicare was a fragile institution vulnerable to death by a thousand cuts. She recalled that those who predicted that the mid-1970s switch from shared-cost to block funding would lead to pressure for extra billing and user fees were ridiculed. Time proved them right. She also warned that the FTA opened up opportunities for private, for-profit medical care, particularly from the United States. As we shall see, her fears have been borne out. (We have shown in Chapter Three that the FTA/NAFTA has been important in destabilizing the fiscal underpinnings of health and social programs, and we have provided concrete examples of how the shrinking policy space is undermining the government's capacity to maintain a strong health-care system.)

The corporate sector views the Canadian health-care sector "as one the largest unopened oysters," a $72-billion-dollar treasure, much of which, up to now, has been largely out of reach. The current climate has brought that bonanza closer to the business treasure hunters. Less than a week after the 1995 Martin budget, the head of Alberta Blue Cross, George Ward, was quoted as saying, "We're finding in Alberta with all the [federal] cutbacks, there are lots of opportunities starting to move out of the public health sector into a private environment."

Public dollars, mainly provincial, financed $52 billion or 72 percent of health spending in Canada in 1993. The private sector dollars financed the other 28 percent—$20 billion. The public portion of health-care spending has been declining. In 1983, it accounted for 76 percent of health-care spending. The public portion has also been shrinking rapidly in relation to the size of the economy, from 6.7 percent of GDP in 1991 to 5.8 percent of GDP in 1993. (Public spending per person dropped from $1,425 to $1,394 while private spending per person jumped from $482 to $502 during this period.)

Overall spending on health care, which has been growing faster than the economy as a whole during the last fifteen years, has now stabilized at 10 percent of GDP, precisely because of the decline in public spending. Private insurance finances those services not covered by public insurance such as private accommodation in hospitals, drugs, dental plans, and cosmetic surgery; and those that are only partially insured, such as eye examinations and physiotherapy. The rapid growth of private insurance as well as individual out-of-pocket expenses has been necessitated because of the slack caused by provincial cutbacks.

The largest single health-care expenditure financed by private insurance is drugs. Drugs are also the only component of private insurance that has grown relative to other areas of private insurance—from 36 percent in 1988 to 40 percent today. What this means is that the rapid growth of private insurance is being driven largely by the even more rapid growth of drug plan spending. The main reason for this is the cost of new patented drugs. Drug costs are the only major component of health spending whose share is rising; the other components have either remained steady or have dropped as a share of total health spending. Drug costs rose $6.7 billion between 1985 and 1993, from 10.5 percent to 15.1 percent of total health expenditures, on a par with physician costs. Most of this increase occurred in the period when the global pharmaceutical companies secured greater monopoly protection for their Canadian drug patents.

Clearly Chrétien, assuming he understands the issue, is not levelling with the Canadian public. When he talks about wanting to get overall health costs down, he really means publicly financed health costs. Health transfer cutbacks to the provinces under the Mulroney government have resulted in a major drop in the portion of health spending funded by the public sector. The Liberal government is accelerating these cuts. Besides eventually eliminating the capacity of the government to enforce national standards, this will lead to provincial governments shifting still more health services into the private sector. The cost of these newly privatized health services will, as they have done, grow more rapidly than the equivalent public services, increasing overall health spending. Thus, to the extent that cuts shift the provision and insuring of the service to the private sector, they actually cause health spending to rise, not fall. This trend is confirmed by Steven Lewis, one of the members of Chrétien's National Forum on Health, writing in *The Globe and Mail*: "a surefire recipe to drive up costs is to let the private sector provide and insure services outside the public system."

Second, the social and economic policies of the Liberal government are worsening the vital social determinants of health—income level and distribution, employment, education, housing. This increases the use and therefore the cost of health services. A 1994 study by three medical researchers at the University of Toronto found that unemployment produced adverse health effects from heart attacks to suicide, from increased hospital visits to more frequent drug use. They estimate that this preventable cause of illness cost the system an additional $1 billion a year.

A recent report by the Federal–Provincial Advisory Committee on Population Health concluded that the most important determinants of a person's health are income level and social status. Men in the top 20 percent of income earners can expect to live on average six years longer than men in the bottom fifth of income earners. Family support services, education, and working conditions are also crucial determinants of health. Years of falling family incomes; mass unemployment, particularly among youth; growing inequality and poverty, especially among single-parent families; weakening social supports—all have put pressure on health-care services. The sacrifice of social programs to the deficit shows that the Chrétien government is not prepared to recognize the interrelatedness of social well-being and the cost of health-care services. In suggesting to CBC's *Morningside* that Canadian spending on health be lowered to European levels, Chrétien did not offer to raise Canadian social spending (which at 18 percent of GDP is low for an industrialized country) to the European average of 23 percent of GDP. In fact, as the budget made clear, his government is moving full speed in the opposite direction.

The most galling contradiction in Chrétien's claim that he wants to control health costs pertains to drugs. In opposition, the Liberals voted against the drug-patent legislation in 1987 and again in 1991. Yet one of his first acts on assuming power in 1993 was to pass NAFTA. Had Chrétien not done this he could have amended or repealed the patent-protection law to restore compulsory licensing, and thereby brought down drug prices. This law is, however, entrenched in NAFTA, which Chrétien has no intention of repealing.

One of the most visible flashpoints in the battle over universal public health care is the Gimbel eye clinic in Alberta. This private clinic receives public funding for providing the "medically necessary service" of cataract surgery. The Alberta medicare plan pays the $600 surgeon's fee; in addition, the clinic charges the patient $700, which it calls a "facility fee." In effect, the public system subsidizes this private clinic. (If the full $1,300 were paid by the patient, this issue would not be so controversial.) The private clinic conducts this lucrative business without having to provide emergency or intensive care units. If need be, it can transfer the patient to the hospital. Thus, the private clinic is not only subsidized directly by the public system, which pays for half the cost of the operation, but it is also subsidized indirectly by having free access to the publicly supported infrastructure to which it does not contribute.

Ralph Klein and Preston Manning think such a subsidy is perfectly fine, and Alberta medicare continues to go along with what amounts to extra billing by the Gimbel clinic: after all, private for-profit medicine is a good thing and should be expanded. Hospitals have a waiting list for cataract operations. If some people want to jump the queue and are able to pay for the privilege, why not let them? It shortens the waiting lists in the public system and thereby improves access for all—everybody is better off.

This argument sounds attractive. Why shouldn't those who are able to pay more do so? (There is no suggestion, however, that those who can afford to should be paying more taxes to be used in the public health-care system.) Yet the Alberta government's support for this type of clinic violates the Canada Health Act; specifically, it violates the principle of universal access because it sanctions access to an essential service based on ability to pay rather than on need. It also undermines the public system. Assume, for example, the wait for this necessary but not urgent surgery is twelve weeks at the hospital and two weeks at the clinic. Money buys a place at the front of the line. At first, those on the hospital waiting list might have their wait reduced to ten weeks; however, the doctor more than likely performs the operation both at the hospital and at the clinic—after all, there is a finite number of eye surgeons. Finding it faster and more profitable at the private clinic, the doctor chooses to spend more and more time there. As a result, the waiting time at the hospital goes up and the public system is weakened.

The federal Minister of Health agrees that Klein's sanctioning of these clinics violates the Canada Health Act and has threatened to withdraw federal payments. However, this clinic has been in operation for several years and to date the minister has done little more than threaten. More disturbing is that she says the government is taking a hands-off approach with the new, leaner block transfer—the CHST. The ambiguous message is reinforced by the finance minister. Martin assures the province that the new block transfer "will give the provinces an overall choice as to where they wish to spend their dollars that we transfer to them." The Liberal government waffles because a decade of budget cuts to federal health transfers, plus those in the Martin budget, have reduced its authority to influence what the provinces can and cannot do.

Klein and Manning have conned their followers—many of whom will be among the hardest hit—into believing that greater involvement by the private sector not only won't hurt the public system but will strengthen it. They start from the simple but false premise, accepted as an article of faith, that because of the size of the government debt we can no longer afford our current universal public health care. Why not let the more efficient private sector provide "non-core" services to those who can afford the privilege of immediate attention, thereby relieving the pressure on the public system. (Klein's deliberate squeezing of the public system has fuelled the outcry for more private-sector involvement.) What are these "non-core" services? Manning would chop the current list of medically necessary services by half. Klein says that there are at least 100 services (although he does not specify which ones) that should be de-insured and provided by the private sector on a user-pays basis. He wants to sell the hospitals that he is closing down to private operators, who would then use them to offer de-insured services on a for-profit basis to those who will pay.

Klein and Manning couch their argument in innocuous language: "two-tier," "affordability," "targeting the neediest," and so on. As Klein says, "This will basically free up the system to address the people who truly need medicare." This has a plausible ring to the uninformed, especially when it includes the promise of lower taxes. But the hard reality is that targeted programs are poor programs and, lacking the support of the population at large, are vulnerable to continuing impoverishment.

Privatization is escalating overall health costs. Klein and Manning propose to lower the average citizen's taxes; but they will take away a much larger amount from that same citizen in direct payments for for-profit health care. These payments will go into the pockets of their corporate friends. Those who cannot afford private insurance or out-of-pocket payment will simply go without the service. Employers will pass on higher insurance costs to the consumer in the form of higher prices, and to the worker in the form of lower wages.

Business interests are drooling at the lucrative opportunities that will come from privatizing medicare. Far from taking pressure off the public system, it will drain scarce resources from that system, which will deteriorate under ongoing starvation. The affluent, who will have high-quality care through self- or employer-provided private insurance, will lose interest in supporting a public system that they have no stake in. Their politically powerful voices will press for further public cutbacks, further underfunding the public system. More people will have decreasing access to a widening range of health services. We need only look at the disastrous U.S. system to see what is in store for us.

Although the most visible threat to health care comes from the free-market zealots, a more dangerous threat is coming from the steady erosion of "medically necessary" services. It is easy to determine that heart surgery is necessary, while a facelift is not; however, the battle is being fought in the huge area in between. In fact, entire areas of medically necessary services have never been covered comprehensively—for example, prescription drugs and dental care. The debate on what is medically necessary in the current climate has become a debate about what services should be cut. We have seen that the Klein/Manning forces want a drastic redefinition. In the past few years provinces have de-insured services such as physiotherapy, eye exams, dental coverage for children, drugs covered by pharmacare plans, and so on. In short, people are no longer fully covered for medically necessary services.

Once these services are deemed no longer necessary and are de-insured, they are ripe for private provision financed by private insurance. At that point, NAFTA requires that the giant American health corporations have the same market access as their Canadian imitators. Moreover, as we describe in Chapter Three, once such access is given, NAFTA makes it impossible to rescind it and return the service to the public sector.

There are many instances of the erosion of free comprehensive medical coverage. Consider the following example of an Ontario patient who is treated in the hospital for a swollen knee: The patient is charged $11 for an injection of cortisone drug, $20 for the elastic bandage that could be purchased at any pharmacy for $6, $30 for medication and, after a wait too lengthy for the treatment to be effective, physiotherapy for which the patient is billed extra. (Physiotherapy purchased privately can be obtained immediately at a still higher fee.) This type of erosion is bound to increase amidst mounting calls for deficit reduction.

The Liberal government, like its predecessor, will protest loudly at the suggestion that it is complicit in the privatization and Americanization of our health-care system. For, while a bank president or a *Globe and Mail* columnist can openly advocate such a course, it would be political suicide for any national political leader. (Even Preston Manning has to reassure his followers that his proposals will not lead to U.S.-style health care.)

Canadians overwhelmingly define who they are—and how they differ from Americans—by their health-care system. Even those who do not fully understand the significance of its five principles know that everyone is covered; that the system is funded largely by taxes; that the vast majority of medical costs are covered; that they can go anywhere in Canada and (with some exceptions) get more or less the same quality of care; and that the quality of service is the same for everyone. They know that health care is not a market commodity dependent on one's ability to pay. It is a right of citizenship.

The Liberal government's actions contradict its soothing words about protecting the basic principles of medicare. Indeed, its actions are facilitating the entry of U.S.-style health care. Needless to say, powerful Canadian corporate interests with close connections to the Liberals have a stake in moving our health-care system in this direction.

Look at the U.S. system and how it is encroaching on Canada. American health care is the most expensive in the world, costing $1 trillion, or 14 percent of GDP. (Rising costs are expected to push it to $1.7 trillion, close to 20% of GDP by the year 2000.) Health care is big business and creates big profits. Hospital company profits are double the average rate of *Fortune 500* companies; drug company profits are five times that average. The hand-wringing about out-of-control health costs overlooks a fundamental contradiction of the American system: the goal of business is to get a larger share of a growing market; a growing market means more revenue; and more revenue for business means higher costs for the users of the system. Business, therefore, has no interest in getting health costs "under control."

American health care is also the least comprehensive. Forty million people have neither sufficient income nor insurance for the luxury of getting sick. Another 40 million Americans are inadequately insured. It is funded 56 percent through private insurance, but a big chunk—44 percent—comes from public dollars. Medicaid, which is supposed to cover all poor people, covers only half the poor population.

The corporate ethos permeates the U.S. industry. As the CEO of a large hospital chain says, "The health care industry is no different than the airline industry or the ball-bearing industry." Wall Street analysts refer to patients as "revenue bodies" and insurance companies owned by for-profit hospitals as "patient-feeder systems." The CEO of a U.S.-owned private medical lab company trying to pry its way into Canada complains that Canadians have an outdated and dysfunctional "not-for-profit mentality." "In order to provide services there has to be a proper return...health care is no different than anything else."

The U.S. has three kinds of hospitals: for-profit, private non-profit, and public. A study of Georgia hospitals found that for-profit hospitals charge an average 10 percent more than non-profits and 20 percent more than public hospitals. They handle hardly any medicaid patients. They turn away such patients or transfer them to underfunded, understaffed, and overcrowded public hospitals. Although it is illegal for any hospital receiving medicaid funds to refuse to treat medicaid patients, many hospitals get around this by discouraging low-income and/or medicaid patients by closing their emergency rooms, which is the way most medicaid patients seek medical attention.

A wave of concentration and integration in the U.S. health-care industry has been under way for the past few years. One trend is for corporations to own the entire range of health-care facilities. The largest for-profit integrated health-care chain is Columbia/HCA Health Care Corporation, with assets of $15 billion. It owns 195 hospitals (half of the country's total for-profit hospital capacity) and 125 outpatient facilities, including centres that specialize in outpatient surgery, home-care agencies, nursing homes, and pharmacies. Columbia is expanding rapidly and has its eye on non-profit and public hospitals, to turn them into for-profit facilities, or simply to shut them down. These integrated for-profit health-care chains are expected to grow rapidly.

The $100 billion-a-year insurance industry is concentrating into a handful of giants: Metropolitan Life, Blue Cross/Blue Shield, Liberty Mutual, Mutual of Omaha. Similar trends are occurring in the newest and fastest-growing segment of the business, the health maintenance organization. Owned predominantly by insurance companies, HMOs are organizations that provide or purchase for employer groups a complete package of doctors, hospitals, drugs, and other health services. Industry analysts predict that by 2000 close to half of all privately insured Americans will belong to one of a handful of mega-HMOs.

The global drug giants are also on a massive buying spree to secure their share of the booming health-care industry. They are taking over companies that manage drug-benefits programs for HMOs and other large employers, ensuring a ready market for their products. Eli Lilly, Smith Kline Beecham, and Merck have each bought out drug management companies for a total of

$12.3 billion. Three other companies—Pfizer, Rhone-Poulenc, and Bristol Myers—have together bought out another.

What does all this mean for the Canadian health-care system? We have seen how the drug industry, in securing extended monopoly protection for its products, has been and will continue to be a major factor in financially destabilizing the Canadian health-care system. Now that they have sent Canadian drug prices skyward, the drug multinationals want to bring to Canada their newly acquired drug-management companies, in effect their hostage formularies, to offer cash-strapped hospitals and provincial drug plans packaged deals at (initially) discounted prices. The Canadian Pharmacy Association is worried that if this system is allowed to take root in Canada "it could adversely affect competition (and prices), and may represent a serious threat to the Canadian generic drug industry."

Another Trojan horse of U.S. corporate medicine is the insurance industry. A good illustration of how it is moving in is the giant Liberty Mutual Insurance Group of Boston. In 1994, Liberty Mutual set up, through its Canadian subsidiary, a for-profit acute-care network of clinics for rehabilitation patients in Toronto called International Managed Health Care (IMHC). The company appointed Dennis Timbrell, president of the Ontario Hospital Association and former Ontario Tory health minister, to chair its board. He was also appointed to the boards of Liberty's Canadian subsidiary and the U.S. parent. Eight months later Liberty Mutual bought Ontario Blue Cross, the private non-profit supplementary health insurance provider owned by the province's hospitals through the Ontario Hospital Association. OHA was selling Blue Cross, which insures 2 million Ontario customers, and an extensive network of claimants—200 hospitals, 2,500 pharmacies, and 2,500 dentists—for between $80 and $100 million. (Timbrell said he quit Liberty's board as well as IMHC as soon as he heard in September that it was going to make a play for Blue Cross.)

Liberty Canada sees great potential for its new acquisition, with the $3.5 billion Ontario market for private insurance expected to double in the next five years, as the province, under fiscal pressure, de-insures services. It will also provide the company with a base for expanding across Canada, as other provinces do the same. The Rae government, despite pressure from the Ontario Federation of Labour and a coalition of health-advocacy groups, pleaded unconvincingly that it was powerless to stop the sale.

Liberty is the largest insurer in the American workers' compensation market, a field that is privatized in many U.S. states. In Canada, all workers' compensation programs are owned and operated by the provinces. Just before it bid on Blue Cross, Liberty hired two consultants—one a former policy advisor to Premier Rae—to conduct a study on options for reforming workers' compensation. The president of Liberty Canada wrote to the prime minister and the premiers informing them of the study. Its stated purpose is "to search out a new model for workers' compensation in Canada that is suitable for the vastly changing health care and workplace environments in the years leading up to and through the historic millennium." The outline proposed a model that links compensation and rehabilitation of injured persons (which happens to be what International Managed Health Care does). Claiming that the present system is not working properly, that it is swamped by debt, the study outline admits to the company's long-term commercial interest in a reformed system (it prefers a public/private mix for obvious reasons), but claims that it is doing the study as a contribution to the public good. Clearly, Liberty is positioning itself on the inside track of likely privatization of provincial workers' compensation programs. With Blue Cross and IMHC, it now has the insurance and rehabilitation capacity it needs to get hold of this oyster.

Another vehicle for the entry of corporate health care is through large management consulting firms such as Peat Marwick, Ernst & Young, Booz Allen & Hamilton, and Arthur Andersen. There are also a number of American management companies that specialize in the health-care industry. One of these, American Practices Management (APM), has been peddling its hospital cost-cutting model in Canada. In the

Alice-in-Wonderland discourse of the business, its model is called "patient focused care" (PFC). Based on its experience with more than a hundred hospitals in the United States, PFC cuts operating costs by 5 to 10 percent, operating space by 15 to 20 percent, and the number of employees by 10 percent, although the cuts to the registered nursing staff can go as high as 27 percent. The biggest saving, however, comes from the use of "multi-skilled health practitioners," a euphemism for less-skilled lower-paid workers doing work formerly done by registered nurses and other skilled practitioners. Examples include: replacing nurses with "patient care assistants" with eleven days' training; teaming as many as four assistants with one qualified nurse; and having housekeepers undertake patient care. Estimates of labour-cost saving from this practice are as high as 50 percent.

Although the company claims that post-restructuring surveys show high levels of employee and patient satisfaction, a survey of a PFC-redesigned facility in Chilliwack, B.C., by the Hospital Employees' Union found that 75 percent of employees said that the system compromised patient safety, 89 percent reported greater stress, and only 20 percent said that their work had become more interesting. A *New England Journal of Medicine* study suggests that hospitals with low qualified nurse to patient ratios have higher mortality rates.

In 1993, American Practices Management director Connie Curran, nicknamed "the bounty hunter" by Manitoba nurses, signed a $3.9-million contract with the Manitoba government to redesign the St. Boniface General Hospital and Winnipeg Health Sciences Centre, promising to save them $45 to $60 million through PFC restructuring. The University of Alberta Hospital has hired Curran to implement a patient-focused care program. Her new colleague in the Toronto office of APM Inc., Michael Decter, deputy minister of health in the Rae government, is involved in the reorganization of the Metro Toronto hospitals.

Our final example of the encroachment of U.S. health-care practices is the importation of the U.S. health management organization, or HMO, model. It is still in the pilot-program stage in Ontario, but other provinces are watching closely. Called Comprehensive Health Organization (CHO), it provides and purchases services for its members on a non-profit, publicly funded basis, with the goal of providing consumer-driven, community-based health care. (Ironically, this is the way the American HMOs started off in the early 1970s, before funding cutbacks forced the shift to for-profit HMOs.) Although it is not allowed to discriminate between members and non-members when it comes to insurable services, it can discriminate when it comes to providing uninsurable services. This creates potential to cut costs by discriminating in favour of healthier segments of the population.

The Comprehensive Health Organization has been designed as a form of publicly financed, managed competition. It is based, according to an Ontario health ministry official, on market principles: "If it has to purchase services, the CHO will shop around between hospitals to get the best bang for its buck." Similarly, individuals will be expected to shop around for the best CHO. Such concepts undermine the principle of universal, accessible, comprehensive health care. In a climate of funding cuts and privatization of services, it is not difficult to envisage a shift to for-profit CHOs. The Ontario health ministry is currently looking at an application from Magna International to set up a CHO for its employees; the Harris government will likely encourage such ventures. This would open the door to participation by U.S. companies, who could not be discriminated against under NAFTA. It is not a huge leap to the entry of the HMO mega-corporations from south of the border.

In April 1995, Jean Chrétien told a meeting of American newspaper editors in Dallas: "We have run an administration that has been straight with Canadians.... We have worked hard to restore integrity to the political process. We have governed...with an emphasis on competence, fairness and honesty." If Canadians were as cynical as most newspaper editors, Chrétien would have found it more difficult to mislead Canadians on this most fundamental of benchmarks by which we define ourselves as a society. His government's pious statements about preserving medicare are repeatedly contradicted by its actions, which are quietly and systematically breaking it down. Where is the point of no return? At what point are the principles of comprehensiveness and universal accessibility and public administration irretrievably violated? If our public health-care system goes, it will likely disappear in small, little-noticed steps. Then, one day we will realize that it has vanished, and that all that is left is the memory of the society we once were.

9

GRIM PRESENT, GRIM FUTURE

"The individuals living in the world created from Reagan through Harris don't make ethical or political choices. Life comes down to acquiring money and going shopping with the proceeds."

Rick Salutin

In a beautiful, state-of-the-art, high-tech school in Cole Harbour, Nova Scotia, a conference is under way on school–corporate partnerships, the newest innovation in cash-strapped public education. The audience is made up of equal numbers of teachers, students (all wearing T-shirts emblazoned with the partnership logo "NovaKnowledge"), and provincial and community business leaders. The purpose is to advance the growing ties between corporate Canada and the nation's schools.

The kids are getting a lesson. Politicians praise the business sponsors and explain that all future schools in the province will be built with private money. They pay tribute to this flagship partnership school co-sponsored by IBM (which received exclusive rights to supply the school with computers) and Maritime Telephone & Telegraph, whose CEO opens the day. The school principal (who is introduced as the school's CEO) touts the student "products" being turned out and takes the opportunity to boost his school's advanced technological capabilities.

Business leaders tell the students that there are no more jobs, only opportunities; it is up to them to be entrepreneurial and create work. They tell the teachers that their reservations about corporations in the classroom are proof that they are a serious impediment to change and the potential of the new economy. Teachers must prepare young people for an economy and a society that are now one. The manager of Pratt & Whitney says that his job is to make money for his international shareholders, period. "I don't care whether unemployment in Nova Scotia goes up or down. All I care about is supplying my company with the right kind of workers and if I can't find them here, I'll go elsewhere."

The students are frightened. They are told that high-tech education is the key to their future, but they can see that there are few jobs out there, high-tech or otherwise. Several say they are trying to act and look young to prolong childhood as long as possible; others fear they will never be able to retire. Student visitors express dismay at the money that has been poured into this facility while their own schools are allowed to run down. Why was this conference not held in my school where "you would have splinters in your backsides from the chairs," one asks, noting that perhaps the growing differences between schools reflects the future. The students do share a smile, however, when the brand-new computer system breaks down and a video on student–business co-op programs must be shown on an old movie screen.

The students and teachers of Cole Harbour are caught in an ideologically driven experiment that is changing the political culture of Canada. Federal and provincial governments are being "reinvented" or "restructured" to divest them of social and environmental responsibilities while granting them new powers to impose a market economy on their citizens. Following a world-wide trend (in 1994, $60 billion worth of state-owned firms were privatized around the world) they are transferring power from the public to the private sector.

The premise of the reinvention of government is that competition between the public and private sectors is good, but in almost all cases the private sector can do better. Government, therefore, should get out of many areas of service, from regulation of the economy and resources to delivering social programs. The attack on the public sector is multi-pronged. Some critics play on the unemployed and contingency workers' jealousies and resentment of those with "security," and disparage public servants as unproductive, lazy, self-serving fat cats with jobs for life. They neglect to point out that most public servants have had their wages frozen for at least five years and are working with resources too diminished to maintain former levels of service after a decade of deep cuts. The critics take advantage of the fact that public services and social programs have been gutted by successive governments to "prove" they are incapable of meeting their original goal.

Others, from ideology or self-interest, use the current economic crisis as a powerful weapon to undermine public services. "Our extravagant ways have caught up with us.... The chickens have come home to roost.... We have to pay the piper.... We have to learn to live within our means.... We can no longer depend on government." These clichés are groundless, but they have a superficially plausible ring, especially when repeated over and over, and rarely challenged.

The unassailable facts documented in Finance Department studies are that during the last twenty years the ratio of public program spending to GDP has remained relatively constant and the real growth in government expenditures has come not from program spending but from interest payments on the debt. Falling revenues due to tax breaks to corporations and the wealthy have contributed to the growth of debt and deficit since 1975; and our social programs look good only when compared to those in the U.S. In fact, Canada now stands near the bottom of the OECD in terms of social spending.

The myths, as repeated continually in the mainstream media, are part of a campaign to reduce Canadians' expectations for their own well-being and that of their families, at work and in retirement. No one has a right to expect a job with security. Families must take responsibility for their members and stop being dependent on government. Children are the sole responsibility of their parents; so, too, is poverty. People at the bottom of the social hierarchy, those on social assistance, have to free themselves from their "addiction" to financial dependency. In spite of the continuous high rate of unemployment, they are held accountable for their own inability to find work.

Restructuring is based on the ideology that government is, by definition, the problem. Public services are merely products, which the private sector could deliver better. Citizens are consumers who should have the "choice" to buy the best health and education "products" they can afford. Families, not governments or communities, are the defining unit of society. (According to Margaret Thatcher, there is no such thing as society in the collective sense, only "individuals and their families.") When we stop assuming we are part of a caring community, our natural entrepreneurial skills will kick in and we'll help the nation become competitive in the new world economy. (President Clinton told Americans in his spring 1995 state-of-the-union address that he is going to "empower" them to become responsible for themselves. In other words, right-wing Republicans have taken over Congress, and he cannot stop them from bashing the poor.)

The reinvention of government is creating a vicious circle. Most wealthy Canadians have long been willing to support government withdrawal from universal publicly funded social programs in return for tax breaks; but it is only recently that many middle-class Canadians have jumped on the bandwagon. The trick is to allow the public service to become so underfunded and run-down that it no longer serves its constituency. The public will then lose faith in the program as they no longer realize a personal benefit from it, and will become willing to withdraw their support. Some parents, frightened for their children, want the

choice to opt out of the public system and buy their kids an educational edge in the market. Baby-boomers, terrified that they
will have no pensions, are buying private plans. Private health-
care plans are booming. The privatization of social security is
well under way.

There is a great deal of profit to be made when governments
running social programs, prisons, transportation systems, police
services, broadcasting, and a whole host of community programs
cede this terrain to corporations. While most Canadians are hard
pressed to identify with the so-called economic recovery, the sector leading the charge against government spending and the
deficit is claiming record profits. A *Globe and Mail Report on
Business* survey showed that the aggregate after-tax profit of the
122 largest corporations in Canada grew by 140 percent in
1994; a *Wall Street Journal* study put 1994 fourth-quarter
earnings of 114 Canadian corporations up 360 percent over the
1993 fourth-quarter earnings — earnings that *The Globe and
Mail* referred to as "torrid...blistering...spectacular...
glorious...and stunning." Corporate profits continued to grow
in 1995.

The companion myth to the lie that public services are failing
is that the private sector delivers a better product. In a paper for
the Canadian Centre for Policy Alternatives, Murray Dobbin
reported that if government had been run like many corporations, it would be out of business. He points out that, for all the
hysteria about government deficits, corporations are much
deeper in debt. The combined debts of about $1,600 billion
owed by corporations, households, and financial institutions is
nearly triple that owed by all levels of government. A growing
proportion of this debt is incurred for unproductive and specula-
tive activity, and taxpayers are often left to bail out the bankrupt
corporations who leave their employees stranded. Moreover,
North American CEOs make obscene salaries in comparison
both to cabinet members and to CEOs of many other countries,
even when they lose money for their companies.

Meanwhile, Canada is developing an entrenched underclass.

In its most recent study of poverty in Canada, the National Council of Welfare sounded the alarm: in 1993, as the economy emerged from the recession and showed a respectable level of export and job growth, Canada's overall poverty rate climbed sharply; the number of poor Canadians grew by almost half a million, mostly children. One in five Canadian children now live in poverty, 51 percent more than in 1989. And more than 90 percent of single mothers under twenty-five are now poor. Although the numbers of seniors living in poverty had fallen steadily in the last two decades, this trend has reversed in the last two years.

The income gap between Canadians is growing. The United Nations still ranks Canada the best country in the world in its human-development index. It measures this using three factors: average income, average longevity, and average education. But on the score that measures income distribution and equality of lifestyle, we fell seven places in the last study. Statistics Canada reports that the gap between high- and low-wage earners increased steadily throughout the 1980s, as contingency work — part-time, low-wage, with few benefits and no security — grew. Analyst Henry Pold found that from 1975 to 1993, part-time jobs grew at more than five times the rate of full-time jobs. The wealthiest 10 percent of Canadian families now hold as much of the income pie as the bottom 60 percent. Even education cannot save all those who have it. The Canadian Council on Social Development says that the number of poor families in Canada in which salary earners have a post-secondary education has doubled in the last decade.

National social programs and other institutions were established to address these very disparities. The Liberal government, however, is transferring so many powers and responsibilities to lower levels of government that the Charlottetown Accord looks like a centralist document. Paul Martin's goal is clear: wherever federal government services can be privatized, they should be; whatever is left over should be given to the provinces or municipalities.

The Tories boasted about decentralization, held a losing referendum on it, and warned Canadians that they were ideologically committed to it. The Liberals, the embodiment of the "one-Canada" ideal, instead of proclaiming aloud their intentions and actions, are decentralizing the country by stealth, behind closed doors. This is a key element of the market economy; governments can be held accountable to the people as long as they maintain responsibility for the social, transportation, cultural, and environmental infrastructure of the nation. However, when they download or privatize these jurisdictions, the public and advocacy groups lose their power to assert any control over them. In many cases, no institution exists to replace the regulating function of government, and the private sector can do as it pleases.

"Scrap Environment Canada," say frustrated environmentalists, fed up with the sham of what one calls the federal department's "revolting" record on national enforcement. (A Washington-based think tank recently declared that Canada has had the second-worst pollution record in the industrialized world during the last twenty-five years.) In the last fiscal year, the first to show these numbers under the Liberal government, Environment Canada caught 169 companies or government agencies breaking the Canada Environmental Protection Act (which is much weaker than its U.S. counterpart), but charged only 15. During the same period, Ontario, with a similar-size enforcement staff, charged 400 offenders and obtained convictions in 345 cases, resulting in fines of over $2.5 million.

Under the budget reduction plan, the department is losing 1,400 employees and $235 million; but there has been little outcry, since the department is already so inadequate in dealing with the patchwork of standards and enforcement measures across the country. Environmentalists did, however, mourn the loss of the annual report, *The State of Canada's Environment*, a comprehensive document that covered every aspect of the environment. It stood as a grim testament to our inactivity in protecting our wildlife, waterways, forests, soil, and air. Activists and scientists ruefully ask how we can claim to be a nation if we cannot even document what we are failing to protect.

As *The Ottawa Citizen* put it, "The federal [environment]

department has little influence on anything you eat, drink or breathe. And it doesn't enforce its own laws. Now it proposes reducing its role further, shifting more responsibilities to the provinces, private businesses and universities...on closer inspection, it looks like the building facade from a movie set."

Natural Resources will lose 9,000 employees, gutting essential resource protection services across the country. Its minister, Anne McLellan, has allowed resource companies to set up a "voluntary" system to meet environmental standards, in place of promised legislation. She has backed the oil and gas industries in fighting her own government's consideration of a carbon tax. She convinced cabinet as well to exempt Canadian oil and gas exports from legislated environmental assessments. Southam News calls her "a preacher for free trade and commerce," so totally is she an apologist for big business.

The Canadian Forest Service has had its budget cut from $220 million to $95 million. This will cause the closing of sixteen forestry centres and twenty federal regional forestry offices, including the oldest forestry research centre, the Petawawa National Forestry Institute, and the elimination of federal support for provincial reforestation programs. Meanwhile, the Regulatory Efficiency Act will allow federal ministers to make special deals with industry sectors or corporations, exempting them from regulations under any federal law, including those regarding the environment. The favoured few will be able to negotiate private contracts with the government, getting around laws that apply to everyone else.

At the Department of Fisheries and Oceans, cuts of up to 70 percent will endanger Canada's world-famous Freshwater Institute and the department's ability to monitor fresh-water pollution and warn us when fish stocks are threatened. Most of the department's 100 award-winning scientists will be laid off, affecting the central and Arctic regions, covering two-thirds of the country, as well as the Great Lakes. Now, contaminants that warp the reproductive system of humans and animals and cause breast and prostate cancer will not be regulated, unless the environment department picks up the project, which it appears unwilling to do. The Liberals are abandoning the responsibility to protect our entire fresh-water system.

Seventy percent of the federal Transport Department is being eliminated. The government is preparing to dissolve the St. Lawrence Seaway Authority and Canada Ports Corp., the agency overseeing federally owned ports, and to transfer responsibility to the provinces. Canadian National Railways and federal airports are being privatized; grain transportation subsidies are being eliminated, which will reroute grain movement to the U.S. rail and port system; freight rate subsidies to Atlantic Canada are gone; the Air Traffic Control System is to be privatized; federally funded firefighters are being removed from fifteen airports; the slack will have to be taken up by local services. Fifty-six weather offices across the country are being closed and the rest auto-mated, a plan the Canadian Airline Pilots Association calls "an accident waiting to happen." Transport Canada officials admit that the experiment to replace human weather observers with technology had "deficiencies," but went ahead in several cities including Edmonton, where in October 1994 a Canadian Airlines Boeing 737 with 120 people on board had to land in hazardous conditions because the information the pilot received was inaccurate.

Funding for federal research in agriculture, forestry, and energy conservation and the National Research Council is being slashed. Federal meat and poultry inspection is being turned over to the provinces. Every year fewer federal correctional officers are left to guard more federal prisoners, resulting in downloading of federal prisoners to provincial institutions.

Federal protections for Canadian culture are being removed: The Canada Council is laying off one-quarter of its staff; budgets to the National Library and the national museums have been slashed by more than 30 percent, forcing them to cut their hours, lay off staff, and charge user fees. The National Film Board, the CBC, Telefilm Canada, and the National Arts Centre are all under assault. The world-renowned Art Bank has been killed. As many as fifty Canadian book publishers, who are losing half their government funding, are likely to go out of business in the next two years. The government has caved in repeatedly to the American entertainment industry in disputes involving the Canadian textbook company Ginn, the U.S. media giant Viacom, and the CRTC protections of Canadian country music.

Canada is disengaging from its role in international aid: it is cutting almost $300 million of promised aid payments to four international development banks in Africa, the Caribbean, Asia, and Latin America; it has cancelled its annual $8-million grant to International Planned Parenthood. It has ended its funding of more than a hundred groups in Canada involved in educating Canadians about global development issues, and has imposed a 15 percent across-the-board cut to all CIDA programs. Trade now officially takes precedence over social, environmental, or human rights concerns in Canada's international relations.

Perhaps nothing symbolizes the change in priorities and values of both the nation and the Liberal Party more than Chrétien and the premiers acting as pimps for Canada's corporate élite as they sell their wares around the world. The prime minister led a blue-ribbon business delegation to China, where they dined with the leaders who had presided over the student massacre at Tiananmen Square. He refused to raise the issue of enforced prison labour or the notorious trade in body parts of executed political prisoners. He brought the CEOs, all smiles and flowered shirts, to Indonesia, where he refused to raise the issue of the genocide of the East Timorese. Bygones were bygones when another group went looking for business in the former military dictatorships of Chile and Argentina, who still have a dreadful record of documented human rights abuses. Says a senior Foreign Affairs official, "We used to go in with lists of political prisoners we wanted released. Now we go in with lists of companies that want contracts."

The Canadian Advisory Council on the Status of Women has been shut down, its national research function lost. The federal Family Violence Initiative, a multi-department project to counter violence against women, will not be renewed after 1996. Cuts to the Canadian Human Rights Commission mean that its six regional offices will no longer investigate complaints. The end of CAP funding leaves no protected funding for battered women's shelters and sexual assault centres. The federal promise to create 150,000 new child-care spaces has been shelved, and the responsibility has been turned over to the provinces and municipalities.

The Liberal government is disengaging from training and employment programs, the centrepiece of its election campaign. A leaked Human Resources Department memo suggests that at least two-thirds of the 454 Canada Employment Centres might be closed. Almost $2 billion has been taken from the Canadian Jobs Strategy and Strategic Initiatives, which will leave the provinces to pick up the slack. The projects hit are those directed toward the most disadvantaged: the illiterate, mentally ill, homeless, ex-cons, aboriginal people, immigrants, youth, visible minorities, disabled, and those on long-term social assistance—society's throwaways.

The Ontario government estimates that federal cuts between 1991 and 1995 have shortchanged more than 200,000 Ontarians eligible for training. The province's community colleges will suffer a direct loss of $20 million in federal monies, and fear that more than five hundred of their teachers will lose their jobs. Ottawa-Carleton, which will take the brunt of the federal public-service layoffs, is shutting down five local training centres serving 1,200 people, most on welfare, several serving visible minority women. Add the $130-million cuts to Ontario training, literacy, and counselling programs from the 1995 federal budget and Mike Harris's cancellation of JobsOntario and there will be very little retraining money left anywhere in a province suffering record high unemployment and potentially heading back into a recession.

The federal government's wholesale retreat from its historic role in these and many other areas, from mining and farm subsidies to tourism, coupled with its retreat from the delivery of social programs, signals a fundamental shift in federal–provincial relations and the redefinition of the nation-state.

On one hand, the Liberal government is abandoning the federal responsibility to maintain national social standards. As in the 1930s, relief for those in need will be under provincial or municipal jurisdiction. To ensure that no future federal government is tempted to reassert jurisdiction over social welfare, the Chrétien government is considering giving the provinces some federal sales (GST) tax points (in addition to continued transfer of personal tax points) in order to allow them to recover some revenues lost through program cuts. This would limit the ability of the federal government to ever re-enter the big-spending areas, such as social programs, and shelter it from debt in future recessions. The provinces would become responsible for the social well-being of their citizens and bear the brunt of the pain.

Decentralization pleases the corporate community, which wants the responsibility for social welfare to rest with the lower levels of government. André Bérard, CEO of the National Bank of Canada, notes that lower levels of government would not have Ottawa's ability to set monetary policy; as such, they would have far fewer spending choices: "It is only by decentralizing the state even more that we can obtain more efficient public services and a permanent reduction in deficits. We should give the power to spend to those who have little power to borrow."

It is true that equalization payments have remained stable, and represent a powerful ongoing role for the federal government; but how long are the wealthier provinces going to be prepared to sacrifice for the poorer, when they are getting nothing from confederation except the bill? What conditions will they impose on maintaining some assistance? Alberta, whose government prides itself on having swallowed the tough medicine of deep deficit cuts, is hardly going to look favourably on giving money to a province that continues to fund social welfare for its citizens. Equalization payments will blunt the impact of the budget cuts to programs for the next few years, but it would be foolish for the have-not provinces to think this will last.

Nor will one province want to support the welfare refugees from another with lower social-assistance standards. Between

March 31, 1993, and March 31, 1994, there was a 29 percent decrease in the numbers of people on social assistance in Alberta and a 6 percent decrease in New Brunswick—the two provinces with the toughest welfare provisions. During the same period, all other provinces experienced an increase in their case loads: 19 percent in Saskatchewan; 9 percent in B.C.; 7 percent in Ontario; 6 percent in Quebec. Without national standards, how long will it be before the more generous provinces refuse to pick up the human slack from the others? An interprovincial race-to-the-bottom is likely once the federal government is out of the national enforcement business. The poorest citizens everywhere will lose.

On the other hand, the Liberal government has launched a project that gives it sweeping controls over the provisions of interprovincial trade and economic policy in Canada. The Internal Trade Agreement (ITA), signed by the federal and provincial governments in June 1994, was negotiated largely by bureaucrats behind closed doors. It did not draw attention from most Canadians, which is a shame, for the ITA is the internal Canadian trade equivalent of NAFTA.

Ostensibly designed to break down interprovincial barriers to trade, the ITA deregulates provincial standards on the environment, health, and safety, and gives corporations the same rights in Canada that they now enjoy in the NAFTA bloc. The agreement challenges high provincial labour, consumer, and environmental protection standards as unfair barriers to trade, and gives corporations direct access to a new forum to frustrate and overturn public regulations. Serving as a corporate charter of rights and freedoms, the ITA limits public-sector activity and restricts the ability of governments and communities to influence corporate activity.

(The fact that all provincial governments—regardless of their political stripes—bought into this deal demonstrates how deeply the ideology of the free market and deregulation has permeated the thinking of the political class in Canada. It also helps explain why voters see so little difference between parties and how the Ontario electorate, for example, could be so fickle as to migrate from Bob Rae to Mike Harris in one election.)

The ITA-implementing legislation was introduced at the same time as the Canada Health and Social Transfer, and stands in stark contrast to it. While the CHST signals a withdrawal of the federal presence in providing for the social well-being of Canadians, the ITA-implementing legislation gives the federal government sweeping new powers to impose an economic market model on the provinces.

It also gives dangerous new powers to the federal cabinet. By granting cabinet the sole authority to impose penalties on provinces found to be in violation of the ITA, the Chrétien government is undermining the legislative and democratic authority of Parliament. Like the Regulatory Efficiencies Act, which allows individual ministers to make private regulatory deals with corporations, and the CHST, which gives cabinet the sole discretion to impose penalties upon provinces violating the Canada Health Act, the implementing legislation of the ITA puts too much power in the hands of cabinet.

In introducing the bill, Liberal MP Raymond Chan made it clear whom it serves: "The government has felt strong and repeated pressure from the private sector to deal with the problems associated with internal barriers to trade and conflicting regulations on cross-border flows of people and capital. We have received representations from the Canadian Manufacturers' Association, the Canadian Chamber of Commerce, the Business Council on National Issues, the Canadian Federation of Independent Business, the Canadian Bankers Association, the Canadian Construction Association, and so on."

He was also clear about its purpose: "Bill C-88 will provide a supportive environment for the economic transition process we are now experiencing.... To grow and prosper, business needs an efficient and open marketplace, an environment that encourages innovation and expansion...competitive advantage...free of unnecessary barriers to trade." The bill authorizes cabinet to "suspend rights or privileges granted by the Government of Canada to the province under the Agreement or any federal law...to modify or suspend the application of any federal law with respect to the province...to extend the application of any federal law to the province...and to take any other measure" it considers necessary to enforce internal free trade.

This empowers the federal government to impose corporate-friendly policies on "rogue" provinces and prevent them from supporting local business and the local workforce. The federal government will have the ability to obstruct a vast range of policy measures proposed by provincial governments. Environmental regulations, labour laws, local procurement provisions, and other policy initiatives could be targeted by Ottawa or a corporation, leading to a "policy chill" in the provinces.

Because social programs are exempt from the ITA, any retaliatory measures against a province could come only out of equalization payments. This means that the federal government could use equalization as a form of blackmail to force a uniform competitive economic model on the provinces at the very time that it is abandoning them in the social welfare field. This explains the apparent contradiction between the two pieces of legislation—one giving the government power, the other taking it away. The reinvention of government is often mistakenly thought to involve downsizing government. In fact, it creates a whole new role for imposing an economic and social model friendly to big business: where it is appropriate to diminish the power of the state, government retreats; where it is appropriate to use state power to impose harsh economic conditions, government advances.

Imagine the provinces several years down the road. Without the powers to implement economic programs that favour their own citizens, but with the sole responsibility for their social well-being on diminishing federal transfer payments, they will have no choice but to cut some programs and services, privatize others, and charge user fees for the rest. An examination of countries and American states that have already gone through this process allows us to project that provinces and municipalities will likely start with "non-essential" services such as libraries, museums, art galleries, recreation programs, zoos, parks, playgrounds and

swimming pools, roads and highways, cultural exchanges and fes-
tivals, public transportation, multicultural projects, cultural and
arts funding, wildlife and wetlands conservation, reforestation,
and garbage and waste clean-up projects.

Next will come the abandonment of the poor and the unemployed. Although most Canadians consider themselves to be
compassionate toward the least fortunate in society, when public
monies become tight and they have limited choices, most will
choose to preserve the programs that benefit them directly. It is
one thing to give generous social assistance to the poor when
there is lots of money to go around, but quite another in times
of high deficits and high taxes. Workfare, punitive conditions on
welfare such as restrictions based on age, lack of physical disability, and residency, and lower benefits to welfare recipients are all
in the cards. Empathy for teenage mothers and their children will
evaporate; unemployed youth will be singled out for punishment. Funding for non-profit housing will shrink. Street people
will be seen as more sinister than an unpleasant reminder of our
collective failure; they will be moved on from public places and
public view more often.

Public servants will be the next scapegoat: anyone with a
"secure" job, particularly paid for out of the public purse, will
attract resentment. ("Why should they have pensions and holidays when I don't?" Canadians will ask.) Their unions will be
singled out as a "special interest group," and governments will
bargain one-on-one with individual workers, creating a contingency workforce in the public sector, cutting full-time work, con-
tracting out services, cutting pensions. The services they deliver
will be severely cut back, causing citizens to be increasingly critical of their quality, and further alienating workers in the public
sector from the general population. ("What are we paying our
taxes for?" citizens will ask.)

Next will come essential services, a showdown between education and health. In the short term, health will win. Although
Canadians are deeply committed to both, fewer than one-third
now have children in school and, as the population ages, that

number will drop. Thus, not all Canadians see a direct benefit from public schools. But all Canadians use public health. If Canadians have to choose between a service that is benefiting them directly and one that they perceive is not (although educating all children is critical to the future of us all), they will choose health. Schools, already targeted by the deficit cutters, will become a prime target for provincial budget cuts. As they are starved for books and computers and art classes and decent buildings, parents will demand charter or private schools and will want to take the tax dollars they pay for public education and use it instead for their own children's schooling.

In the end, health care won't escape either. Governments will make a big deal of the distinction between essential and non-essential services. As the dollars shrink, essential services will become fewer. Private clinics will spring up to fill the vacuum. In public hospitals, front-line health-care workers will have their wages frozen, be hired without security or benefits, or be replaced by non-qualified workfare personnel. Canadians will take out more private insurance to protect them from the costs of the growing number of non-essential services. ("Why are we paying taxes to the public system when it no longer serves our needs and the waiting lists are so long?" they will ask.)

Angry citizens will blame their politicians and start to demand recall of MPs, balanced budget amendments, and lower taxes. More and more of their income will go to private social insurance and user fees, and they will resent anyone appearing to get a free ride; prime among these will be immigrants. Hostility to "big government" will grow, as citizens sense a loss of control over their futures. ("If government can't do anything for me any more, let me be free from the pretence," they will say. "Give me back my tax dollars and I will buy my own services.") Private charities will be called on to fill the gap left by the withdrawal of government support. Advocacy groups for the poor, farmers, seniors, the unemployed, aboriginal peoples, immigrants, children, and sectoral associations and unions, particularly in education and health, will eye one another like animals competing at an inadequate drinking hole. Class divisions among us will grow.

These scenarios are not fiction; they are not speculation. They are documented fact, in Canada and in other parts of the world. Take for example, California.

Two decades ago, California was the American dream; today it is a living laboratory of what can happen to a community when its members lose their commitment to one another and to common goals. With the 1978 Proposition 13, California voters approved a whopping 60 percent cut in their property tax and virtually prohibited their municipal governments from raising taxes. Now, to raise taxes, the government must go to the people on a case-by-case basis for referendum approval—some require a full majority, others, a two-thirds majority. Since it is next to impossible to get such agreement on anything, California's political system has become totally paralysed. Cities and towns starved of funds have had to be bailed out by the state government, plunging it billions of dollars into debt.

Journalist Peter Schrag describes what the lack of public revenues has done to the state. Children's protective services have been gutted; public health hospitals and mental health facilities have been closed; libraries are closed or kept open only on certain days with volunteer labour. As thousands of professors are fired from the University of California and California State University, student tuition fees have skyrocketed—from $800 a year a decade ago to $4,000 now; to enrol for classes, students have to line up all night. Roads and freeways are left unrepaired—California is dead last in state spending on per capita highway repair. While per capita tax revenues have been effectively frozen, client rolls for state services—schools, prisons, Medicaid, and welfare—have increased faster than the population, leaving huge structural gaps and government deficits, as the state has had no option but interim borrowing.

Orange County has declared bankruptcy and the state has had to resort to IOUs instead of cash to pay its public servants. The county is unable to pay its $1.1-billion loans debt; it must sell its libraries, court buildings, drug-treatment centres, and perhaps even its prized airport to stave off default. In a referendum in June 1995, however, its residents voted against a sales tax increase that would have cost its average (wealthy) taxpayer $50 a year. Los Angeles County must eliminate 18,000 public service jobs, and sell its huge USC Medical Centre, libraries, parks, and health clinics. Jails are freeing inmates early to clear space.

California was among the top ten states in per-pupil spending for schools in 1969. It is now fortieth. Its schools are among the most crowded in the country; many operate without libraries, counsellors, nurses, art, music, physical education or computers. In a typical San Juan high school, "students pass through hallways that seem like subterranean tunnels, dark and damp...the old heating pipes running beneath the room generate steam that buckles the floor and gives the room a constant hothouse atmosphere. The windows are steaming and the textbooks are warping." California school libraries carry books predicting that "one day man will walk on the moon."

The state is dividing between those who can pay for private services and those who can't. Says Schrag, "As tax-supported services (except for prisons) decline, for lack of either political support or a dedicated revenue source, the sense of civility that comes with them declines as well." A decade ago, the state spent three times as much on higher education as it did on prisons (13 percent to 4 percent); today, prisons are winning (9 percent to 8 percent). The growing anger that caused California voters to cut education and health services to landed immigrants in the last state election is a reflection of the gap between those who vote—only 27 percent in a recent primary—and those who need the services. (Increasingly, as all over the United States, Californians consider democracy to be irrelevant to their lives, and have stopped voting.) The gaps widen, old against young, white against minority, rich against poor, tax payer against "tax user."

The terrible irony for Californians is that the very reason for the tax revolt—to enable ordinary citizens to take on government and win—has totally backfired. Proposition 13 was sponsored by millionaire Howard Jarvis and the state's real-estate industry, which was the chief beneficiary of the cuts to property tax. Two-thirds of the savings went to corporations, landlords, and commercial interests. Meanwhile, arts and community groups and children's advocates have to beg for money in individual referenda, the vast majority of which fail. Government has become almost incomprehensible to both citizens and legislators.

Ralph Klein's Alberta is hard on California's heels. Klein's radical restructuring of government proves that Liberals and others who swear that the provinces will pick up services repudiated by the federal government, and won't allow standards to fall below a certain minimum, are dead wrong. In fact, just the opposite is the case. Freed from the constraints of national regulations, provinces like Alberta are engaging in a deadly game of competitive poverty with their citizens.

Since coming to office in 1993 with the backing of only 27 percent of eligible Alberta voters, Klein and his Conservative government have gutted public spending so deeply, and privatized government services so fast, that the Fraser Institute recently gave them an award as the jurisdiction with the lowest levels of taxation and government spending among all Canadian provinces and forty-three American states. The cuts are stunning: 12.4 percent to education; 18 percent to health care; 16 percent to advanced education; 18.3 percent to family and social services; 30 percent to environmental protection; 48 percent to municipal services, including police and firefighting. Almost $1 billion a year is being cut from government spending, all departments have been told to cut 20 percent from their operating budgets, and 6,000 public servants, who had already accepted a 5 percent wage roll-back, have been laid off. As many layoffs are still to come.

It is essential to assess these cuts in conjunction with those announced by the federal government. For instance, while the federal Liberals gutted the departments of the Environment and Natural Resources, the Alberta Tories have slashed the province's environment budget by one-third, and eliminated the

Environment Council of Alberta, the Provincial Roundtable on the Environment and the Economy, the Water Resources Commission, and the Alberta Environmental Trust Fund. The two levels of government have abandoned the obligation to regulate corporate environmental abuse. The Klein government supports the position of industry that it should be self-regulating; the environment minister has declared that he is setting up alternative private-sector "regulatory organizations...to take over former environment department duties." (This is a perfect illustration of how provinces who don't want to maintain standards once the federal government has withdrawn its authority are free to drop them altogether.)

Similarly, cuts to federal transfer payments for social programs in Alberta of $1 billion over the next two years must be factored in to the pain being suffered by citizens. Even if the Klein government were to end provincial cuts—a very unlikely scenario—it would still have to cut program spending to accommodate lost federal revenues. The most vulnerable members of Alberta society—seniors, the unemployed, the poor, and children—will continue to be hardest hit.

Alberta's seniors' incomes have declined by 12 percent in just two years. Those in subsidized housing face rent increases of 25 percent to 30 percent of their incomes. Those with an annual income of over $10,400 have had their benefits reduced; those with incomes over $18,000 have lost all their benefits, including property tax credits, health premiums coverage, and dental, drug, and eye-care subsidies, adding more than $1,500 to the financial burden of older people living on the margins of poverty.

Klein has scapegoated the poor and the unemployed. Welfare rolls have been chopped by 40 percent, cutting off more than 45,000 welfare recipients, many of them single mothers. The Department of Social Services has been ordered to cut its case load by 3,000 a year regardless of need. Welfare rates have been slashed by 20 percent, making them the lowest in the country. A single person deemed employable now receives assistance equal to 36 percent of poverty-line income. Poverty in Alberta has jumped: in 1982, the province had the lowest rate of poverty in the country; a decade later, it had the highest. It dropped slightly in 1993 (the latest statistics available) because so many poor had left the province. British Columbia estimates at least 20,000 Albertans have fled there, many using a one-way ticket supplied by the Alberta government. Those who stay are forced to turn to non-profit agencies, themselves trying to survive deep funding cuts, and food banks trying to cope with increased demands as high as 50 percent.

The Klein government has defied the rules set up under CAP to protect the poor and ensure national rights. Mothers must find work when their babies turn six months rather than two years, or be cut off assistance. The thirty-day warning for welfare cut-off has been scrapped. Teenagers under the age of eighteen, with or without parents or a home, are no longer eligible for assistance; the government is talking about extending ineligibility to those under thirty. Welfare no longer pays for diapers, child car-seats, telephone or utility hook-ups; welfare recipients must accept workfare jobs offered at $6 an hour or lose their benefits. Unqualified workfare employees are replacing health-care professionals in hospitals, putting the safety of patients in jeopardy.

The government has made it clear that only the disabled will qualify for welfare in the future. Government House Leader Stockwell Day boasts, "In many ways we're already ahead of the Americans. We have deadlines here where there is no more social assistance." At the most recent provincial Tory convention, delegates made their views on welfare explicit. One called for blood tests for people on social assistance to ensure that they are not spending their welfare money on cigarettes. "Many children go hungry because their parents are addicted to nicotine," she explained. When the child welfare branch of Alberta Family and Social Services refused to pay the fee for counselling a six-year-old girl who had been repeatedly raped by her twelve-year-old male babysitter, Family and Social Services Minister Mike Cardinal blamed the mother, who was on welfare. Saying she should have chosen her babysitter more carefully, he wondered out loud where the father was.

The suffering of poor people is palpable. The Alberta Association of Social Workers says that families "can no longer pay rent and buy food, children are embarrassed in school at lunchtime because of inadequate/nonexistent food, inadequate clothing, and inability to participate in fee for service school activities." In the spring of 1994, the government suddenly decided to charge parents for kindergarten and was surprised when thousands of children did not turn up when school opened in the fall. The Tory convention labelled the Alberta Teachers' Association "totalitarian" for objecting to this move.

Teenagers thrown off welfare are turning to prostitution, theft, and drugs. Single mothers are thrown off welfare if they miss even one résumé-writing training session, even if they had to stay home because their child was sick. Single people, receiving only $165 a month in "shelter allowance," are living in cockroach-infested rooming houses. Mark Kennedy of *The Ottawa Citizen* describes the situation of twenty-nine-year-old Karen S., a single mother of two living on welfare since her husband "beat her bloody" several years earlier. Both children are hyperactive, one with attention deficit disorder, which makes him flee his school every day and run home to his mother. First, Smith's welfare cheque was cut by $200 a month. After rent and utilities were paid, she had about $40 a month to feed herself and her children. Her solution? She just stopped eating for weeks at a time. Recently, she was deemed employable and therefore ineligible for any assistance; the cheques stopped immediately.

The Klein government has also targeted health care: $750 million is being taken out of the system in three years. Hospitals are being closed all over the province; the government has announced it will close half of its hospital beds by 1997. Thousands of nurses have been laid off, and thousands more have been shifted from full-time to casual status, losing their security and benefits. The remaining nurses are being forced to accept wage freezes after roll-backs of over 5 percent.

Mental hospital and health clinic budgets have been severely cut and patients are sent into the community to cope without resources. Seniors are being moved from hospitals to community "foster homes," where they are cared for by unsupervised and unqualified staff. Five of the seven remaining hospitals in Edmonton are being closed, supposedly to shift care from institutions to the community. The government is replacing the 1,250 hospital nurses with 4 community health nurses.

Specialists are leaving the province, fed up with the lack of fully functioning medical teams or follow-up care for their patients. Waiting periods for operations grow longer; emergency departments are closed or working beyond capacity with waiting times from six to twenty hours. Many patients have lost toes and fingers unnecessarily because of the delay in emergency treatment. The government wants to de-license nurses, health-science technicians, dentists, and psychologists in favour of a "generic" health-care worker who will require fewer qualifications and earn lower wages. One hospital wants to call its nurses "patient hostesses." Less qualified personnel are replacing health-care professionals in old-age homes and hospitals. "Continuing care aides" with only four hours of training are administering medications in seniors facilities; cleaning and maintenance staff bathe, feed, and shave patients in understaffed hospitals.

Care for Albertans has plummeted. New mothers are sent home from hospital the day they give birth. Women having radical mastectomies are in and out the same day with no follow-up home care. A man dying of cancer was sent home from hospital with no home care; he didn't qualify because he had a wife. A man had to care for his very ill, fragile ninety-year-old mother, including administering enemas, in a city hospital, as the nursing staff were overworked. A daughter slept on the floor in her mother's nursing room after her mother's hip surgery, as the staff couldn't provide even minimal care.

The lone nurse on duty in a pediatric ward was called to emergency, leaving the maintenance man in charge of the floor. In another, a nurse was forced to put a child with pneumonia into a stroller and roll the child around with her on her rounds. A two-year-old child died while in transit to a distant hospital because her local facility was swamped. At the Sturgeon hospital near Edmonton, an eleven-year-old boy was admitted with a concussion, a fractured pelvis, and internal injuries after being hit by a car. Because of budget cuts, no pediatric nurse was on duty from 11 p.m. to 7 a.m., so the boy's parents had to stay with him through the night to check on his vital signs, monitor his intravenous drips, and record all information on a chart. This is now standard practice, under the hospital's "24-hour care by parents" program.

A patient admitted to a hospital was put in a bed that had not been changed since the previous occupant had died; the bedsheets were still soiled with his body fluids. An elderly pensioner was flown by air ambulance from Medicine Hat to Edmonton for a liver transplant, but he was told to find his own way from the airport to the hospital. Because he was so late arriving, the liver was given to another patient. The man was then told he had to make his own way back to Medicine Hat. He was able to borrow only enough money to get him to Calgary, and had to go without food for the entire trip. His wife had to borrow money so she could drive the 300 kilometres to Calgary to pick him up.

Trudy Richardson of the United Nurses of Alberta says that Albertans are no longer consumers, but victims of public health care. Ralph Klein just shrugs. "Maybe some will [die]...that would be unfortunate. But that might have happened anyway." His government passed legislation allowing the government to sue "wrongdoers" for their full health coverage if they are at fault in accidents. Moreover, according to the government's own estimates, Albertans will be paying nearly 50 percent more in medicare premiums by 1998 for this much reduced health-care system.

Given the state and cost of public health care in Alberta, it is no surprise that some Albertans are now receptive to Ralph Klein's plan to privatize. The latest provincial Progressive Conservative annual convention voted to turn closed hospitals over to the private sector, and Klein is openly courting investment from giant American health-care corporations. (It is important to remember that, under NAFTA, once a public service is privatized, it is next to impossible to return it to the public sphere.) He wants to allow wealthy Americans to go to the front of the line in private clinics and hospitals, and believes wealthy Albertans should have the "choice" to pay for superior and more immediate care.

Private clinics are operating and growing in the province and are hustling business in other provinces. One potential client/customer was told by a well-known eye clinic that she had to sign a petition in favour of legislation extending private clinic rights in the province before she would be served. Another, an elderly woman suffering from macular degeneration, which has left her nearly blind, attended a lecture with a number of other seniors. She received a free eye examination in exchange for signing up with the clinic. She was told by the clinic ophthamologist that her problem was cataracts: for $1,265 per eye, he could perform an operation that would largely restore her sight. At the urging of her nurse daughter, the woman contacted a public-sector ophthamologist who confirmed that she had no cataracts and her vision had deteriorated too far to correct.

The Klein government is forging ahead with legislation to deregulate and privatize many areas of government service, including health, and, in the words of political scientist Laurie Adkin, to "transform the Government of Alberta into a holding company for an assortment of private companies which will be selling services previously provided and managed by the government." Public servants who speak out for their rights and those of the public are branded as radicals and suspended without pay. Klein loves the confrontational nature of this fight, and has assured the people of his province that he will finish his revolution with or without their approval.

The Alberta blueprint for reinvented government is being watched closely by other provinces and by the federal government. Ontario's Mike Harris idolizes Klein and has stated his intention of duplicating his program. Jean Charest says that Alberta's experiment is the future of the country. But Albertans are not finding services any cheaper; they are simply paying user fees for services they used to get for free, and they are buying private social security insurance to top up a public system being forced to fail. Gutted social programs are discrediting the whole public service, and citizens are openly demanding tax cuts. It is no coincidence that the national tax revolt started in Alberta.

Private families, primarily women, are being forced to take over the care of the sick, the young, and the old. The private sector is offering the "choice" of superior education and health to wealthy Albertans. The poor and unemployed, cast as villains, are left to fend for themselves. The federal government's decentralization plans and block funding arrangement suit Klein's agenda very well: his government applauds the Canada Health and Social Transfer, saying it will enable Alberta to complete its revolution. Klein had no intention of following national guidelines in any case; the CHST merely ends the pretence that we are a nation with common values and rights.

The students of Cole Harbour, Nova Scotia, take note of the world the adults are bequeathing them. So do the students of Alberta. They are learning their lessons from their elders: what counts are individualism, competitiveness, adaptability, self-reliance, survival. The state is removing itself from their lives; in its place is the private sector, whose primary function is to sort winners from losers in the most effective way possible. Says one, "I feel I'm entering a war zone. I sure know I'm on my own."

10

RECKONING

We are now in the midst of a social revolution twenty years in the making. Corporate interests have captured the political agenda. They have put government and its citizens on trial. They have put the dream of the just society on trial. The democratic rights of Canadians are being subverted. With the complicity of the Liberal government, Canada is moving toward rule by corporations.

The corporate agenda has been spearheaded by a relatively small consortium—academics, think-tank researchers, corporate leaders, senior bureaucrats, lobbyists, politicians, media managers and commentators. The policies are deliberate and identifiable, as are their consequences. They are supported by like-minded individuals and organizations throughout the industrialized world, including international organizations such as the World Bank and the International Monetary Fund, which have been a breeding ground for the world-wide dissemination of neo-liberal ideology.

It is not a conspiracy, although the agenda has been advanced in countless meetings behind closed doors. The policies are knowable, if not always apparent in their execution, as are their consequences. The agenda is grounded in the perception by the élites of their common interests and how to achieve them, with little consideration for their effect on society at large. If the protection of their wealth requires that the Bank of Canada, free of democratic accountability, keep the country in a state of chronic depression with millions of people unemployed, so be it.

The language of neo-liberalism dominates everyday discourse: deregulation, privatization, free trade, free markets, restructuring, downsizing, limited government, reinvented government, competitiveness, globalization, structural adjustment, inevitability, fiscal responsibility, tight money, sound currency, personal responsibility. The market, law professor Neil Brooks says, has been socially and politically constructed "not by the invisible hand of some omnipotent law-giver; it has been directed by the sleight of hand of the economically powerful."

Instead of big business leaders and their political water boys being held responsible for these destructive policies, the Canadian people are accused of being coddled by unaffordable social programs, of being insufficiently trained and uncompetitive. The corporate oligarchy has subverted democratic structures, sabotaged the social agenda, and just about killed the dream of a just society.

The enormity of this social crisis has left many Canadians personally demoralized and politically immobilized. We ask ourselves how we can reverse the tide, how we can begin to mount a defence against such an accumulation of power. It must start with a reclamation of the Canadian experiment; we must reclaim our collective memory, or what some call our "narrative."

The political schizophrenia apparent in Canadian society today is a symptom of a loss of purpose in our national life. Poll after poll shows that Canadians hold their politicians in contempt. We say, "It doesn't matter what they say or what party they belong to, they are all the same. They all lie." What we mean is that politicians govern but they do not rule. Corporations rule. The international investment community rules. Global financial institutions rule.

Perhaps we are mourning. Our democracy is under siege, our history fading. Our ancestors invested great trust in their governments to forge a nation-state, knowing that, left to market forces alone, Canada would not make it. But the covenant between the

Canadian people and their governments has been broken and politicians won't admit it. We are being compelled both by outside forces and by our own economic and political élites to abandon our own values and accept their monoculture of values. As Indian writer Vandana Shiva explains, world corporate monoculture abhors diversity and promotes uniformity of thinking. It sells itself not as a globalized local tradition of corporate America, but as a universal system inherently superior to local systems. Monoculture spreads, not because it produces more, but because it controls more. It is the global-market narrative that has caused a sea change in the political culture of Canadians.

What is the Canadian narrative? In social terms, John Kenneth Galbraith reminds us that a civilized society is one in which "there must not be a deprived and excluded underclass. The good society does not allow some of its people to feel useless, superfluous and deprived." Canadians sought to build a society, imperfect as it was and is, in which everyone is included by citizenship.

How did we let the Canadian narrative go so easily? Was it lost, stolen, abandoned? Was it proven false? Did we lose a sense of faith in its "rightness"? Did we stop caring? We cannot claim to be a people if we so willingly forsake the values and institutions upon which our culture was built. Neo-liberal proponents will say, without a shred of evidence, that this narrative bankrupted Canada and made us a lazy people. Do we really accept that the search for social justice destroyed our initiative, our place in the world? Or could it be that our narrative had to be discredited by those who stand to profit by its demise before it could be replaced by another inimical to democracy?

Can we reclaim our narrative, and weave it into the realities of a new century? We cannot and should not build walls around our country. We are part of a global community, and we must build different global institutions with a different mandate. If, however, we cannot protect our own democracy and do not fight for the public governance of our institutions, we lose our claim to being a people, relinquish our national purpose.

Next, we need to roll back corporate power in our society. Without this, any alternatives we put forward are weightless, easily ignored or dismissed as unrealistic. This is a long-term challenge that demands ongoing commitment, but it is the only way to reclaim democracy in our public institutions and the media, to tame the market so that it serves the many and not the few, and to move again toward the just society that has been held captive for twenty years.

This task requires that we disarm the capacity of corporate interests to dominate the media with their propaganda; revoke the corporate privilege of evading taxes and claiming huge financial handouts from the state; pre-empt the corporations from playing workers and communities off against one another in a destructive "race to the bottom"; and refuse the corporations the luxury of subverting environmental health, and workplace safety regulations. We must also disarm the banks and the money managers so that they can no longer disrupt the economy; disarm the media managers, lobbyists, and backroom dealmakers; and stop corporations from buying political parties and bureaucracies. It also requires that we expose the neo-liberal ideology as a false god that cannot deliver on its promises of general prosperity, employment and stability. It is a self-serving agenda that advances inequality, instability, and the disintegration of our nation.

At this time in our nation's history, there is no political party with the capacity to address the issues of corporate rule. Before the corporate agenda took hold, in the era of the social agenda, people used political democracy, largely embodied in successive Liberal governments, to build economic democracy on a foundation of social and economic citizenship rights. (Ironically, discrediting government pushes many Canadians toward parties advocating extreme versions of the market-based solutions that caused the problem in the first place.) We now have to focus part of our work on building a political party that puts forward a real platform for dismantling corporate rule. This is the challenge for those trying to rebuild the NDP, and for social Liberals struggling with their party's recent behaviour.

Dozens of Liberals have (privately) expressed to us their ardent disagreement with the social-policy direction of their government and sadness at the betrayal of their party's social legacy. When thirty-year parliamentary veteran Warren Allmand voted against the Canada Health and Social Transfer, he made it clear that he felt the Chrétien government was betraying the Liberal Party's legacy: "It was the Liberal Party that built up these programs. I was there when we built them up. I voted for medicare. I voted for the Canada Assistance Plan. I voted for reducing old-age pensions to age 65. And I don't intend to be part of a team that tears down what we built up."

Allmand remained true to himself, his values, and his Liberal past. For Allmand and other social Liberals, progressive social policy is synonymous with Liberalism. But until they acknowledge the reality of how their government has capitulated to corporate rule, they will be voices in the wilderness, slowing, but not stopping, its inexorable progress.

As the Liberal Party flagrantly breaks the promises it made in the Red Book and during its years in opposition, it deepens the cynicism of those who question why they should even vote; and confuses others, who see that the dismantling of the nation-state is sad, but who cannot believe that Liberals would knowingly hurt Canadians. For the federal government to pretend that it can remove itself from the enforcement of national social and environmental standards without consequence on the day-to-day lives of Canadians is deceitful. Like all governments, the Chrétien Liberals could have chosen a different economic and social model.

By buying into the corporate-dominated global economy and by exchanging the Canadian social inheritance of sharing-for-survival for the American social inheritance of survival-of-the-fittest, the Chrétien government is sabotaging Canadian democracy. For there *are* other powerful models of international community that would allow, even encourage, nation-states to maintain a strong public social security system, a fully employed workforce, and a healthy domestic economy. But we are not given such options. Jean Chrétien raises the issue of national sovereignty before the G7, but refuses to take any measures that would counter the very trends he pretends to decry. Instead, Canada spearheads the creation of an OECD multilateral code to totally deregulate the flow of private investment across borders. Instead of meeting with representatives of the world's poor and unemployed in preparation for the Halifax summit, he listened instead to the International Chamber of Commerce's call for the G7 to dismantle their labour laws and cut their social safety nets to "encourage the world's unemployed to look harder for work."

Transnational corporate rule is a recipe for the greatest social divisions and unrest of modern times, and the Liberal Party will be held accountable to history for buying into it. Individual Liberals who disagree with their party's recent conversion have a role to play in making it accountable, and must speak out. They do not need to accept this expropriation of power by Chrétien and his cabinet. They can mobilize at the grass roots; speak out publicly; fight the challenge to party democracy; split the party if necessary. Social Liberals need to confront the issue of electoral financing and the power of corporate money in the upper echelons of their party. They could add their voices to those of Canadians calling for reform of the electoral system itself, perhaps even a referendum on the next federal ballot, allowing Canadians to vote for proportional representation.

History won't remember those who were content merely to conform; it will recognize those, like Warren Allmand, with the courage to break ranks for the sake of their country, and their party. True, the party is riding high in the polls and there is no parliamentary opposition to challenge its about-face; but when the global economy, and the shaky principles of market dominance upon which it is built, fails, and it will surely fail, Liberals who take no action now will have ensured that the rebuilding tomorrow will be done by others.

In the long run, however, rebuilding requires a change in the political culture, and this will only be realized by Canadians prepared to challenge the corporate ideology that has overwhelmed us. No party, particularly not the Liberal Party, given its history, can fight this battle for us. Even the best political representatives to federal or provincial legislatures cannot deliver until we build a democratic culture in which political parties will be truly accountable to their citizens.

This mighty corporate juggernaut is neither inescapable nor irreversible. Change is possible. Choices are available. It is not our intention in this chapter to lay out a detailed blueprint of alternative economic and social policies. For one thing, resources on alternatives exist in abundance, in both of our organizations and in many others. Our problem lies not in finding solutions but in building a common political purpose and a vision for the future of the country based on popular democratic control.

The impetus for this vision is not going to come from government for the foreseeable future, so, as in the 1930s, Canadian social and environmental movements will have to pick up the slack. There is no easy set of actions that will reverse the current trends in the short term, and any suggestion to the contrary would be dishonest. We should not be impatient. If we are correct that the new right took twenty years to build support for their view in the culture, we must realize the work that lies ahead for us.

We will work at the personal level and organize in our communities. We will also work at the national level; for though the nation-state is not perfect, it is the only political institution big enough to set economic, social, cultural, and environmental policy that works on behalf of its people as a counterweight to corporate power, but small enough to be responsive when citizens exercise their democratic choice. Many policy options are available to Canada: we could make the Bank of Canada accountable to Parliament and its mandate of full employment; abrogate NAFTA; manage and regulate the economy; introduce a progressive tax system; reform party financing and elections, including introducing proportional representation; restrict lobbyists; strengthen the social security system; set up public investment funds; and so on.

As well, however, we will work at the international level. We need to understand the changing nature of the global economy.

No nation-state can operate alone; we need a new and fair global trading and financial system to replace Bretton Woods, the International Monetary Fund, the World Bank, and the World Trade Organization. We must promote the formation of global citizen and environmental movements to establish international standards for the care of our planet, human rights, and social justice.

We keep being told that Canada is going through a bad time, and that if we are patient all will soon be well. Let us confront that corporate lie: it is a matter of ideology, a clash of values, a contest of interests. The global economy is designed by and for those with a great deal to gain from it. It is fuelled by deep inequities, excessive consumerism, and ecological crime. The global economy is creating an unbalanced world in which race and class warfare are rife. It also poses a direct challenge to democracy. Tommy Douglas said, "Let me remind you what fascism is. It need not wear a brown shirt or a green shirt—it may even wear a dress shirt. Fascism begins the moment a ruling class, fearing the people may use their political democracy to gain economic democracy, begins to destroy political democracy in order to retain its power of exploitation and special privilege."

To rebuild democracy, we Canadians must start in our communities and move out across sectors, across communities, across countries, across race, gender, and age lines. Employed and unemployed, city and rural, we must find one another and recognize that we are a movement in opposition to corporate rule. Our goal must be to change the hearts and minds of enough people, here and around the world, to rebuild democracy.

We must take on the responsibility of returning Canada to the path toward the just society. We must fight to restore the political climate in which the just society can thrive, just as others before us fought to create it. Citizens must become politically active on a scale so large that it is considered un-Canadian: in our unions, our churches, our advocacy groups, our political parties, our professional groups. We must demand the restoration of democracy in government, the accountability of politicians, and the subordination of corporate interests to the needs of citizens. We must create a climate in which no political party dares to backtrack on the democratic pursuit of the just society.

Those of us opposed to the global economy must stand in clear opposition to it. The corporate and political élites of the new economy have absolutely clear goals. *They* look like the revolutionaries, with their talk of stripping government in the name of individual freedom. We must not accommodate the forces that want to dismantle our social infrastructure. We must not buy their analysis or use their language. Fair trade, full employment, co-operation, cultural diversity, democratic control, fair taxation, environmental stewardship, community, public accountability, and social justice are the touchstones for the restoration of the just society.

Nor should we accept prevailing propaganda of inevitability. To say that we have no choice is intellectual terrorism. Although the corporate agenda is dominant throughout the world, different nations have reacted differently to its pressures. Many European nations have been successful in insulating their people from its worst excesses. Citizen movements are springing up everywhere to counter unjust corporate globalism and work with citizens in other nations to create alternative international social, economic, and environmental models.

Ultimately, our hope rests on the faith that people living under a system that is unstable and incapable of delivering on its promises will eventually reassert democracy. The global fight against corporate rule will finally be won by people and their governments acting collectively to reclaim control over transnational power and to reverse its brutal legacy. For Canadians, the heart of the fight, and ultimately the test of its success, will be the struggle to protect the public services and universal social programs that our parents and grandparents fought so hard to create, in which we thrive, and upon which our national narrative was built.

CHAPTER NOTES

1: Building the Just Society

Several excellent political texts served as background material for this chapter: Allan Moscovitch and Jim Albert's *The Benevolent State: The Growth of Welfare in Canada* (Garamond Press, 1987); Allan Moscovitch and Glenn Drover's *Inequality: Essays on the Political Economy of Social Welfare* (University of Toronto Press, 1981); Denis Guest's *The Emergence of Social Security in Canada* (University of British Columbia Press, 1980); Rodney Haddow's *Poverty Reform in Canada, 1958–1978* (McGill-Queen's University Press, 1993); Linda McQuaig's *The Wealthy Banker's Wife* (Penguin Books, 1993). Political scientists William Christian, Colin Campbell, and Duncan Cameron have written excellent pieces describing the Liberal Party's division into social and business factions. See *Political Parties and Ideologies in Canada* (McGraw-Hill Ryerson, 1974) and *Canadian Parties in Transition*, edited by Alain Gagnon and Brian Tanguay (Nelson Canada, 1989). Diana Ralph of Carleton University's School of Social Work kindly helped guide our research.

Distinguished authors and historians who provided background documentation include Richard Splane (the "father" of CAP), Leonard Marsh (author of the noted report on social security), Donald Creighton, W.L. Morton, William Kilbourn, Kenneth McNaught (on Mackenzie King and J.S. Woodsworth), Blair Neatby, and Pierre Berton, particularly his outstanding chronicle *The Great Depression, 1929–1939* (McClelland & Stewart, 1990).

Gerald Caplan gave us insight into the early years of the CCF in his book *The Dilemma of Canadian Socialism: The CCF in*

Ontario (McClelland & Stewart, 1973). Peter Newman captured the Pearson years in *The Distemper of Our Times* (McClelland & Stewart, 1968), and Christina McCall wonderfully documented Liberal history in *Grits: An Intimate Portrait of the Liberal Party* (Macmillan, 1982) and, with Stephen Clarkson, *Trudeau and Our Times: The Heroic Delusion* (McClelland & Stewart, 1994). Pierre Trudeau and Thomas Axworthy contributed to our understanding through *Towards a Just Society: The Trudeau Years* (Penguin Books, 1990).

2: The Hostile Takeover

Many documents used in this and other chapters are mentioned in the body of the text and are not repeated here. Many good books have been written on corporate power. Three that were useful include: Richard Barnett and John Cavanagh, *Global Dreams: Imperial Corporations and the New World Order* (Simon & Schuster, 1994); J.K. Galbraith, *The Anatomy of Power* (Houghton Mifflin, 1984); *The United Nations: World Investment Report*, 1994. On the marriage of the new right and the corporate interests see Pat Marchak, *The Integrated Circus* (McGill-Queen's University Press, 1991). On corporate think tanks, see the work of David Langille on the BCNI, particularly "The Business Council on National Issues and the Canadian State" in *Studies in Political Economy*, Autumn 1987. Also, Murray Dobbin, "Thomas d'Aquino: The De Facto PM," *The Canadian Forum*, November 1992; Alan Earnst, "From Continentalism to Neoconservatism: North American Free Trade and the C.D. Howe Institute," *Studies in Political Economy*, Autumn 1992; and on the Fraser Institute, see John Crane, *Directions for Social Welfare in Canada* (University of British Columbia Press, 1994).

3: The Cornerstones

The main statistical sources were Statistics Canada: *National Accounts; Employment Earnings and Hours; Exports by Country; Balance of International Payments; The CALURA Report;* and

Intra-Corporate Ownership. The Bank of Canada Review was also a useful source of statistical information in this chapter. Much has been written on the FTA/NAFTA; recent work includes Duncan Cameron and Mel Watkins (eds.), *Canada under Free Trade* (Lorimer, 1993); Laurence Martin, *Pledge of Allegiance* (McClelland & Stewart, 1993). There is excellent material on the free trade debate in Tony Clarke, *Behind the Mitre* (HarperCollins, 1995). On monetary policy and the Bank of Canada, see Linda McQuaig, *Shooting the Hippo* (Viking, 1995); Michael Babad and Catherine Mulroney, *Where the Buck Stops* (Stoddart, 1995); William Krehm, *A Power Unto Itself* (Stoddart, 1993); Harold Chorney et al., *The Deficit Made Me Do It* (CCPA, 1992); Pierre Fortin, "Strategies for Deficit Control," *Canadian Business Economics*, Fall 1994; various articles by Jordan Grant, chair of the Bank of Canada for Canadians Coalition; transcripts of the Commons Finance Committee pre-budget hearings; and Duncan Cameron, editorials in *The Canadian Forum* and brief to the Finance Committee, June 1995. The Galbraith quote at the end of the chapter comes from *Journey Through Economic Time* (Houghton Mifflin, 1994). Materials from a conference, "Civic Society, Globalization, Nationhood and Well-Being," York University, April 3-4, 1995, particularly tables provided by Marvin Novick, were also useful.

4: The Battleground

Many individuals assisted our thinking in this chapter. We are grateful to the numerous Liberals, inside the House of Commons and in the party at large, who spoke with us in personal (mostly private) interviews. Political scientist Robert Jackson gave us insight into the inner workings of the free trade struggle in the party. We would like to note the excellent work of journalists Edward Greenspon of *The Globe and Mail*, Mark Kennedy of *The Ottawa Citizen*, Linda Diebel of *The Toronto Star* and writer Ron Graham, who provided insight into the Liberal Party in many different articles. Graham also gave us helpful background material in *One-Eyed Kings: Promise & Illusion in Canadian Politics* (Collins, 1986).

We used Jean Chrétien's own words and thoughts in *Straight from the Heart* (Key Porter Books, 1985), and Roy MacLaren's in his autobiography, *Honourable Mentions* (Deneau Publishers, 1986). The proceedings of the Aylmer Conference, *Finding Common Ground* (Voyageur Publishing, 1992), were important source materials.

5: The Reversal

In preparing this chapter we had access to an extensive media record of the period, including press reports and audio and visual tapes of interviews and the transcript of the leading economists, conference. The voluminous work of Noam Chomsky on media was insightful as an analytical framework for this chapter. Here we cite two references: *Necessary Illusions* (Anansi, 1991); and (with Edward Herman) *Manufacturing Consent: The Political Economy of the Mass Media* (Pantheon/Random House, 1988). See also James Winter, particularly *Common Cents* (Black Rose, 1992); and Stephen Dale, "Why the Press Downplayed the Alternative Budget," *CCPA Monitor,* June 1995.

6: Barbarians at the Gate

The most important reference sources for this chapter were the documents and discussion papers that came out of the *CCPA-CHO!CES Alternative Budget, 1995* project in which hundreds of people from scores of organizations participated. Besides the budget itself, working papers of the policy groups, including employment by Andrew Jackson, taxation by Hugh McKenzie, and macro-policy by Jim Stanford, were particularly valuable. Also very useful were briefs by a number of organizations to the Commons Finance Commitee and the Human Resources Development Committee. They include: the Canadian Labour Congress, the Canadian Autoworkers, the National Union of Provincial and General Employees Union, the Metro-Toronto Social Planning Council, the Paying for Canada Coalition, the Bank of Canada for Canadians Coalition, the Canadian Council on Social Development, the National Council of Welfare, the National

Anti-Poverty Organization, and the Caledon Institute. We have drawn material on the impact of the CHST from two Canadian Union of Public Employees publications: *Undoing Health Care*, April 1995; and *Our Country Under Attack*, May 1995. We would also acknowledge the invaluable work of Neil Brooks, Osgoode Hall Law School, on taxation, and the role of the public sector. His essay *Left vs. Right: Two Ways of Looking at the Public Sector, the Deficit and the Tax System* will be published by the CCPA in the fall of 1995. Also, see Diane Bellemare and Lise Poulin-Simon, *The Cost of Unemployment* (CCPA, 1994).

7: Sliding Through Gethsemane

The transcripts of the Human Resources Development Standing Committee hearings on the Social Security Review were a useful reference for this chapter, as was the committee's final report, *Security Opportunities and Fairness*, February 6, 1995. To examine Lloyd Axworthy's thinking we also benefited from the video transcript of the Queen's University Forum on Social Policy. A number of documents have been important to our understanding of the social security system; they include Armine Yalnizyan et al., *Shifting Time* (Between the Lines, 1994); and the Ecumenical Coalition for Economic Justice, *Reweaving Canada's Social Programs*, 1993.

8: Punishing the Innocent

This chapter has benefited from detailed information provided by the Canadian Health Coalition, the Canadian Union of Public Employees, the National Federation of Nurses Unions, the United Nurses of Alberta, and the Hospital Employees Union of British Columbia. We are also indebted to Stephen Leary, Hugh Armstrong, Trudy Richardson, Kathleen Connors, and Colleen Fuller.

9: Grim Present, Grim Future

We wish to acknowledge a number of advocacy and research organizations whose material was helpful in this chapter. These include the Canadian Teachers' Federation; the Canadian Centre for Policy Alternatives, particularly Ed Finn's work on the CCPA regular publication, *Monitor*; the Canadian Labour Congress; the Public Service Alliance of Canada, particularly the *Report on PSAC Hearings into Public Service Delivery*, 1994; the National Action Committee on the Status of Women; the Canadian Association of Sexual Assault Centres; the Alberta Teachers' Association; the United Nurses of Alberta; the National-Anti Poverty Organization; the Canadian Conference of the Arts, the Canadian Union of Students Overseas; the Council of Canadians, particularly the research of David Robinson; and the Ontario Network of Employment Skills and Training Projects.

University of Alberta political scientists Laurie Adkin, Gurston Dacks, Joyce Green, and Linda Trimble provided excellent background on Alberta. Analyst Murray Dobbin was helpful in a number of areas to do with the public sector. Journalists whose work was very helpful include Tom Spears and April Lindgren of *The Ottawa Citizen*, Mary Janigan of *Maclean's*, Peter Schrag of *Harper's* magazine, and Anthony Johnson of SouthhamStar Network.

INDEX

C